School of American Research
Southwest Indian Arts Series

DOUGLAS W. SCHWARTZ, GENERAL EDITOR

SCHOOL OF AMERICAN RESEARCH
SOUTHWEST INDIAN ARTS SERIES

Mimbres Painted Pottery
J. J. BRODY

Jewelry of the Prehistoric Southwest
E. WESLEY JERNIGAN

Indian Rock Art of the Southwest
POLLY SCHAAFSMA

INDIAN ROCK ART
OF THE SOUTHWEST

This publication was made possible by generous support from

THE WEATHERHEAD FOUNDATION

INDIAN
ROCK ART
OF THE
SOUTHWEST

Polly Schaafsma

SCHOOL OF AMERICAN RESEARCH
Santa Fe

UNIVERSITY of NEW MEXICO PRESS
Albuquerque

Library of Congress Cataloging in Publication Data

Schaafsma, Polly.
    Indian rock art of the Southwest.

    (Southwest Indian arts series)
    Bibliography: p. 347
    Includes index.
    1. Indians of North America—Southwest, New—Art.
2. Indians of North America—Southwest, New—
Antiquities.   3. Petroglyphs—Southwest. New.
4. Rock paintings—Southwest, New.   5. Southwest,
New—Antiquities.   I. Title.   II. Series.
E78.S7S28   709′.01′1   79-9127
ISBN 0-8263-0913-5

SCHOOL OF AMERICAN RESEARCH
Santa Fe
    Douglas W. Schwartz, General Series Editor
    Phillip Brittenham, Managing Editor

UNIVERSITY OF NEW MEXICO PRESS
Albuquerque
    Elizabeth Gard, Series Editor

COMPOSITION: University of New Mexico Printing Plant

PRINTING AND BINDING: Bookcrafters

Fifth paperbound printing, 1992

Contents

Foreword   ix

Preface   xi

1. Introduction: Images on Stone   1

2. Techniques: Brush and Hammerstone   25

3. Hunters and Gatherers   33

4. Hohokam Rock Art of Southern Arizona   81

5. The Anasazi   105

6. The Fremont of Utah   163

7. The Mogollon   183

8. Pueblo Rock Art After A.D. 1300   243

9. Navajo and Apache Rock Art   301

10. Concluding Remarks   343

References   347

Lists of Illustrations   367

Index   373

The "scientific world view" to which we are all captive makes it difficult to reach meaningfully into the metaphysical esoteric areas of the past—or for that matter, the present—but at least we can be certain that in pre-Hispanic art, as in the art of other non-Western peoples, things are rarely what they appear to be at first glance.

Peter T. Furst (1972:351)

Foreword

Pecked and painted on cliffs, boulders, and cave walls throughout the Southwest are thousands of examples of rock art. On first consideration these seem only a bewildering array, including meandering lines, ghostly rows of anthropomorphic forms with large staring eyes, winged human figures, mountain sheep pierced with spears, bulging heads capped with antennae, lizard-men, humpbacked flute players, and Spanish soldiers on horseback. Yet after several years of field research, thoughtful analysis, exacting chronological placement, and ethnographically based interpretation, Polly Schaafsma has found in this material an amazing degree of order. She sees each figure as a work of art, and a sensitive reflection of the culture. Using this approach, a striking richness in form, function, meaning, and cultural relationships is discovered in the rock art of the Southwest Indian.

With an art critic's clarity of description, a scientist's caution, and the support of rich illustrative material, Ms. Schaafsma begins with the history of rock art research and an examination of the basic analytical tools of its study, the concept of style, problems of interpretation, and the intricacies of chronological interpretation. The major part of the volume describes and traces the known rock art styles of the Southwest from their earliest examples at about 2000 B.C. up to and including the historic period. It is presented within the context of its cultural setting, beginning with the hunter-gatherer period and proceeding to the Hohokam desert dwellers, the mountain and lowland Mogollon, the plateau Anasazi, and the relatively recent Athabaskan. What emerges is a new way of viewing the overall configuration of southwestern cultural history. But this art form is so intimately related to ritual life that one is constantly impressed with the complexity of prehistoric ceremonial systems. In the historic period, for example, when the sky in ceiling paintings of the Navajo is presented, the reader is transported into those great overhanging cliff shelters to peer at the Navajo-conceived night sky, only to become aware that it is not the sky we are familiar with, rather one drawn by another culture's cognitive map.

ix

From its inception in 1907, the School of American Research has maintained a strong interest in both the art and anthropology of the Southwest. Its early support of Indian artists like María Martínez and researchers such as Kenneth Chapman helped to encourage both the production of Southwest Indian arts as well as a scholarly interest in them. This book grows from, and reaffirms, that tradition. It is the third volume in the School's Southwest Indian Art Series, which documents and examines from an anthropological perspective the full range of prehistoric southwestern Indian arts. This series, supported and encouraged by the Weatherhead Foundation, began in 1977 with the publication of J. J. Brody's *Mimbres Painted Pottery*, followed in 1978 by E. Wesley Jernigan's *Prehistoric Jewelry of the Southwest*. The series serves three important audiences: Indian artists, who we hope will find visual and conceptual links to the traditions from which they have always worked; southwestern scholars, for whom the series draws together source material and contemporary research into a new synthesis; and the knowledgeable general reader interested in the quality, variety, and history of southwestern Indian art. Currently under development are additional volumes on prehistoric weaving, drypainting, historic jewelry, historic weaving, and painting. When completed, this series should provide a comprehensive statement on the origin, history, development, meaning, and beauty of the Indian arts of the American Southwest.

Navajo rugs and Pueblo pottery long have been recognized throughout the world as quality examples of artistic achievement. But the art of the southwestern Indians has for over two millennia contained so much more of excellence. In this volume on rock art the reader is given the opportunity to understand something of the formal diversity, historical complexity, and stylistic variation of another aspect of this regional art tradition. In each chapter, beauty is presented as it is seen from the perspective of other value systems, through mysterious forms, dramatic rhythms, and tapestry of meanings. In so doing, Polly Schaafsma has made a significant contribution to our appreciation and understanding of an intriguing element in the multi-dimensional mosaic of southwestern Indian art.

Douglas W. Schwartz, President
School of American Research

Preface

Drawings on rocks are probably man's most enduring art form. In the arid Southwest, where rock surfaces are nearly always available, rock paintings and petroglyphs document about 3,000 years of artistic endeavor by Native Americans. This art is divisible into styles that follow geographic and cultural boundaries and that show immense variation in content and in aesthetic development. The enormous diversity in Southwest rock art reflects the complexity of Southwest prehistory and of the ideologies and ritual and social functions in which rock art played a part. I have approached rock art as an archaeological resource because so viewed it can add a significant new dimension to knowledge of the prehistoric southwestern peoples.

Eventually regional research and studies at the local level will modify and bring into sharper focus what has been said in this volume. Our understanding of how these drawings on rock functioned and the significance of the iconography is still in preliminary stages. Dating methods need to be refined. And there are still gaps in the information, some geographical.

As for any art, words are of limited descriptive value. The aesthetics of any given style or particular painting or petroglyph can be fully understood only through visual inspection, and for this reason I have used as many illustrations as possible. Adequate visual material allows the reader to evaluate for himself interpretations given in the text. As in any work dealing with art, the photographs and drawings herein are one of the more important parts of the book.

The photographs made specifically for this volume were taken by Karl Kernberger, who has hauled his camera equipment up and down cliffs, over talus slopes, and through canyons all over the Southwest for the sake of rock art. Other photographs for study and illustration were contributed by the New Mexico State Planning Office and the Donald Scott File. Special thanks are due the Peabody Museum at Harvard and Mrs. Donald Scott, who allowed the School of American Research to retain the Scott files in Santa Fe for the writing of this volume. Other photographs and institutions from which illustrations were obtained are named in the photo credits. Maps, charts, and drawings were made by Wes Jernigan, assisted by Aaron Heldt, who worked with painstaking care on difficult material.

I am particularly indebted to Douglas W. Schwartz and the late Wanda Driskell for their valuable suggestions and encouragement as work on the manuscript progressed, and to Jerry Brody, Watson Smith, and Joe Ben Wheat, who also carefully evaluated the first draft of the text and offered their comments. Others who have contributed information and assistance include Jack Campbell, Howard Davidson, Tom Dickerson, Charles Di Peso, Campbell Grant, Julian Hayden, Harry O. King, Pat Neitfeld, Christy Turner, Gwinn Vivian, Klaus Wellmann, and Leland Wyman. The final typing of the manuscript was done by Barbara Stanislawski.

Without the enthusiastic cooperation of numerous people throughout the Southwest, many important sites would have been inaccessible or would have remained unknown for the purposes of this book. Assistance in fieldwork, which included guiding us to sites, hospitality, and the occasional loan of a vehicle, was provided by Edward Abbey, Kee Begay, Deedee Blank, Roy Blank, Edward Bull, Lou Cawley, Jack Cawley, Robert Childress, John Davis, Marguerite Davis, Dody Fugate, Paul Fugate, Harry Hadlock, Sally Hadlock, Peter Koch, David Laing, Jennifer Laing, Clay Miller, Jody Miller, Pat Vivian, and Leo Threadgill. In addition I had the cooperation of National Park Service personnel at Canyon de Chelly, Navajo, Organ Pipe, Petrified Forest, and Saguaro national mounments and at Canyonlands National Park.

A special note of appreciation is due the members of my family, Curt, Hoski, and Pieter, who usually accompanied me in the field, and especially to Curt for his willingness to discuss problems at length and for his advice and support throughout.

INDIAN ROCK ART
OF THE SOUTHWEST

1

Introduction:
Images on Stone

For several thousand years the Indians of the American Southwest have been using as canvas and drawing board the rock surfaces of canyon walls, rock-shelters, and talus boulders that characterize the arid terrain of this region. The drawings produced by the application of paint (rock paintings) or the cutting away of the rock surface (petroglyphs) are examples of what is known as rock art. They were made for many purposes by the peoples who have occupied this area, from the early hunter-gatherer populations to the present-day Pueblos, Navajos, and Apaches (Figs. 1, 2).

These images pecked into or painted on stone are a valuable component of the archaeological record—graphic images that often derive from the various aspects of prehistoric cosmologies and mythic systems. Some prehistoric ideologies of the Southwest have been carried into the ethnographic present by the modern descendants of the prehistoric peoples, but other such systems, with the exception of what can be learned through the visual imagery of the petroglyphs and rock paintings, have been almost totally lost. Rock art, then, is an important means of reaching some understanding of the sacred dimension and certain related practices of the prehistoric period.

In addition, rock art provides other kinds of information for the archaeologist. It is a sensitive tool, seen through its many stylistic manifestations, for identifying cultural relationships, patterns of communication,

Figure 1. Petroglyph made by hunter-gatherers, Arroyo Hondo, Taos County, New Mexico. Circles about 4 inches in diameter. New Mexico State Planning Office; photograph, Curtis Schaafsma.

Figure 2. Navajo horsemen and deer, Canyon de Chelly, Arizona. Horses approximately a foot long. Photograph, Karl Kernberger.

evidence of trade, and other types of cultural contact. Changes in style and content of rock art are often indications of the adoption of new ideologies and religious practices, which in turn reflect other shifts within the cultural matrix.

The age of the oldest rock drawings in the Southwest has not been determined; but 2,000 years of work can be safely documented, and at least another thousand years should be added to account for those petroglyphs attributable to the preceramic cultures at a hunting-and-gathering level of existence. Even this estimate may eventually prove conservative. The time period involved and the regional diversity in culture and environment are factors contributing to the variety of rock art styles in this area.

Southwestern rock art styles fall basically into two categories, representational and abstract (Figs. 3, 4). Sometimes, however, elements of both occur together within a single style.

Representational art in the Southwest is almost always concerned with the depiction of life-forms such as human figures, anthropomorphic supernatural beings, quadrupeds, birds, snakes, and so on. Occasionally plants are represented. Representational art is rarely naturalistic. Elements depicting figures from the natural world, rather than approaching the subjects with realism, are stylized to a greater or lesser degree. This stylization results in a limited number of distinctive figure types for any given class of subject matter. *Abstract* elements or styles are divorced from the real-life image either completely, with no representation of this type intended, or sufficiently so that any resemblance to the real world is lost to the uninitiated.

Style names, as used here and elsewhere in rock art studies (Heizer and Baumhoff 1962; Hedges 1973; Grant 1967), sometimes include "abstract" or "representational" as descriptive terms.

An evaluation of southwestern rock art from an aesthetic point of view indicates that there is no correlation between the degree of sophistication in the art and the level of cultural development of the authoring group. Indeed, noteworthy artistic achievements were attained by the hunter-gatherers as well as by horticulturalists living in large towns.

In this volume, the many rock art styles that occur in Utah, Arizona, New Mexico, and the adjacent parts of northern Chihuahua and West Texas are described and discussed within the context of the various cultures that produced them. Wherever possible, the ways in which the art functioned and the meanings various elements and symbols may have had are also considered.

Figure 3.   Life-size anthropomorphic figures and animals, Temple Mountain Wash, Utah. Photograph, Karl Kernberger.

Figure 4. Chihuahuan Polychrome Abstract Style paintings at Hueco Tanks, near El Paso, Texas. These paintings are attributable to the Archaic period. Photograph, Karl Kernberger.

A HISTORY OF ROCK ART STUDIES

The American Southwest is only one of many places where rock art occurs. Throughout the world, rock drawings are both monuments to man's achievements as an artist and documents of various aspects of his social and religious life, reflecting his myths, beliefs, and magical practices.[1] Probably the oldest rock art known is that of the Ice Age hunters of western Europe. Much research has been conducted and many books written on the spectacular paintings from the European caves, and thus these ancient masterpieces immediately come to mind when the subject of rock art is broached (Breuil 1952; Ucko and Rosenfeld 1967).

Rock art in the United States is only now emerging as a subject of general concern to archaeologists and Indian art historians. In many geographic regions, such as the Southwest, however, rock drawings are by far the most readily accessible and prolifically occurring products of prehistoric artistic endeavor, and the literature that has accumulated on the subject over the years is considerable.[2]

In the Southwest, the area of our concern, salvage projects in the early 1960s initiated a continuing study of rock art. Rock art research was conducted in Glen Canyon in southern Utah and northern Arizona and on the Pine and San Juan rivers in northern New Mexico and southern Colorado before the Glen Canyon and Navajo dams flooded these drainages (Turner 1963; P. Schaafsma 1963). A subsequent rock art project was carried out along the upper Rio Grande before the construction of Cochiti Dam above the pueblo of Cochiti (P. Schaafsma 1975).[3]

Nevertheless, in the Southwest as elsewhere in North America, rock art studies have lagged behind other archaeological research. There are several reasons for this. Archaeologists, preferring to deal with excavations and the data thus obtained, have chosen to ignore rock art rather than add this seemingly enigmatic body of material to their burden of analysis. In some instances, the lack of associated cultural remains has made it difficult to date or assign rock art to a specific cultural period. Underlying these problems is the rather diffuse bias on the part of many archaeologists that rock art, unlike other cultural remains, lacks order, a definite structure or patterning that can be used as a guideline for analysis. A certain amount of this prejudice may have arisen from the earliest rock art studies, in which investigators were primarily concerned with trait or element tracking. This approach was not fruitful and served to fracture and obscure the stylistic complexes that later scholars have found to be the primary tool for ordering the immense and varied body of raw data of rock drawings. As a result, the subject was conveniently tabled, and an integrated body of information on rock art comparable to that available on other types of archaeological remains has been lacking.

Fortunately, recent rock art research has served to dispel this prejudice. The fact that rock art is structured, in the same way that all archaeological data conform to discernible patterns, has been well established.

THE STUDY OF ROCK ART: A THEORETICAL FRAMEWORK

Basic to a meaningful approach to the study of rock art is an understanding of how rock art is structured. Variation in the patterns within the art can then be described and used to inform the archaeologist of meaningful variation within the broader cultural context. Second, how the art relates to the total cultural complex needs to be considered. Finally, interpretation of the content of the art may be attempted, particularly if ethnographic information is available.

The Concept of Style

The recognition of rock art styles is basic to the ordering of data concerning rock art. That "human behavior is not capricious but is patterned" (Martin and Plog 1973:24) is a fundamental premise, of course, that has always underlain systematic investigations of human activity, and it has been well demonstrated that the art of any cultural group conforms to the confines of a style or a limited range of styles. The recognition of styles in rock art and the use of these styles to correlate rock art with particular prehistoric cultures is not new to rock art studies. Perhaps one of the earliest instances of documented recognition of the correlation between art styles and prehistoric cultures is to be found in a comment by Crimmins:

> In January, 1925, we wrote to Dr. Fewkes that the study of the petroglyphs on Senator A. B. Fall's ranch at Three Rivers, New Mexico, led us to believe that many of them were made by the pre-Pueblo Indians, as they were similar in design to the pictures on

the pottery of the Mimbres Indians. Dr. Fewkes wrote us as follows: "So far as known to me, this is the first time in the history of archaeological research in the Southwest, that pictographs have served as guides to locate native cultures in the Pueblo region." (1929:38)

Following this, a number of rock art studies recognized the concept of style (Steward 1929; Morss 1931; Cressman 1937; Haury 1945b). These investigations have been followed by recent works that take for granted the utility of this concept and that relate rock art styles to specific prehistoric or historic cultural groups (Baumhoff, Heizer, and Elsasser 1958; Heizer and Baumhoff 1962; Turner 1963; Grant 1965, 1968; Newcomb and Kirkland 1967; P. Schaafsma 1963, 1971, 1972; Burton 1971; Hedges 1973; Heizer and Clewlow 1973). In the organization of data into style categories, a number of different methods have been used, the simplest being based on mere inspection of the material. More exact methods have involved the use of statistics and factor analysis in order to measure the occurrences of given elements or to determine how certain traits cluster for the purpose of describing definite figure types (Heizer and Baumhoff 1962; Von Werlhof 1965; Burton 1971).

It is worthwhile, perhaps, to examine the meaning of the word *style* and to clarify its use in rock art studies. Among the major components of style in regard to rock art are the element inventory and the specific figure types making up this inventory. A figure type is the specific form and characteristic mode of expression of any given element. Important in the development of figure types are the major design components and the shapes employed. Second, the forms used and the relationships between the elements of a panel work together to create an overall aesthetic quality of expression that in many instances is an important aspect of style. The various technical means employed in creating designs also contribute to the general sense of style and its aesthetic consideration (P. Schaafsma 1971:3).

Schapiro (1953) noted that style is studied more often by the archaeologist as a diagnostic means than for its own sake as an important constituent of culture. Further, he points out that the characteristics of styles vary continuously and resist systematic classification into perfectly distinct groups, but that precise limits are sometimes fixed by convention for simplicity in dealing with historical problems. Common to the approach of the art historian or anthropologist is the assumption that every style is peculiar to a period of culture and that in a given culture or epoch of culture there is only one style or at least a limited range of styles. Therefore, style can be used with confidence as an independent clue to the time and place of origin of a work of art. Thus its use as an archaeological tool is justified.

The style concept is not a static one, however. Once a style has been described and its range of distribution determined, it is necessary to understand the significance of this information in a wider archaeological context. Regional variation also may be present within the bounds of the style, and it is the aim of the archaeologist to explain this variation, or even the lack of it, rather than merely describing it. In order to do this, one must have some idea of how rock art is articulated with the prehistoric cultural system of which it is a part.

The major subsystems of a cultural system have been classified as technological, sociological, and ideological (Binford 1962), and the functioning of any of these so-called subsystems leaves behind material evidence that reflects the nature of the component. *Art* is an artifactual or material record of the ideological component of a prehistoric social system.

With this understanding, rock art studies can proceed on at least two different levels of investigation—regional and local. It has been proposed that the term *interaction sphere* be used to deal with regional configurations in an archaeological context (Struever 1972). The concept of the interaction sphere is applicable to areas of stylistic uniformity. Stylistic uniformity results from a panregional information exchange network, and the degree of homogeneity in a region depends on the efficiency of the intergroup communications (C. Schaafsma 1973:12, 26–27). A shared repertoire of rock art elements, figure types, figure complexes, and aesthetic modes—hence *style*—thus signifies participation in a given ideographic system and, in turn, in a given communication network. The spatial and temporal distribution of a style, once determined, can be used as an aid in defining the range of the communication network and hence the sociocultural system being considered. Regional differences within the style may denote regional variation within the culture.

At the local level, minor variation within a style, such as different element inventories between contemporaneous sites, may indicate that these sites served different needs. This brings us to the subject of how rock drawings functioned for the people who made them. The means to understanding this are several.

The Function of Rock Art Sites

How rock art sites functioned is a major concern in reconstructing the lives of prehistoric groups when these sites are present in the cultural inventory. Information may be limited to the contents and the situation of the site itself. Or it may be known how it correlates with other contemporaneous prehistoric remains (habitation sites and trails) as well as with geographic features such as hilltops, canyon junctions, and water sources. In most instances the rock art of a specific cultural group exhibits patterned modes of distribution. Using this kind of information, Heizer and Baumhoff (1962) and Grant (1968) have made a convincing case that the Great Basin Abstract petroglyphs of Nevada and eastern California were made in connection with hunting rituals. Likewise, White (1965), Zahniser (1970), Kearns (1973), and others have attempted to correlate Hohokam rock art sites with a number of different kinds of Hohokam remains (see pp. 96–99).

A consideration of the location as well as the contents of Paleolithic paintings in Europe has led scholars to suggest that these ancient works, dating over thousands of years, were done for a multitude of reasons. As summarized by Ucko and Rosenfeld:

> There is nothing against assuming that Palaeolithic art, as is also the art of many living "primitives," is the result of many different interests. Within any one cave, therefore, it is possible to imagine that many . . . possibilities . . . apply: that some representations were the work of children (perhaps some of the floor engravings), that some were used in acts of sympathetic magic (perhaps some of the representations pierced with holes), that some were placed in particular situations in order to please (perhaps some of the open-air low reliefs), and that some were illustrations of myths and traditions (perhaps those which contain imaginary creatures, anthropomorphs and unexpected combinations of animal species). It is very possible, however, that some and perhaps many Paleolithic representations were made for reasons which still totally escape the modern observer. (1967:239)

Ethnographic documents of modern tribes in Africa and Australia substantiate the multiuse interpretation set forth by Ucko and Rosenfeld on the basis of archaeological evidence (Frobenius and Fox 1937:22–24; Moore

1971:117–19). The fact that many Australian sites are currently in use or are subject to ethnographic interpretation has contributed to an understanding of how rock art sites have been used by people everywhere. Specifically, these sites have provided models for suggesting how hunter-gatherer sites may have functioned in the Southwest.

In the Southwest, however, the use of ethnographic analogy can also be much more specific. Ethnographic documentation on the use of rock art sites by recent Pueblos and Navajos can by extension aid the archaeologist in understanding the function of prehistoric or protohistoric sites of these same people. Or, individual rock art elements may be interpreted ethnographically. For example, modern Pueblo use of the hand print, a common element in rock art (Fig. 5), has suggested its meaning in certain prehistoric occurrences.

In sum, the combined use of ethnographic analogy, both generally and within a single ongoing culture, and analysis of sites and their relationships to other remains has suggested many uses and functions for southwestern rock art before historic times. The creative activity of painting and carving designs on stone was not narrowly focused, nor do these remains as a rule represent doodling and play, as is sometimes postulated. Rather, they were more often integrated with a wide range of needs, just as artistic enterprises permeate many facets of all modern cultures.

Symbolism and Interpretation

The relationship between rock art and its cultural matrix is all very well, but of surpassing interest to most general readers are the questions: What does it mean? Are these rock drawings a language awaiting interpretation? Interpreting rock art designs is intriguing yet difficult, often impossible. As a result, other, more fruitful approaches to rock art have been devised.

Whenever an interpretation of rock art by the archaeologist is possible, it is usually made so through the use of the ethnological record, just as ethnographic accounts contribute to an understanding of the function of rock art sites. Certain general interpretations have been arrived at by comparing elements in the rock art with various aspects of shamanistic symbolism. A number of basic shamanistic beliefs recur throughout the world, and the elements of these beliefs are present in the native religions of this continent. Rock art from a number of different places in North America has been examined from the point of view of shamanism (Hedges 1975; Wellmann 1975; Vastokas and Vastokas 1973). In many instances, figure complexes and

Figure 5. White hand prints, Tsegi Phase, Inscription House, Arizona. Photograph, David Noble.

symbolism found in the rock art of the Southwest seem to be explainable within the context of shamanic beliefs and practices.

Further, ethnographic sources are especially useful in those instances in which we are dealing with prehistoric or protohistoric records of the same Indian cultures that exist in the Southwest today, such as the Pueblos and Navajos. In many cases, specific supernatural beings can be identified in the rock art of these peoples, and even some of the more abstract symbolism of ritual design can be interpreted with a reasonable degree of certainty.

Nevertheless, it is also true that ethnographic sources should be used with caution. Fewkes (1973:64) observed that among the Hopi the meanings of many designs have been lost and that a single design can have a variety of meanings. He found, for example, that the circle is the totemic signature of the earth people but that it also means other things. Thus he did not try to interpret the circles in the designs of the prehistoric pottery with which he was dealing. He also pointed out that most of the ancient pottery symbols were incomprehensible to the modern Hopi priests, although the priests suggested many—and differing—interpretations for the designs.

Ellis and Hammack (1968:35), in referring to the concentric circles from Arrow Grotto, state that this ancient symbol is so standardized in Pueblo explanation as possibly to warrant designation as a glyph—the outer circle representing the light around the sun, the second the sun himself, and the dot his umbilicus (Fig. 6). Several years ago, however, while visiting some petroglyphs near the Hopi reservation, I was informed by a knowledgeable Hopi that this symbol represents the earth, the center circle or dot standing

Figure 6. Concentric circles painted in white in rock shelter beside Arrow Grotto and Feather Cave near Capitan, New Mexico. Both sun and earth symbolism seem to be present in this simple figure. Circles 6 to 8 inches in diameter. New Mexico State Planning Office; photograph, Curtis Schaafsma.

for the water in the earth's center. Nevertheless, it should be pointed out that in this particular instance the apparent contradiction may be superficial. Heyden (1975:143) expresses the opinion that sky and earth were inseparable in ancient myth and thought in Mexico, and he cites the fact that Sahagún (1969, IV:172) refers to the Sun-Earth as one. That this duality is also present in Pueblo thought is made explicit by Ellis and Hammack (1968) in their reference to Arrow Grotto as a combined earth and sun shrine.

An interesting case of symbol diffusion on the Great Plains that serves as a model along the lines of which change in symbolic meaning occurs has been described by Spier (1921). Among the Plains tribes, there was a wider distribution of rites and regalia, including symbols, than there were shared features of organization and mythological beliefs. This situation occurred because objective phenomena were readily diffused between neighboring tribes, but the borrower would not necessarily have the opportunity or desire to learn the esoteric connections and complex web of meanings of the borrowed goods. The new user was often satisfied with an explanation of a ceremonial object furnished by his own beliefs (Spier 1921:517). In this way, symbolic meanings were constantly changing as they were passed on between even similar groups of people.

The baffling nature of the content of rock drawings continues to spark the imagination of the uninitiated, providing a kind of Rorschach test in which the observer projects onto the drawings meanings that coincide with cultural biases and personal and popular fantasies. Among the most common of these "folk interpretations" is that a particular petroglyph or painting represents a map to treasure buried somewhere in the vicinity. Finding a "story" that can be "read" in the depictions is also common. There are also the very popular volumes that see in rock art, as well as in other archaeological remains, evidence of sunken continents or ancient visitors from outer space.

One of the most persistent misconceptions is the notion that all Indian rock art is, in fact, a form of writing. Although this possibility has been considered by various writers for some time, a recent book by Martineau (1973) develops this thesis most explicitly. It is his contention that rock art is rock writing—a pan-Indian system akin to sign language, applicable everywhere, regardless of cultural affiliations or the time in question. This system he attempts to "crack" by the application of the tools of cryptanalysis. His hypothesis, however, is not substantiated by archaeology. The fact that universal meanings are lacking for symbols commonly found in rock drawings has been admirably discussed by Renaud (1936:5), Cain (1950:54), and recently by Heizer and Clewlow (1973:51–52).

Dating Rock Art

One of the major problems presented by the study of rock art is that of dating the art. Several approaches, in some cases used together, have made possible the chronological ordering of southwestern rock art styles as they are described in the following pages. The ability to date a particular site absolutely is rare, but various methods provide means of relative dating.

Patination is an important means of determining the relative ages of petroglyphs made at different times on the same cliff or boulder surface. Patina is the formation of a black or brown stain of hydrous iron and manganese oxides on rock surfaces (Grant 1967:43). When a petroglyph is made, the design is pecked or scratched through this surface so that the original color of the rock is exposed. On this exposed surface, a new layer of

Figure 7. Rosa Representational (A.D. 700–1000) and Gobernador Representational Style (A.D. 1700–1775) petroglyphs in the Largo Canyon drainage, northwestern New Mexico, showing differences in degrees of patination and superimposition. New Mexico State Planning Office; photograph, Curtis Schaafsma.

patina immediately begins to form. The older the figure is, the darker it becomes. If two or more figures on a surface were made at different times, the more recent one will be lighter in color (Fig. 7). Because patina varies with the composition of the rock and its exposure to sun and rain, however, the degree of patination alone is not an absolute guide for dating.

Superimposition is another way to determine the relative age of rock art. Designs were sometimes painted or pecked on top of older ones, and in some cases the figures of several different styles and periods were made in the same spot. When the superimpositions are petroglyphs, the difference in patination between the periods of work will indicate, at least roughly, whether much or little time elapsed between the points at which they were made. Where designs were pecked or painted over others of the same style and no age differences are apparent, we may be dealing with a narrower time span.

Vertical placement of styles on a cliff face or within a rock-shelter can also be an important indication of age. In the river canyons of the Colorado Plateau during early prehistoric times, for example, petroglyphs were sometimes made from the tops of sand dunes lying against the cliffs. The dunes were often removed later by floods, and petroglyphs were made by subsequent canyon occupants in the scars left by the dunes. Thus vertical stratigraphy is present today, with the oldest work on top. Similarly, ledges in rock-shelters and along cliffs often enabled early artists to reach locations now inaccessible, and the work of later cultural groups, made after the ledges fell, is often present below.

The association of habitation debris with rock art is sometimes very helpful. In the Southwest, rock art often occurs with habitation sites of the Hohokam, Mogollon, and Anasazi horticulturalists. Frequently these sites can be placed within a given time frame by the pottery types present. In late Anasazi sites very specific dates are sometimes obtainable for the rock art that was made from the rooftops of cliff dwellings. Some of this originated within the fifty-year period between A.D. 1250 and A.D. 1300.

One of the most useful means of ordering the chronology of certain rock art styles has been the comparison of rock art figures with those on datable artifacts such as pottery or clay pipes, or wall plaster in the ruins themselves (Figs. 8, 9). A major stylistic break occurring in the mural art of the Anasazi around A.D. 1300–1350 has assisted in dating a comparable change in the Anasazi Pueblo rock art.

Limitations on absolute dates are sometimes provided by the content of the art itself. The first appearance of the bow as a hunting weapon, replacing the spear and the atlatl, is dated in Arizona as early as A.D. 200. It spread eastward across New Mexico, reaching West Texas between A.D. 600 and A.D. 1000 (Grant 1968:50–51; Newcomb and Kirkland 1967:40). The appearance of the bow in rock art, particularly in the northern Chihuahua and West Texas region, has been helpful in establishing the earliest possible date for these paintings. Conversely, styles in which the spear is emphasized must be earlier in date than those in which the bow is depicted.

The horse is another element with obvious temporal restrictions. The presence of this animal in a rock art panel indicates beyond any doubt that one is dealing with art of the historic period. First brought to this continent by the Spaniards in the sixteenth century, the horse was becoming popular among the Apaches of New Mexico by the first half of the seventeenth century (Clark 1966:8). Horses became a favorite motif in Apache rock drawings, presumably at this time or shortly thereafter; they first occur in Navajo art in the early eighteenth century.

Finally, some of the late rock art of the Navajo depicts specific historical events, such as the Spanish expedition into Canyon del Muerto that ended with the tragedy at Massacre Cave in 1805 and the Ute invasion of the same

Figure 8. Bighorn sheep, Jornada Style, below Cook's Peak, Mimbres River drainage, New Mexico. Figure about a foot tall. New Mexico State Planning Office; photograph, Curtis Schaafsma.

Figure 9. Bighorn sheep on Classic Mimbres Black-on-white bowl. Photograph, Fred Stimson.

canyon in 1858. Presumably the paintings of the Spaniards and their horses and the charcoal drawings depicting the encounter with the Utes were made within a few years of the events themselves (see Chapter 9).

AIMS AND CONSIDERATIONS

This volume describes the many rock art styles of the Southwest, beginning with the oldest and ending with those of the historic period (Fig. 10). The styles are examined in their archaeological contexts. Wider stylistic relationships, the origin of styles, traditions through time, and stylistic variation are also mentioned, and their significance is considered within the cultural framework. Whenever possible, the functions that the rock art sites may have served and the meaning of the designs are considered. This study will demonstrate the usefulness of rock art as a tool for widening our understanding of prehistoric cultural systems in the Southwest.

A framework for the whole discussion is provided by the cultural classifications of southwestern archaeology (Fig. 11). The earliest cultural level to which rock art can be ascribed is a hunter-gatherer adaptation, variously referred to as the Desert Culture or the Western Archaic (Davis 1963; Martin and Plog 1973:69–80). This period dates in the Southwest from approximately 5500 B.C. to the beginning of the horticultural period around A.D. 1 in Arizona and most of New Mexico and persisting later by several hundred years in eastern New Mexico and West Texas. Rock art assigned to this period is found throughout much of the Southwest and is estimated to date from possibly as late as A.D. 700–800 in the eastern part of the area and to go back in time at least as far as 1000 B.C. and perhaps earlier.

There is evidence to suggest that various regional manifestations of the Western Archaic were the progenitors of the horticulturalists who followed around A.D. 1, with the possible exception of the Hohokam. Although corn was being grown in the Southwest as early as 2000 B.C., not until much later did horticulture become a way of life. It took many hundreds of years before domesticates became significant enough to effect a change from a nomadic, hunting-and-gathering existence to a sedentary, farming one. When this occurred, the resulting increase in the population of the Southwest produced a corresponding increase in the quantity of archaeological remains, including rock art.

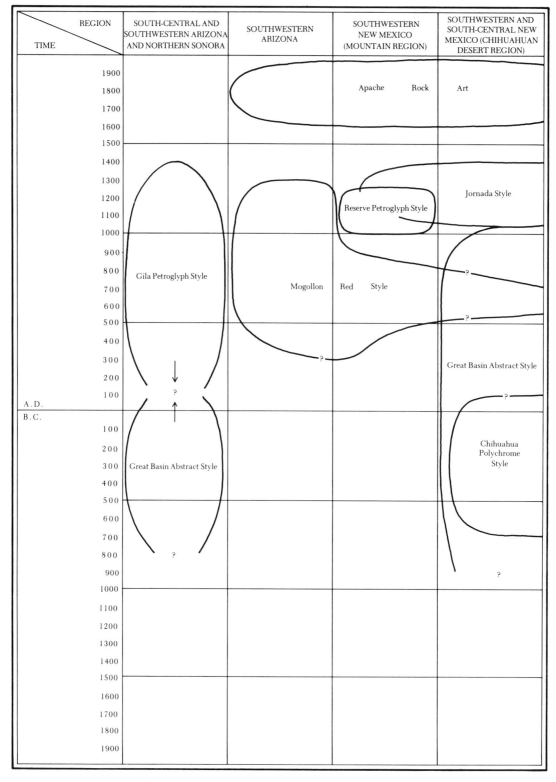

Figure 10. Space-time chart showing the distribution and approximate dates of Southwestern rock art styles.

EL PASO–CARLSBAD WEST TEXAS CHIHUAHUA	EASTERN UTAH (WEST OF COLORADO RIVER)	NORTHERN ARIZONA SOUTHERN UTAH	NORTHWESTERN NEW MEXICO	NORTH CENTRAL NEW MEXICO (RIO GRANDE DRAINAGE)
Apache Rock Art		Historic Navajo Rock Art		
			Gobernador Representational Style	
		Rio	Grande	Style
Jornada Style		Tsegi Painted Style	Anasazi Rock Art Styles Designations Lacking	
	Northern and Southern San Rafael Styles	Kayenta Representational Style		
		Virgin Representational Style		
	Classic Vernal Style	Cave Valley Style (Western Utah)		
Mogollon Red Style		Chinle Representational Style (Arizona)	Rosa Representational Style	
Diablo Dam Petroglyph Style				A.D.
				B.C.
Candelaria Painted Style	Barrier Canyon Anthropomorphic Style	San Juan Anthropomorphic Style		
Pecos River Style (Peripheral)				
?				
Miniature Paintings		Glen Canyon Linear Style		Great Basin Abstract Style
?				
Chihuahua	Polychrome Style			
	?	?		
		?		
Great Basin Abstract Style				?
?				

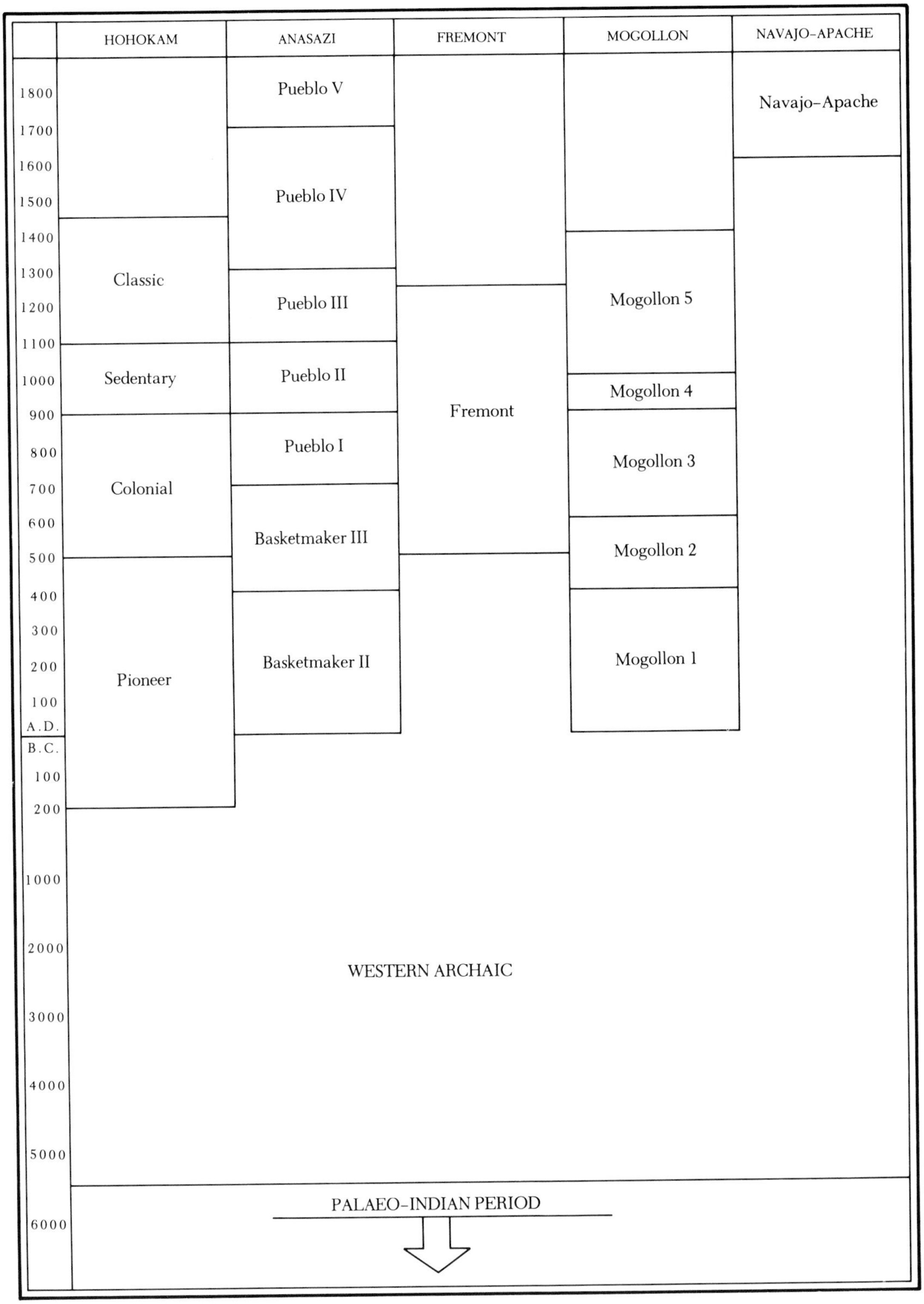

	HOHOKAM	ANASAZI	FREMONT	MOGOLLON	NAVAJO–APACHE
1800		Pueblo V			Navajo–Apache
1700					
1600		Pueblo IV			
1500					
1400	Classic			Mogollon 5	
1300		Pueblo III			
1200			Fremont		
1100					
1000	Sedentary	Pueblo II		Mogollon 4	
900					
800	Colonial	Pueblo I		Mogollon 3	
700					
600		Basketmaker III		Mogollon 2	
500					
400					
300		Basketmaker II		Mogollon 1	
200	Pioneer				
100					
A.D.					
B.C.					
100					
200					
1000					
2000		WESTERN ARCHAIC			
3000					
4000					
5000					
		PALAEO–INDIAN PERIOD			
6000					

Figure 11.   Chart of southwestern chronology. The vertical time range before A.D. 1 has been shortened.

The major southwestern horticultural traditions are the Hohokam, the Mogollon, and the Anasazi (Map 1). The Hohokam occupied the river valleys and Lower Sonoran desert life zone of southern Arizona, and the Mogollon occupied the highlands to the east in southern Arizona and New Mexico, and also the Chihuahuan Desert as far east as West Texas and adjacent parts of Chihuahua. The Anasazi lived in the higher elevations of the Colorado Plateau across southern Utah and northern New Mexico and Arizona. These cultural traditions had their beginnings sometime around A.D. 1 or slightly before and existed for fifteen hundred years or more. Each is distinguished by distinctive developments in architecture, ceramics, and other cultural remains, and each produced its own styles of rock art.

At the same time, the Fremont culture, dating roughly between A.D. 700 and A.D. 1200 in Utah on the northern periphery of the Southwest, developed an art style based on Anasazi motifs from the south. Some of the most spectacular petroglyph sites in the Southwest are of Fremont origin, and the Fremont rock art is included in this review.

The archaeological record of the Hakataya of western Arizona differs significantly from that of the Hohokam, Mogollon, and Anasazi. Contemporaneous with horticultural groups elsewhere in the Southwest, these ancestors of the modern Yumans added corn and ceramics to their cultural inventory about A.D. 650 (Willey 1966:Fig. 4-6). Nothing is known of their rock art, so it could not be included in this study.

The cultures of the Mogollon and the Hohokam ended as recognizable configurations sometime in the fifteenth century. The Anasazi, referred to as Pueblos in more recent times, persisted, albeit with certain changes. Many of these changes occurred during the fourteenth century, introduced by innovations from the Mogollon, who at that time still occupied adjacent regions in southern New Mexico. It is significant here only to point out that at that time a new rock art tradition was adopted by the Pueblos in lieu of the old Anasazi art. The new configuration has been consistently maintained for more than six hundred years and is manifest today in the ceremonial art of the Pueblo world. It has also served as the basis for the ritual art of the Navajo and the Apache, Athabaskan latecomers to the Southwest.

This volume concludes with a discussion of the rock art of these recent groups. The earliest Navajo rock paintings and petroglyphs date from the 1700s and are located in the San Juan River drainage of northwestern New Mexico. These works are ceremonial in nature and are ancestral in style and content to modern Navajo drypainting. In the twentieth century, Navajo rock

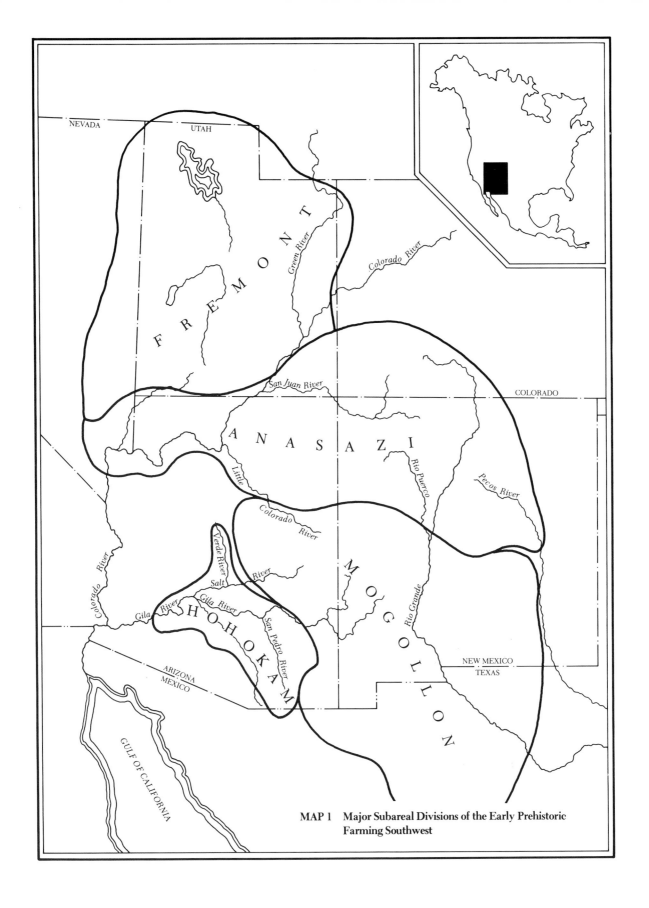

NEVADA

UTAH

F R E M O N T

Green River

Colorado River

COLORADO

San Juan River

A N A S A Z I

Little

Colorado River

Rio Puerco

Pecos River

Verde River

River

Salt

Colorado River

Gila River

Gila River

H O H O K A M

San Pedro River

M O G O L L O N

Rio Grande

ARIZONA

MEXICO

NEW MEXICO

TEXAS

GULF OF CALIFORNIA

MAP 1   Major Subareal Divisions of the Early Prehistoric
Farming Southwest

art has become secularized and influenced by contact with Western culture. Apache rock art is less well known and discrete styles have not been identified, although sites attributable to this widely dispersed group are found throughout southern New Mexico and Arizona.

In sum, the modern ceremonial art of the southwestern Indians is preceded by hundreds of years of tradition, documented by the thousands of rock drawings scattered across desert and mesa. The importance of these drawings on stone to our understanding of culture history and art in the Southwest cannot be underestimated.

NOTES

1. To mention just a few references, rock art has been documented in studies from Siberia (Okladnikov 1969), Central Asia (Ksica 1960), various parts of Africa (Culwick 1931; Cunnison 1951; Mori 1972; Pager 1975; Fosbroke and Marealle 1952; Goodall, Cooke, and Clark 1959), Arabia (Anati 1970), India (Wakankar 1962, 1976), Australia (Moore 1971; Lommel 1976), Panama (Harte 1960), the Caribbean Islands (Fewkes 1903b; Frasseto 1960; Huckerby 1914), South America (Pollak-Eltz and Bull 1975; Von der Osten 1946; Pederson 1963; Gardner 1931), Baja California (Meighan 1969; Grant 1974; Crosby 1975), and Canada (Dewdney 1959; Dewdney and Kidd 1962; Vastokas and Vastokas 1973; Swauger 1962).

2. Some of the first observations on the scope of the rock art in this country were made in J. W. Powell (1881:75), and these were followed shortly by the classic works on American rock art by Garrick Mallery (1886, 1893). Following Mallery, the only major publications on the general subject for almost seventy years are Julian Steward's *Petroglyphs of California and Adjoining States* (1929) and "Petroglyphs of the United States" (1937). The next major overview of North American rock art is Campbell Grant's recent volume (1967), soon to be followed by Wellmann's treatise (in press).

Earlier regional studies include publications by Jackson (1938) and Gebhard (1960) on Texas rock art, Cain (1950) on Washington petroglyphs, Cressman (1937) on Oregon petroglyphs, Gebhard (1951) on Wyoming rock art, and Shumate (1960) on central Montana rock art. Since the publication in 1962 of Heizer and Baumhoff's volume on the rock art of eastern California and Nevada, rock art studies have been on the increase, particularly in the western states. In California, Heizer and Baumhoff's study was followed by a survey of the rock art of the entire state (Heizer and Clewlow 1973) and by regional studies by Grant on the rock art of the Chumash Indians (1965) and in the Coso Range (1968) and by Hedges (1973) on southern California in general. Newcomb and Kirkland (1967) presented the second comprehensive study on rock art in Texas, which integrates and amplifies Jackson's basically descriptive work. The recent volume by Swauger (1974), *Rock Art of the Upper Ohio Valley,* is a major contribution to the study of rock art of the eastern United States. A listing of many additional references to rock art studies throughout the United States, Canada, and Latin America is present in Heizer and Clewlow (1973:48–49), and Meade (1968) has published an annotated bibliography of rock art north of Mexico.

3. Further studies of southwestern rock art include the early work of Guernsey and Kidder (1921), Morss (1931), Steward (1941), Haury (1945b), Cosgrove (1947), and recent investigations by Clark (1974), White (1965), Pilles (1974), and Smith (1974). Statewide rock art surveys have also been conducted in Utah and New Mexico (P. Schaafsma 1971, 1972). Numerous other specific studies of the rock drawings of particular sites add substantially to the broad data base established by the regional investigations.

2

Techniques:
Brush and Hammerstone

Rock drawings were made in a number of different ways, and the method or combination of methods chosen to execute designs on rock is one aspect of style. There are two major technical categories: rock paintings, and petroglyphs, or designs cut into rock. The ambiguous term "pictograph," which has a long history of usage in the literature and may refer to either rock paintings alone or to both painted and cut figures, is not used in this volume.

ROCK PAINTINGS

Rock paintings are usually found on the light-colored rock surfaces of protected places such as rock-shelters and beneath overhangs where there is little or no patina (Plate 1). Of the colors used for these paintings, red, white, black, and orange are the most common, with red predominating. Yellow and pink also occur from time to time. Green and blue are rare but are occasionally found. The colors used were determined by the materials available as well as, at least in some cases, by ritual requirements.

Paint consists of three major components: the pigment or coloring agent, a binder used to stabilize the paint and cause it to adhere to the surface to which it is applied, and the vehicle, the means by which it is made fluid (Hibben 1975:36).

The pigment, consisting of a lump of clay or other mineral, was ground up in preparation for mixing with the other ingredients. The paints used in southwestern rock paintings have not been tested for their constituent parts, but the pigments used in the kiva mural art of the Hopi ruins of Awatovi and Kawaika-a have been analyzed in detail; for an excellent discussion of the results, see Watson Smith (1952:22–24). Astonishingly similar results are reported from Pottery Mound by Hibben (1975:36–48). It is reasonable to suppose that the pigments used in rock paintings did not differ appreciably from those of the mural paintings.

The various shades of red can probably be ascribed to the use of the mineral hematite, or red iron oxide. Limonite was probably the source for yellow, while orange was in all likelihood obtained from a combination of these. Malachite is the most obvious source for green pigment and azurite for bright blue. Turquoise paint may have been obtained from grinding up turquoise itself. White clay was often used for painting, although silica, gypsum, chalk, or calcium carbonate are other possible sources indicated by the mural paint analysis. Clays stained with other minerals produce various pastel shades, and these were used for rock painting, particularly by thirteenth-century Anasazi; colors include subtle shades of pinks, salmon, lavender, and pale green. An organic material such as charcoal or another form of carbon would have been a readily available source for black paint.

The vehicle and binding agent were combined into a single fluid to which the ground pigment was added. It is likely that water was commonly used to create the desired consistency of the paint, but the binding medium used in the mural paints has never been determined because there is no evidence of it left. Judging by what is known from ethnographic sources, the binding medium was probably any one of a number of organic substances. The Hopis, in painting ceremonial objects, use saliva generated by chewing a variety of seeds that contain a vegetable oil; sometimes, but not always, water is added (Smith 1952:30). Smith also reports the use as a binding agent of yucca juice or syrup, water and white bean meal, piñon gum for preparing blue and green paints, and the whites of eagle eggs (1952:31).

Once the paint was mixed, it could be applied in several ways, and the rock surface, particularly when sandstone was involved, was sometimes smoothed and abraded in preparation for receiving the painting (Fig. 12). Brushes, possibly made from the ends of yucca leaves that had been chewed to remove the pulp and leave the strong vertical fibers, seem to have been used for painting small solid areas, clear lines, and fine details. Wider areas

Figure 12. Painted and incised Navajo supernaturals in a Delgadito Canyon shelter, northwestern New Mexico. The rock surface had been smoothed in preparation for the depiction of the figures. Further rubbing and partial loss of the figures has subsequently occurred. Figures about a foot tall. Photograph, Karl Kernberger.

Figure 13. Detail of anthropomorphs in Plate 1. Several techniques were used to produce these large figures. The thin background paint on the torsos was smeared on with the fingers. Lines of complex detail and dots in thicker paint were probably applied with brushes and fingertips. Photograph, Karl Kernberger.

27

may have been painted with a corn husk wrapped around the finger (Smith 1952:31). The use of the finger itself for painting is evident in the finger streaks left in areas painted in this manner (Fig. 13). This technique was often used to create a thin application of paint over a large area. Dots, an element commonly found in abstract paintings or as a decorative device on the human form, were usually painted with fingertips dipped in paint. Whole hand prints are also common (Plate 2). Occasionally a negative or stenciled design occurs, like the star crosses in Figure 14, which were made by spraying paint around a form. Hands are the most usual motif painted in this way. Finally, dry lines were produced by drawing directly on the rock with a stick of charcoal or a lump of soft pigment. Lines or areas of solid coloring done with a dry medium are usually less definite and very sketchy compared to painted ones.

PETROGLYPHS

Petroglyphs are more common than paintings. Throughout many regions of the Southwest these figures occur by the hundreds. Dark exposed surfaces of highly patinated sandstone and basalt cliffs and talus boulders were often selected for making petroglyphs because of the effective contrast between the original rock surfaces and the newly cut designs.

The usual method of making petroglyphs was by *pecking* (Figs. 15, 16). This was often done by means of a direct blow with a hammerstone, a tool sometimes found in association with petroglyph sites. Direct percussion does not provide precise control over the placement of the resulting peck mark or dint (Turner 1963:2). When a hammerstone was used in conjunction with a chisel, results were finer, as greater control could be exercised over the size of the dints and their spacing (Fig. 17). Another aid to achieving accurate results in the finished design was the occasional practice of lightly incising or pecking a preliminary outline. The remains of these outlines are sometimes still visible.

Even taking into account variability attributable to individual artists, differences in pecking techniques to some degree characterize different styles. Large dints and uneven outlines, for example, may be typical of one petroglyph style, while another may fairly consistently exhibit small and very even dinting.

Whether small solid figures or large outline figures were made was largely a stylistic choice within the pecking technique. Because of the greater

Figure 14. Seventeenth-century Navajo horned mask and arc of stenciled negative star images, Carrizo Canyon drainage, New Mexico. Mask approximately 15 inches across. New Mexico State Planning Office; photograph, Karl Kernberger.

Figure 15. Detail of early Anasazi flute-playing animal pecked in sandstone, northwestern New Mexico. New Mexico State Planning Office; photograph, Curtis Schaafsma.

29

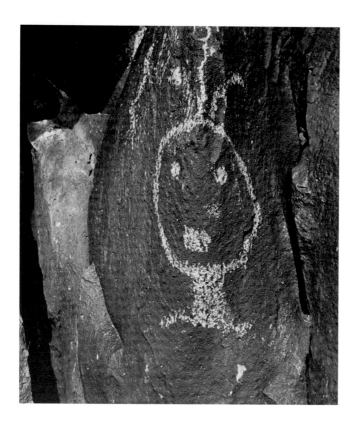

Figure 16. Pueblo IV face on corner of basalt boulder. The rock is hard and the figure shallowly pecked. La Cienega, Rio Grande Valley, New Mexico. Face about 8 inches high. New Mexico State Planning Office; photograph, Curtis Schaafsma.

Figure 17. Eighteenth-century Navajo bat, Blanco Canyon, New Mexico. The figure, about a foot across, is carefully pecked in the sandstone by indirect percussion. New Mexico State Planning Office; photograph, Curtis Schaafsma.

Figure 18. Masks, bear paw, and historic lettering incised in sandstone cliff at El Morro National Monument, New Mexico. New Mexico State Planning Office; photograph, Curtis Schaafsma.

amount of work involved, solid figures tend to be smaller. Outline figures, on the other hand, are sometimes very large and may approach life-size. Further, the use of unpecked interior space allows the addition of many details or decorative elements.

Another method of making petroglyphs is to *incise* or scratch designs into the rock with a sharp tool. Incised designs are often found on soft sandstone surfaces lacking a heavy patina, and they are characteristic of historic petroglyphs in the Southwest (Fig. 18). Designs rendered by this method lack the boldness of the pecked figures; but more fluid and expressive lines result, and greater detail is possible. Although incising tends to create a linear style, in some cases large areas were abraded, resulting in solid patterns.

In some examples, two or more techniques were used together. Scratched or incised details, for example, were sometimes added to both pecked and painted figures. In other instances, pecked figures were also painted.

The reasons for the different technical methods chosen by prehistoric artists are not always clear, but a major determinant in this matter frequently seems to have been the regional character of the available rock or the character of the particular rock to be decorated. Petroglyphs dominate, for example, in parts of southern Arizona and in the Rio Grande Valley of New Mexico where open talus slopes strewn with patina-blackened boulders are a major landscape feature. On the other hand, shallow caves and overhangs in light-colored rock were selected for rock painting. Thus painting is the characteristic rock art technique found in the mountains of southwestern New Mexico, where small overhangs in the rhyolite cliffs present the best surfaces for decoration.

On the Colorado Plateau, however, where vast stretches of highly patinated, smooth sandstone cliffs are readily available along with numerous rock-shelters, certain stylistic complexes may be made up predominantly of either petroglyphs or paintings. This suggests that other factors, such as ritual prescription, function (hence location, which often has a bearing on the nature of the rock), and even fashion, may also have influenced the method used. An intensive regional survey to determine how technical aspects of rock art correlate with such variables as style, subject matter, and site situations would be informative, particularly on the Colorado Plateau, where both rock-shelters and highly patinated cliffs and boulders were available for rock art.

3

Hunters and Gatherers

Around 5500 B.C. in the Southwest, hunting and gathering replaced Paleo-Indian big-game hunting as the dominant adaptive life-style (Irwin-Williams 1973). Primary representatives of this way of life were members of the Western Archaic or Desert Culture.

The terms "Western Archaic" and "Desert Culture" can be regarded as generic: generalizations that refer to a number of distinct ecological adjustments representing specific adaptations to a diversity of arid environments (Davis 1963:202). Certain adaptive mechanisms and features of social organization, however, were held in common by all Western Archaic groups. Baskets and flat milling stones are the most characteristic artifacts, the economic orientation centering around the gathering of nuts and seeds that were commonly parched and ground to a fine flour or paste for eating. Vegetables were gathered, and small animals, as well as larger game such as deer, antelope, and mountain sheep, were important in the diet. The gathering of wild food as a way of life demanded a seasonal pattern of movement corresponding to the availability of the food supply. Accordingly, houses were impermanent structures, and natural shelters such as caves and rock overhangs were frequently used (Willey 1966:55). There was little accumulation of material goods. Upon leaving a camp, a woman would often leave her milling stone overturned, with the mano beneath, in a convenient location to be used upon her return at some later date.

Under these conditions, the population remained small and unconcentrated. The effective social unit is thought to have been a small kin-related group of between twenty-five and fifty people (Martin and Plog 1973:72). Intergroup communication was undoubtedly brought about by reciprocal visiting, trade, food-sharing ceremonies, and marriages, to mention a few possibilities.

This level of existence has been documented from most parts of the Southwest, where it persisted for several thousand years preceding the horticulturalists. It is to this basic cultural complex that the earliest known rock art in western North America can be attributed. In many regions of the Southwest, the rock art is a major component of the Archaic archaeological record, and a study of this art contributes significantly to our knowledge of this period. Rock art serves as a sensitive guide to identifying cultural changes and defining regional relationships. Most important, it also contributes to information on the group itself.

Regional variation within the Western Archaic, based on differences in point types and other tools of the stone-making technology that presumably reflect variation in adaptive strategies, has been described by various investigators, and a recent synthesis has been proposed by Irwin-Williams (1967). Regional boundaries within the Western Archaic in the Southwest are probably best defined in southern Arizona and New Mexico. Southwestern Arizona is included in the Amargosa Culture or what has recently been defined by Irwin-Williams (1967) as the Western Sector of the southwestern Archaic. Irwin-Williams's Western Sector includes all of western Arizona, the southern tip of Nevada, and the southern half of eastern California. Her Southern Sector includes southeastern Arizona and southwestern New Mexico and covers what is generally understood as the Cochise Culture. She does not venture east of this into southern New Mexico and adjacent parts of West Texas and northern Chihuahua, but the Archaic component there was first described by Lehmer (1948:71–75) as a "poorly known Cochise-related Hueco Phase." Wheat (1955:30) takes issue with relating this region to the Cochise, stating that it differs from the Cochise in many ways and has relationships to the south and east. At any rate, as a region within the Archaic, it seems to be distinct.

In northeastern Arizona and northwestern New Mexico, Irwin-Williams sets her Northern Sector, which extends into the adjacent parts of Utah and Colorado. Most of Nevada, Utah, and western Colorado fall within the confines of what she defines as the Desert Culture. As used by Irwin-Williams,

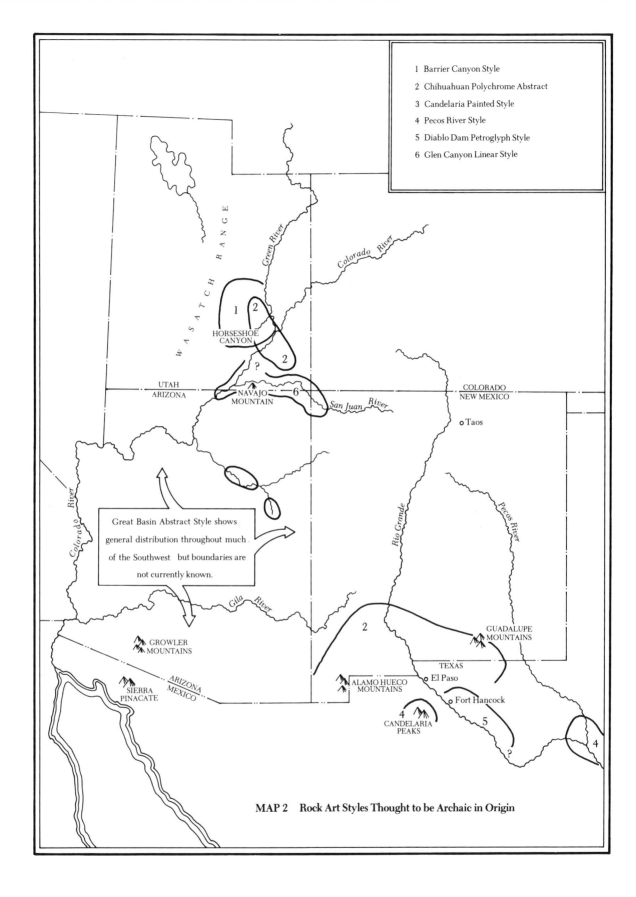

1 Barrier Canyon Style
2 Chihuahuan Polychrome Abstract
3 Candelaria Painted Style
4 Pecos River Style
5 Diablo Dam Petroglyph Style
6 Glen Canyon Linear Style

WASATCH RANGE

Green River

Colorado River

1 2
HORSESHOE
CANYON

2

?

UTAH
ARIZONA

NAVAJO
MOUNTAIN

6

San Juan River

COLORADO
NEW MEXICO

o Taos

Colorado River

Rio Grande

Pecos River

Great Basin Abstract Style shows
general distribution throughout much
of the Southwest but boundaries are
not currently known.

Gila River

GROWLER
MOUNTAINS

2

GUADALUPE
MOUNTAINS

TEXAS

SIERRA
PINACATE

ARIZONA
MEXICO

ALAMO HUECO
MOUNTAINS

o El Paso

o Fort Hancock

4
CANDELARIA
PEAKS

5

?

4

MAP 2   Rock Art Styles Thought to be Archaic in Origin

this is a more restricted definition of a term that was originally defined by Jennings (1953) as any Western Archaic manifestation.

Within the Southwest there are a number of rock art styles for which Archaic origins are suggested (Map 2). These are widely distributed throughout the region and exhibit considerable variation in content, style, and technique. To date, the manner in which these styles correspond to regional variation within the Western Archaic as established by other cultural artifacts is not always clear. Nevertheless, rock art is one of the most outstanding remains of the hunter-gatherers who occupied this area.

THE GREAT BASIN ABSTRACT STYLE OF THE SOUTHWESTERN ARCHAIC

The oldest rock art attributable to the Western Archaic in the Southwest is abstract in content. The petroglyphs described below are not fundamentally different in any way from the Great Basin Abstract Style as originally described by Steward (1929:220) and later by Heizer and Baumhoff (1962). This abstract rock art was the work of hunter-gatherers in the Great Basin, sometime between 1000 B.C. and A.D. 1500. Because of the basic similarity of the abstract petroglyphs of the Southwest to those of the Great Basin, I have retained the original style name first given by Steward in order to avoid an unwarranted proliferation of names and resulting confusion (Fig. 10). On the other hand, there are minor regional variations in content as well as temporal extent within the style as it occurs in the Southwest.

Abstract Petroglyphs of the Western Arizona Desert

The first group of abstract petroglyphs for consideration are those of the western Arizona desert, included in Irwin-Williams's Western Sector. These are contiguous with other manifestations of the Abstract Style as it occurs farther west and north into the Great Basin itself.

On the basis of observations by Hayden (1972), it appears that petroglyphs in the Abstract Style are not commonly found in western Arizona. They are, nevertheless, well represented at a few known sites, one of which is located in the Growler Mountains (Figs. 19–22). Designs are pecked in heavy, clear lines through the black patina on small scattered boulders, and two distinct types of decoration are present. All the designs, with the

Figure 19. Curvilinear abstract designs from a petroglyph site in the Growler Mountains, Yuma County, Arizona.

Figure 20. Large abstract petroglyph designs between 2 and 3 feet tall with both recti-linear and curvilinear components. Each design fills most of the rock facet on which it occurs. Note the symmetry exhibited. Growler Mountains, Arizona.

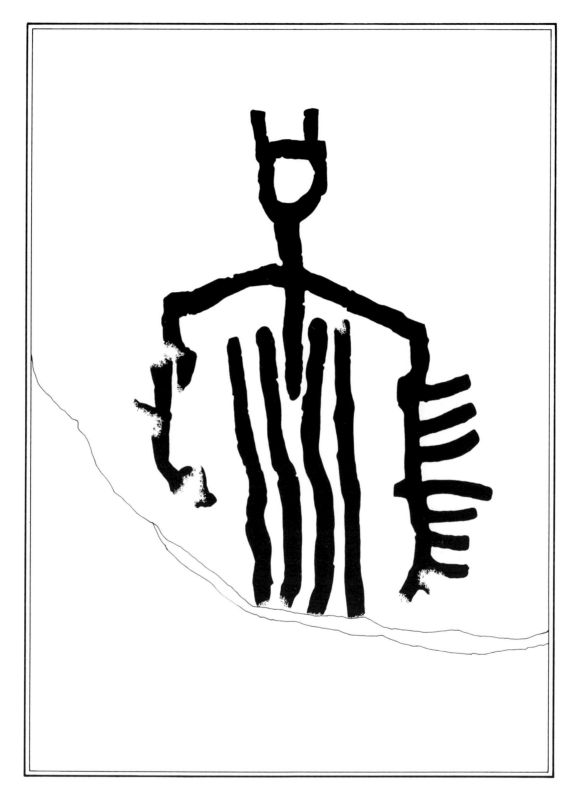

Figure 21. Anthropomorphic petroglyph figure approximately 2 feet tall, Growler Mountains, Arizona.

Figure 22. Curvilinear abstract designs and a gridiron superimposed by more recent figures of the Hohokam Gila Petroglyph Style, Growler Mountains, Arizona.

exception of the few examples of Hohokam-type figures, bear the same degree of weathering discoloration and thus appear to be contemporaneous. One type is composed primarily of curvilinear elements. These elements tend to cover one or more surfaces of a boulder and consist of circles, triangles, agglomerations of circles, wavy lines, and curving and meandering lines, the last sometimes serving to tie everything together in a somewhat haphazard manner (Fig. 19). In other cases, however, only one or two large contained patterns are found on a rock's surface, and these more spectacular and distinctive designs have both rectilinear and curvilinear components (Fig. 20). Limited series of parallel lines are a characteristic motif, and the circular and rectangular gridiron (Steward 1929:196, 198) and the rake are typical ways in which the parallel-line motif is used. Crosshatched designs resembling net bags are depicted, and large abstracts with vertical symmetry are also found. A single large anthropomorph is clearly part of this style complex (Fig. 21); he is shown holding a rake and his body is indicated with parallel lines.

Another site at which circular gridirons, rakes, and related motifs predominate is Tinaja Romero in the Sierra Pinacate of northern Sonora, where these motifs are located together in substantial numbers on the cliff above a water catchment or tank. According to Hayden (1972:74–75), this is one of only two known petroglyph sites in the entire 600 square miles of the Sierra Pinacate.

Related glyphs in the adjacent Colorado Desert of California, west of the Colorado River (Jaegar 1957:84), are assigned to the Amargosa Culture (Hedges 1973:16). It would seem that this entire region made up what was referred to earlier as a communication or information exchange network.

As for dating the material under discussion, association with the Amargosa Culture would give a maximum date of 5000 B.C. (Hedges 1973:16), but there is a certain amount of evidence to suggest that the Growler Mountain petroglyphs are somewhat more recent than this. The Abstract Style itself has estimated beginning dates around 1000 B.C.; the rectilinear component of the style is thought to have even later initial dates (Heizer and Baumhoff 1962:233). Evidence for an upper limitation in dating is found in the petroglyphs themselves. On one boulder, several Hohokam-style figures are superimposed over a group of curvilinear designs and a gridiron (Fig. 22). The gridiron and the curvilinear elements are technically similar and have the same amount of moderate patination, while the Hohokam figures are pecked in wider lines and are considerably lighter in color. Several hundred years must have passed between the carving of these two groups of petroglyphs to account for the differences in the patinas visible today. As Hohokam work dates no later than A.D. 1450 (see Table 1), the Abstract Style designs must have been made early in the first millennium, at the very latest.

TABLE 1.
Hunters and Gatherers

Periods		Phases	
Pioneer	300 B.C.–A.D. 550		
		Vahki	300 B.C.–A.D. 1
		Estrella	A.D. 1–A.D. 200
		Sweetwater	A.D. 200–A.D. 350
		Snaketown	A.D. 350–A.D. 550
Colonial	A.D. 550–A.D. 900		
		Gila Butte	A.D. 550–A.D. 700
		Santa Cruz	A.D. 700–A.D. 900
Sedentary	A.D. 900–A.D. 1100		
		Sacaton	A.D. 900–A.D. 1100
Classic	A.D. 1100–A.D. 1450		
		Soho	A.D. 1100–A.D. 1300
		Civano	A.D. 1300–A.D. 1450

Quite different observations have recently been made by Hayden (1972) on these same sites. He proposes that the Tinaja Romero petroglyphs and those in the Growler Mountains are part of the "Hohokam School." He suggests that the gridirons described previously may be a stylized representation of shells, made by the Hohokam during trips to and from the Gulf of California to obtain this material, perhaps as records of shell expeditions. This is an intriguing hypothesis, but the higher degree of patination on the gridirons than on the Hohokam work on the same panel and the repetition of the gridiron and similar motifs in the Great Basin Abstract Style in California (Steward 1929; Heizer and Clewlow 1973: Figs. 230, 232, 236, etc.) argue against it.

In regard to the Great Basin abstracts of California, Heizer and Clewlow (1973:5) suggest that petroglyph making involved magic and ritual centering around food-gathering activities. The idea that petroglyph sites in the Great Basin of Nevada and California were made for purposes of hunting magic has been extensively tested by Heizer and Baumhoff (1959, 1962), Von Werlhof (1965), and Grant (1968). These authors feel that the location of sites in spots appropriate for game taking lends this thesis a high degree of probability. Sites are located along prehistoric game trails leading to water holes near hunting blinds and in narrow gorges where game could be ambushed.

This type of study has not been made in western Arizona. The Arizona sites described herein do occur on trails and at or near water, but these occurrences in themselves are not conclusive. Hedges states that there is no clear evidence that the Colorado Desert petroglyphs were associated with hunting activities and notes that major sites, like those in Sonora and Arizona described here, are located at dependable water sources with trails and campsites in association. He concludes that it is not clear whether petroglyph sites are associated with water, trails, camps, or simply general human activity. Another interesting possibility is that in this region small sites associated only with trails may have functioned as trail shrines (Hedges 1973:16).

Abstract Style Petroglyphs of the Chihuahuan Desert

Moving east into the Chihuahuan Desert of southern New Mexico, West Texas, and northern Chihuahua (Map 2), the region of Lehmer's Hueco Phase, one encounters several styles attributable to the Western Archaic. Among them are abstract petroglyphs once again in the Great Basin Abstract Style (P. Schaafsma 1972:90–95; Jackson 1938). In the intervening region is Irwin-Williams's Southern Sector, the area of the Cochise Culture, but rock art sites belonging to the Western Archaic have not been identified there.

In an earlier study (P. Schaafsma 1972) the Abstract Style petroglyphs in the Chihuahuan Desert were attributed to Mogollon of the region before A.D. 1000. This association was based on the presence of abundant Mogollon refuse at certain of these sites; on the fact that there is no noticeable difference in patination between the most recent of these designs and those of the post–A.D. 1050 Jornada Style, a later Mogollon representational style that sometimes occurs at the same sites; and finally, on the presence of specifically Mogollon elements in context with the abstract designs. I am now of the opinion, however, that this style in this region has its origins with the hunter-gatherers and that a continuity in art between the Archaic people and the pre–A.D. 1000 Mogollones is in evidence. The numerous superimpositions that occur among the petroglyphs of this style, together with the contrast in the degree of patination between the oldest examples and the more recent ones, indicate that the style was used over a long period of time.

Figure 23.   Abstract Style petroglyphs on dike near Carrizozo, New Mexico. New Mexico State Planning Office; photograph, Karl Kernberger.

Figure 24.   Abstract Style petroglyphs with barred and bisected ovals, San Diego Mountain, New Mexico. New Mexico State Planning Office; photograph, Karl Kernberger.

Sites consisting primarily of Abstract Style petroglyphs are among the largest petroglyph sites in the Southwest. Near Carrizozo, New Mexico, petroglyphs in this style extend for roughly one-half mile along a basaltic dike, and the rocks are heavily decorated throughout (Fig. 23).

The petroglyphs are often irregular, defying categorization, or they may be so confused by superimpositions that they cannot be described. Many discrete elements, however, can be isolated. Single zigzags, pairs or sets of parallel zigzags, wavy lines, varied irregular complexes with curvilinear or rectilinear components or both, concentric circles, circles with dots, sunbursts, one-pole ladders (a single long line bisected at right angles by two or more shorter lines), rakes, and "nets" are present at most of these sites. Circle clusters, rows of circles, connected circles, varied grid patterns, small barred ovals, and sawtooth elements occur a little less frequently (Fig. 24). Although abstract elements predominate, representational figures (such as stick-figure anthropomorphs, other life-forms, and tracks) seem to be an integral part of this petroglyph complex, at least in its later and perhaps Mogollon phases (Fig. 25). The outlined cross, a formal and therefore anomalous design, is contemporaneous with the more elemental figures.

Variation between sites or regions is noticeable. There are differences in the way elements are arranged and in stylistic emphases, the latter ranging from wholly curvilinear configurations to strongly rectilinear ones. The Carrizozo site, for example, is unusual in that along with a large number of imposing rectilinear geometric designs, there are numbers of repetitive designs such as sets of parallel lines, wavy lines, rakes, triangles, circles, and even anthropomorphs (Fig. 23).

A general characteristic of the Abstract Style petroglyphs in New Mexico is their occurrence on all sides of the surface of a boulder or outcropping. At some sites, one finds designs on the faces of cracks just wide enough to have allowed the artist to maneuver. Seemingly related to the tendency to play with the form of the rock is the occasional deliberate adaptation of the design to the shape of the surface being decorated. Pecked outlines around the edges of rock faces sometimes occur. Often rock features such as bumps or holes were incorporated.

Only the most general observations can be made about the function of these petroglyphs. A number of large petroglyph sites are found in the vicinity of springs. Other cultural remains at the same spots indicate that these locations were campsites at which petroglyph making was an important activity. A typical site of this type is near a large spring on the slopes of

Figure 25. Abstract Style petroglyphs and representational forms from the Tres Ojos range, Samalayuca, Chihuahua.

Alamo Mountain, on which most of the food-producing plants in the locality grow. Great Basin Abstract and Jornada Style work are extensively represented, and the small campsites and the cultural debris (including both ceramics and lithic material) are undoubtedly the remains of both groups of Mogollon, the earlier Archaic hunter-gatherers, and, finally, Apaches. The lithic tool inventory includes pulping planes, grinding surfaces, an occasional bedrock mortar, and manos and metates, indicating that food gathering as well as food preparation took place here. It is clear that Alamo Mountain and its spring were visited by many desert inhabitants on food-gathering expeditions, and the tradition of petroglyph making seems to have been maintained. The exact purpose it served in this context is little more than conjecture. Territorial designation having to do with rights to that particular desert spring and ritual use in connection with food-gathering ceremonials, are hypothetical functions that could be investigated at all cultural levels.

Abstract Style Petroglyphs in the Upper Rio Grande Valley and the High Plains of Eastern New Mexico

Almost no research and very little documentation have been done on the Abstract Style petroglyphs that occur in the northern Rio Grande Valley (Figs. 26, 27). Their complete distribution is unknown, and in localities where they occur, they have been overshadowed by the more compelling and relatively recent Pueblo designs. Recently, however, it has been demonstrated that the Abstract Style complex does exist in the northern Rio Grande region. It occurs on the San José River, and it has been recorded in Arroyo Hondo, Taos County (P. Schaafsma 1972:171–76), and in the vicinity of the ruin of San Cristobal Pueblo in the Galisteo Basin (Lang 1976). Designs are similar to those described above and include rakes, dot complexes, repetitious linear motifs, zigzags, circles, and one-pole ladders. Occasionally, elements follow boulder contours and in doing so enhance the shape of the rock. The designs are heavily patinated. In Arroyo Hondo they are superimposed by Pueblo designs dating between A.D. 1000 and A.D. 1200. They were formerly noncommittally described as a group, "Taos 1" (P. Schaafsma 1972); it is now suggested, on the basis of their apparent age and similarity to Archaic sites elsewhere, that they are probably the work of the hunter-gatherers of the region and that at the latest they are Basketmaker II in date (see p. 107 for Anasazi period sequences). North of Arroyo Hondo, the association of a Basketmaker II site with abstract rock art suggests that this style was still

Figure 26. Abstract Style petroglyphs in the northern Rio Grande Valley decorating lichen-covered boulder, Arroyo Hondo, Taos County, New Mexico. New Mexico State Planning Office; photograph, Curtis Schaafsma.

Figure 27. Barred Abstract Style element echoes the shape of the rock upon which it has been pecked, Arroyo Hondo, Taos County, New Mexico. New Mexico State Planning Office; photograph, Curtis Schaafsma.

being made at that time. Reinhart (1967:467) proposes that Basketmaker II artifacts may be older in the Rio Grande Valley than in the San Juan area. By Basketmaker III times, the San Juan Anasazi were making their impact felt on their Anasazi neighbors to the east (Reinhart 1967). San Juan Anasazi style paintings at a Basketmaker III site in the Galisteo Basin confirm this observation (Lang 1976).

This same complex of Abstract Style petroglyphs extends eastward from the Rio Grande Valley to the high plains, from southern Colorado to east-central New Mexico. Again it is hypothesized that hunter-gatherers were responsible (P. Schaafsma 1972:185–88).

The Chihuahuan Polychrome Abstract Style

Another rather widespread rock art style of the Western Archaic is the Chihuahuan Polychrome Abstract. These paintings are distributed in the caves and rock-shelters throughout the Chihuahuan Desert of southern New Mexico from the southwestern border of the state, east to the Guadalupe Mountains, and south below the Texas border. Paintings of this type have also been found in eastern Utah. This style complex was earlier described as Polychrome Abstractions (P. Schaafsma 1972:61–71) in a survey of New Mexico's rock art. These paintings are similar in terms of design inventory to the Great Basin Abstract Style petroglyphs, and it is possible that they are but a variation within the tradition. Nevertheless, they are discussed here separately because of their distinctiveness as paintings. Also, as opposed to being distributed along thousands of feet of basaltic dike, rimrock, or talus boulders, they are concentrated within the confines of rock-shelters.

Clays, other minerals, and charcoal were probably used to produce the colors, which include yellow, red, orange, black, and white. One or more of these colors might have been used in the painting of a design. Individual elements were placed on the walls of the shelters in a rather haphazard manner, each design being more or less independent of the rest (Fig. 4). Series of short parallel lines and zigzags are the most characteristic basic design components. The parallel line groups are either freestanding or joined across the top to form rakes (Fig. 28). If the pendant lines are short, the impression is one of a fringe rather than a rake. Zigzags are painted either horizontally or vertically and vary in size from those with segments a foot long to those with segments only a half-inch in length; the latter are particularly characteristic.

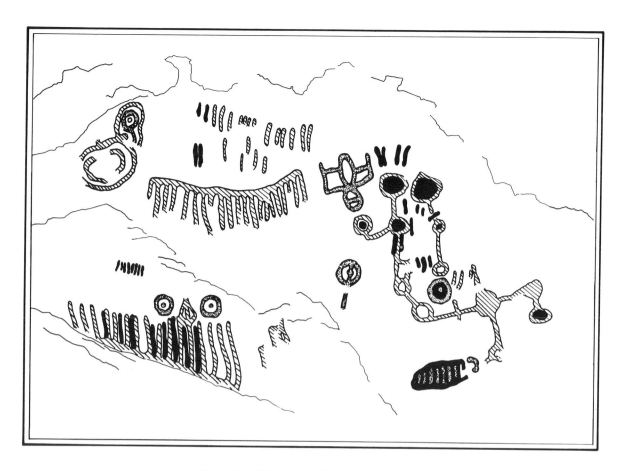

Figure 28. Chihuahuan Polychrome Abstract Style designs from the Mimbres Valley in southern New Mexico. The elements are painted in black, red, and orange.

Zigzags occur singly or in double sets, or they may be crossed to create diamond chains and nets. Two or more colors were sometimes used in the complex examples. Circles, ovals, sunbursts, dots and dot designs, and areas of solid wash are also typical. Circles may be joined by straight lines; in the southern sites, sunbursts are often located so that they radiate from natural holes in the rock walls (Fig. 29). A few stick-figure humans are also depicted.

A very large site with Abstract Polychrome paintings in the Alamo Hueco Mountains of Hidalgo County in southwestern New Mexico consists of three cavate rooms, all filled with paintings, under a single overhang. Variation in the degree of weathering and small differences in the elements and their arrangement in each of the rooms suggest that these paintings were made over a period of time. Paintings in the first room are faded, and many of them are covered with heavy travertine deposits. Some of these deposits have

Plate 1. Paintings in the Great Gallery, Horseshoe (Barrier) Canyon, Utah. Anthropomorphs approximate life-size. Photograph, Karl Kernberger.

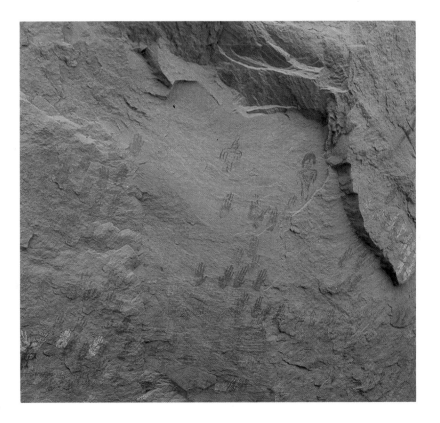

Plate 2. Mural of painted handprints in several colors, Painted Cave, Buttress Canyon, Arizona. Note the small anthropomorphs in red and green at the top. Photograph, Karl Kernberger.

Plate 3. A colorful display of superimposed paintings in Painted Grotto, Guadalupe Mountains, New Mexico. New Mexico State Planning Office; photograph, Karl Kernberger.

Plate 4. A single carefully painted anthropomorph, approximately 2 feet tall, is the focus of this Barrier Canyon Style composition which occupies the same shelter as the pair in Fig. 25. The long fringed objects on either side could not be identified, but the snake above the anthropomorph's head is extraordinarily life-like. Torso decoration may be a skeletal motif suggesting ribs. West of Green River, Utah. Photograph, Karl Kernberger.

Plate 5. Barrier Canyon Style paintings, Sego, Utah. These uncanny figures display a good deal of variation and they approximate life-size. Photograph, Karl Kernberger.

Plate 6. Anthropomorphic figures popularly known as the "Holy Ghost" panel, Great Gallery, Horseshoe (Barrier) Canyon. The largest figure is slightly over life-size and was painted by a spatter technique. Further decoration has been incised over the painting. Photograph, Karl Kernberger.

Plate 7. Striped anthropomorph and others, the Bird Site, the Maze, Utah. Figures approximate life-size. Photograph, Karl Kernberger.

Plate 8. Right-hand side, main panel at the Bird Site in which harvest elements are present. Two of the small figures in profile appear to carry burden baskets. Photograph, Karl Kernberger.

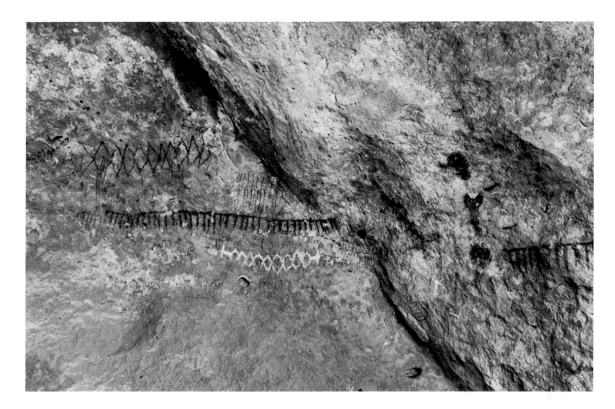

Figure 29. Chihuahuan Polychrome Abstract paintings in a cave in the Alamo Hueco Mountains of southwestern New Mexico. Note the painted lines radiating from a natural hole in the rock. To the left below another hole has been rimmed with white paint. New Mexico State Planning Office; photograph, Karl Kernberger.

been worn slick by subsequent human traffic within the shelter. Designs are scrawled across the shelter walls, but the whole is vaguely united by a large zigzag extending for 20 or 30 feet around the top of the wall (P. Schaafsma 1972:Fig. 53).

The paintings in the next two rooms are more vivid (Fig. 29). They are also more controlled in arrangement, with greater adherence to vertical and horizontal axes. Long rakes and zigzag motifs, closely placed, resemble textile patterns, and again a large zigzag at the top of the vertical wall in the center room serves as an integrating device. An element that looks as if it might represent a long ripe seedpod occurs in the last and, from all appearances, most recently painted room. A similar and well-preserved design is superimposed over the faded paintings in the first room. This occurrence seems to verify the general impression that although they are similar throughout, the paintings at this site were not all done at the same time.

In addition, some relatively recent appearing hand prints in orange are superimposed over the abstract elements, and a large cloud terrace in black is painted on the ceiling of the middle room. These suggest that the site was subsequently visited by late Mogollon inhabitants of the region, whose remains are found in nearby caves in these mountains (Lambert and Ambler 1964). Bedrock mortars in the ledge in front of the cave and the lithic scatter on the slope below are of undetermined cultural affiliation. The shelters themselves, however, lack fill or indications of fires and appear never to have been occupied. They were probably used ceremonially by the hunting-and-gathering population of the locality or even by regional groups or organizations extending beyond the band (Service 1971:62–63).[1]

From the point of view of artistry, color, and overall effect, the Painted Grotto, a shelter in the Guadalupe Mountains of southeastern New Mexico, is by far the most exciting of these sites (Fig. 30; Plate 3) (Gebhard 1962; P. Schaafsma 1972). Paintings similar to those just discussed cover the back wall of the cave; but in this instance there are many superimpositions, and the paintings in yellow, red, and orange are numerous and solidly massed. Yellow and white dots in lines or blocky patterns were printed with paint-covered fingertips and appear like strings of jewels across the background of polychrome rakes, sets of parallel lines, and zigzag motifs. Rows of small white triangles also span the painted area to unite the complex. Solid elements, vaguely anthropomorphic in form, and others resembling plant stalks, seedpods, and triangular and harp-shaped flowers (Gebhard 1962:221) give added emphasis. The whole is like a vibrant, colorful tapestry. The solid elements are distinctive, and of these only the seedpod motif is present in the sites to the west. Among the unusual designs are fringed or tasseled concentric ovals. The possibility that certain of these motifs are in fact intended to be stylized representations is reinforced by comparison with Australian Aboriginal art, in which diamond chains and parallel zigzag designs denote seedpods and tree grubs, respectively (McCarthy 1938:28).

Additional sites with Abstract Polychrome paintings very like those from southwestern New Mexico occur in the Upper Sonoran life zone in eastern Utah (Keller et al. 1974). The paintings, well preserved in large sandstone rock-shelters, are typical expressions of the style (Fig. 31). The Grand Gulch site in the San Juan drainage is particularly significant because it provides information demonstrating that the paintings are almost unquestionably of Archaic origin. The shelter itself is unstable and is filled with rubble. The abstract paintings are confined to a high area of the wall and ceiling of the

Figure 30. Fringed concentric ovals, rakes, and possible flower elements in a detailed view of the Painted Grotto. New Mexico State Planning Office; photograph, Karl Kernberger.

Figure 31. Polychrome rakes, zigzags, circle, and plant designs in the Abstract Style, Grand Gulch, southeastern Utah. Photograph, Audrey Hobler.

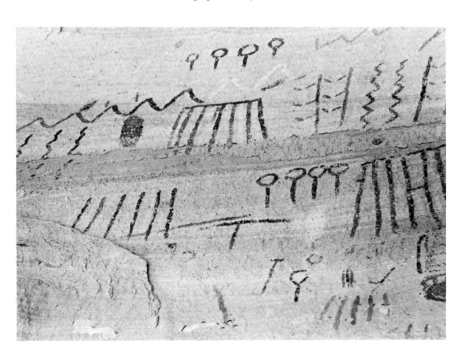

Figure 32.   Chihuahuan Polychrome Abstract Style paintings in red and black, San Rafael Reef, eastern Utah. Photograph, Karl Kernberger.

cave, to which access was formerly available along a ledge that subsequently fell. In the scar of the fallen ledge are numerous paintings of Basketmaker anthropomorphs, which probably date after A.D. 1 and possibly as late as A.D. 700 in this region.[2]

Thus the abstract paintings are clearly older than the Basketmaker paintings. It is notable that there is a complete stylistic break between the two, suggesting that a major ideological shift had taken place. A second northern site with excellent Polychrome Abstract paintings is located just west of Green River in east-central Utah (Fig. 32). Barrier Canyon Style paintings (see p. 109) occur in a separate location within the same shelter.

The significance of these Abstract paintings in the north is not fully understood. Assuming that they are roughly contemporaneous with those in the south, they suggest a general connection or homogeneity between hunting-gathering populations of the Southwest at the time they were made, just as is indicated by the widespread occurrence of the similar Great Basin Abstract Style petroglyphs.

REPRESENTATIONAL ROCK ART OF THE SOUTHWEST ARCHAIC

Although in some regions the old Great Basin Abstract Style of the Western Archaic persisted into the beginnings of the horticultural periods, in the El Paso region and in eastern Utah, representational styles believed to be the work of Archaic groups possibly sometime after 500 B.C. either replaced the Abstract Style or were added to the Archaic repertoire. Presumably the advent of these representational styles reflects diversity and changes taking place in the ideographic system at the end of the Archaic Period. Representational art is also of particular interest in that in some instances it graphically conveys the concept of the supernatural realm held by these early peoples, as well as providing occasional glimpses into their everyday lives.

Representational Hunting-Gathering Art of the El Paso Region

The prolific Chihuahuan Desert region (in the general vicinity of the Rio Grande from El Paso south to the Big Bend) presents, in addition to the Abstracts, an almost confusing array of representational rock art believed to be the work of late hunter-gatherers in the area. In the El Paso region, miniature life-forms are sometimes present along with the Polychrome Abstract paintings and other style complexes. At least two such miniature figures are present at the base of the Painted Grotto mural. One is a winged anthropomorphic figure, no more than an inch tall; the other is an animal about 3 inches long. Other miniatures were reported by Mera (1938) from elsewhere in the Guadalupe Mountains, and they also occur near Fort Hancock, southeast of El Paso. As at Painted Grotto, mythical anthropomorphic figures are depicted in these instances. The cultural affiliation of these paintings is unknown, but they more closely resemble the work of hunter-gatherers than that of the horticulturalists of the region.

There are, in addition, simple and crude paintings of human forms that resemble in general type those of the elaborate Western Archaic Pecos River Style paintings to the southeast (Newcomb and Kirkland 1967:37–80) and that are believed to date before A.D. 600 (a beginning date has not been established). A recent article by Bilbo and Sutherland (1975) describes these and other anthropomorphic and zoomorphic figures scattered throughout the West Texas region that are believed to be Archaic in origin, but as yet these seem to constitute a miscellaneous group.

The most significant representational Archaic rock drawings in this general region are the paintings from the Candelaria Peaks in northern Chihuahua (Fig. 33) and the petroglyphs of men, spears, and animals north of Fort Hancock at Diablo Dam (Figs. 34, 35) (Jackson 1938:35–37). They may be varied expressions of a single art tradition or complex. Although they are stylistically and aesthetically distinct, both the paintings and the petroglyphs have in common an emphasis on long spears with tanged, basally notched projectile points. In the case of the petroglyph examples, these spears have been likened to the Archaic Shumla point (Sutherland and Steed 1974:3), whose distribution centers to the east around the Pecos–Rio Grande confluence (Suhm and Jelks 1962:247). Present also in both the paintings and the petroglyphs are broad-shouldered anthropomorphs, frequently shown with spear in hand. Emphasis on the depiction of spears and spear points or both is unusual in southwestern rock art, and their size and number, as well as the innovative use of this motif in the petroglyphs, suggest that they had taken on supernatural significance.

The petroglyphs of this complex at the Diablo Dam site, henceforth referred to as the Diablo Dam Petroglyph Style, are numerous and are characterized overall by pecked, bold, solid designs. The broad-shouldered anthropomorph was mentioned previously. Some of these figures are horned, signifying supernatural, perhaps shamanic power (Furst 1974a:135; and this volume, pp. 71, 239). Others have points emerging from the tops of their heads. The point alone is a prominent element, one of the depictions of which is 24 inches long (Sutherland and Steed 1974:11). In some cases the point itself takes on anthropomorphic aspects and appears to be a very stylized man with raised arms. The man becomes the point, or vice versa, and again shamanic power is implicit. Along with these elements are numerous figures of square-bodied deer and mountain sheep, commonly pierced by a spear. One cannot escape the feeling that this is a site with magical power, that it was an important hunting shrine.

Other art styles in the vicinity include Abstract Style petroglyphs, over which Diablo Dam petroglyphs are occasionally superimposed, and Jornada

Figure 33. A partial reconstruction of a panel in the Candelaria Painted Style from East Candelaria Peak, Chihuahua. The sheep are later additions to the original group and superimpose the men with spears. The latter are between 3 and 6 inches tall.

Figure 34. Man, spear points, deer, and sheep in the Diablo Dam Petroglyph Style, near Fort Hancock, Texas. Man approximately 10 inches tall. Several badly eroded figures have been omitted from this reconstruction.

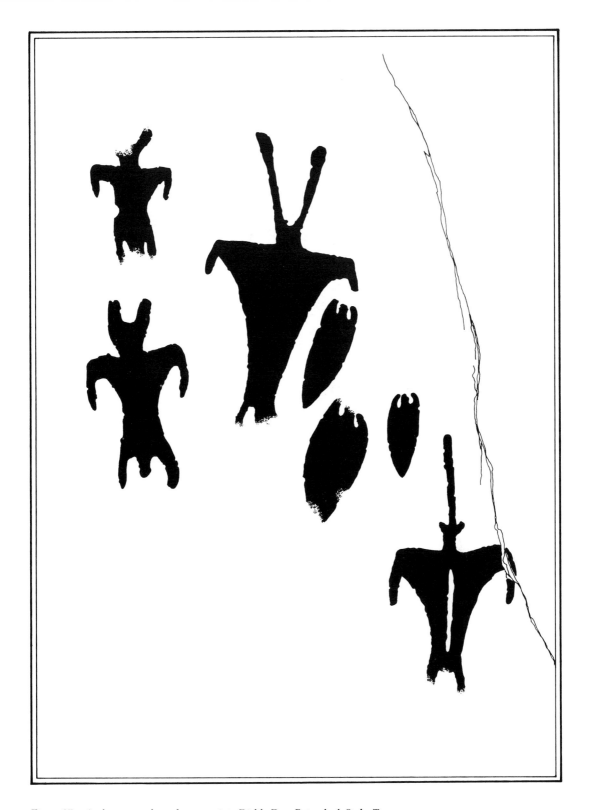

Figure 35.   Anthropomorphs and spear points, Diablo Dam Petroglyph Style, Texas

Style elements, suggesting that this locality was frequented for many centuries by the region's inhabitants.

In contrast, the paintings referred to here as the Candelaria Painted Style are delicate renderings of very small, exquisite human figures holding spears and either standing still or cavorting across the granite surfaces (Fig. 33). More than seventy of these figures appear in one panel (Davis and Toness 1974), but unfortunately many are faded and partially obscured by designs painted by later visitors to the site. The spear-holding men are of two types. Most skillfully painted are those in motion. They vary between 3 and 6 inches in height. The body shape tends toward a crescent, and this form together with the thin, expressively painted arms and legs lends an almost insectlike and dramatic sense of movement to these figures. They are not painted with an orientation to a basal groundline but may be positioned in almost any direction. The variety of poses and the action portrayed are unique in southwestern rock drawings and are comparable to those in the well-known East Spanish Style paintings of Europe and related work in the deserts of Africa (Christensen 1955:Fig. 326). Several of the leaping Candelaria figures wear headdresses of long feathers or crescent-shaped objects, and their long spears have ornate points. Taking into account differences in technique and stylistic emphases, the points depicted here could be the same type as in the Diablo Dam petroglyphs. The static, standing figures have trapezoidal bodies and are typologically like the Diablo Dam figures. They hold their spears upright, and many of the spears exceed the height of the men. The spears are painted in fine double or triple lines and have feathers and elegant tips.

The complexity of the painting suggests that more detail and subject matter may have originally existed, but the faded condition of the paint, combined with the delicacy of the designs and the fact that they are superimposed by larger paintings in orange, red, and black, makes it difficult to see more.

The superimposing designs consist primarily of larger figures of mountain sheep painted in light red. These are similar in certain respects to those described previously from the site at Diablo Dam. They have rectangular bodies, fine, linear, stylized legs, and small pointed heads. Their most interesting feature is their horns, which are shown in frontal perspective. This type of representation is unusual in the Southwest. Several of these bighorn sheep were later repainted in black. Small black stick figures of men with bows seem to be contemporaneous with the repainting and date after the introduction of the bow into the area, between A.D. 600 and A.D. 1000 (Newcomb and Kirkland 1967:40).

The possible interrelationships of the two styles described here are not fully understood. A historical or cultural relationship is postulated, but contemporaneity is not necessarily implied. If the Shumla point did serve as the prototype for the point depictions, the paintings and the petroglyphs could date as late as A.D. 700–800 (Suhm and Jelks 1962:247). Estimates of a bottom date for this point type are lacking. In the absence of indications of great age, such as heavy patination, I suggest that the Diablo Dam petroglyphs date late within the Archaic Period. Also of interest in terms of relative dating is the observation that elements of the Diablo Dam Petroglyph Style superimpose Abstract Style designs at Fort Hancock and other sites.

The Barrier Canyon Anthropomorphic Style

Rock paintings believed to be the production of pre-Fremont hunting-and-gathering peoples in the northern Southwest are the Barrier Canyon Anthropomorphic Style paintings of eastern Utah (Figs. 3, 13, 38–48 and Plates 1, 4–8). They constitute a major style grouping. The number of known sites is about twenty, and they are located in the rugged, arid canyon country of the Colorado Plateau in the drainage of the Colorado River (Figs. 36, 37) (P. Schaafsma 1971:68).

This region was also occupied by the San Rafael Fremont between A.D. 700 and A.D. 1200, and the paintings have been classified by some archaeologists as Fremont (Gunnerson 1969). In an earlier study of Utah rock art, the problem of the cultural affiliation of these paintings was examined in depth (P. Schaafsma 1971:128–35), and it was felt that evidence supported the probability that the Barrier Canyon Style artists were hunter-gatherers immediately preceding the Fremonters of the region.

The dominant motif in the Barrier Canyon Style is the dark, tapering, immobile anthropomorphic form, painted in a dark red pigment. These figures are frequently ghostly in appearance, hovering in rows against a sandstone backdrop within arched alcoves and rock-shelters (Figs. 38, 39). The number of figures at a site may vary from a single anthropomorph to dozens. Isolated compositional groupings, centered on one or two large human forms, flanked by smaller ones or tiny birds and quadrupeds, as well as by zigzags or unidentifiable objects, sometimes occur (Fig. 40 and Plate 4). In

Figure 36. Canyon of the Colorado Plateau harboring Archaic rock art, San Rafael Reef, Utah. Photograph, Karl Kernberger.

Figure 37. A skeleton landscape of bare sandstone, canyons, and lonely buttes, The Maze, Green River drainage, Utah. Barrier Canyon Style paintings were made in sheltered locations in the canyon depths. Photograph, Karl Kernberger.

Figure 38. Spectral human forms in water-streaked alcove, Sego, Utah. Figures approximate life-size. Photograph, Karl Kernberger.

Figure 39. Dark red anthropomorphic figures hover on cliffs in the Great Gallery, Horseshoe (Barrier) Canyon. Photograph, Karl Kernberger.

Figure 40.   Pair of Barrier Canyon Style figures west of Green River, Utah. The anthropomorphs are accompanied by fringed circular objects and snakes, and tiny birds fly around the antennae of the figure on the right. Anthropomorphs about 2 feet tall.

other instances a number of these figures may be painted together as a group or arranged in long lines across the cliff. Large staring eyes, bulging heads, and the absence or near absence of arms and legs serve to emphasize the spectral aspect of these beings. Some border on the fantastic (Plate 5). Headgear may take the form of horns or "antennae" painted in delicate thin lines. Many figures wear a crown of white dots, and occasionally white dot patterns decorate their faces and bodies. Stripes and textilelike decoration are also depicted on the torso, as if robes were intended. Figures with arms may hold snakes or plants, and as mentioned above, zigzags and small naturalistic portrayals of animals may occur at their sides (Fig. 41). Some are accompanied by dogs (Fig. 42). At a site west of Green River and in the Maze, bears are also depicted.

Figure 41.   Detail of a Sego anthropomorph showing its abstract head and the small quadrupeds on the shoulders. Chalked outlines are one form of defacement that has occurred here in recent years. Photograph, Karl Kernberger.

Figure 42.   Paintings in Horseshoe (Barrier) Canyon. These figures are comparatively simple. The large dog at the left, approximately 18 inches long, is a commonly occurring motif. Photograph, Karl Kernberger.

The paintings of the Great Gallery in Barrier Canyon, better known as Horseshoe Canyon, are among the finest in the style. The long wall of the shelter is covered with dozens of richly decorated anthropomorphs, many of which are life size (Figs. 13, 39, 43–46 and Plates 1, 6). In a number of instances the surface of the rock was smoothed in preparation for receiving the paintings, and several techniques were used to achieve the varied and elaborate textural effects. The tall ghostlike being in Plate 6 was created by a spatter technique; the indefinite result contributes to his ethereal appearance. Possibly, however, it is a fur robe that is represented. The paint on the torsos of other anthropomorphs (Figs. 13 and 44) was applied with the artist's fingers, a method of painting that created a thin background on top of which lines and dots were applied in thicker paint. In several cases, lines were incised through the more heavily painted areas, and the feeling of a rich textile resulted. In some instances, the body area is divided into panels elaborated with stripes or wavy lines or both. One Great Gallery anthropomorph has animals in the area of the chest, and another has smaller, mummylike figures incorporated into panels on the torso. Other solidly painted figures are adorned with linear patterns of white dots (Figs. 45, 46). Tiny birds and quadrupeds are grouped at the heads, shoulders, or sides of a number of these anthropomorphs. The skull-like aspect of the heads in Figure 43 is readily apparent.

The triangle of delicately painted mountain sheep (Fig. 46) forms an unusual group. The sheep are portrayed in different running positions and below, more crudely painted, is a dog that appears to be chasing them. To the right are two men apparently holding spears and engaged in combat. The expressive use of line to denote action in the figures of the sheep and the two men contrasts with the surrounding immobile mummylike forms, although they were all clearly done by the same hand.

Other notable paintings (Figs. 47, 48 and Plates 7, 8) are located at the Bird Site in the Maze in the Horse Canyon drainage near the junction of the Colorado and Green rivers (Fig. 37). The main panel is a composition consisting of a long row of figures that are very elongate and that approach life size (Plates 7, 8). Again there is evidence of surface preparation prior to making the paintings. Unlike the Great Gallery anthropomorphs, most of those in the Maze have thin arms or legs or both. Stripes and wavy lines decorate their bodies, and zigzag lines are drawn beside them. As elsewhere, these figures are accompanied by tiny birds and animals. Motifs concerning the harvest also are present (Plate 8). Two smaller figures, expertly rendered as

Figure 43.   A segment of the Great Gallery mural depicting a number of large mummylike figures variously decorated. Figures approximate life-size. Photograph, Karl Kernberger.

Figure 44. Detail of anthropomorphic figures, Great Gallery. Photograph, Karl Kernberger.

Figure 45. A group composition consisting of a major central figure with three attendants. Lines of white dots and white crowns adorn these awesome beings in the Great Gallery. Photograph, Karl Kernberger.

Figure 46. Small mountain sheep, a dog, and conflict as well as the usual mummylike figures are part of this Great Gallery panel. The striped figure (upper right) occurs in other large sites where many figures are depicted. Photograph, Karl Kernberger.

Figure 47. Isolated composition consisting of an elongate human form with bird and upright quadruped, the Bird Site. Anthropomorph between 2 and 3 feet tall. Photograph, Karl Kernberger.

Figure 48. Small painting of a single anthropomorph, the Bird Site in the Maze. The figure is distinguished by his feathers and his large eyes resembling white spectacles from which fall lines of white dots. To his left is a plant form. Photograph, Karl Kernberger.

silhouettes, seem to wear burden baskets and carry in their hands objects that resemble tools for gathering wild grains (P. Schaafsma 1971:129). The last figure on the right in this group is approached by a large bird and has rabbits running down his arm. What appears to be ricegrass, the seeds of which were a major food source at the hunter-gatherer level, sprouts from a finger. Another small composition at this site consists of a human figure about 15 inches tall that is approached by tiny birds and quadrupeds; again, wild plants are included in the group. In addition to what appear to be grasses, there is a stalk of what may be yucca fruit.

A comparison can be drawn between the Barrier Canyon Anthropomorphic Style and the paintings of the Archaic Pecos River Style in Texas (P. Schaafsma 1971:Fig. 132).[3]

These two art complexes share certain stylistic emphases as well as some very specific and unusual details. Considering the distances involved, the significance of these similarities is puzzling. In a recent article, however, Schroedl (1977:260–62) points out that parallels in the realm of nonutilitarian objects exist between the Grand Canyon split-twig figurine complex in southern Utah and the Pecos River region in Texas that suggest a relationship between these two regions. Schroedl regards the Barrier Canyon Style paintings as a probable component of the late Grand Canyon figurine complex in southern Utah. Excavation in Cowboy Cave in the vicinity of the Great Gallery on a Barrier Creek tributary revealed painted sandstone and clay figurines with counterparts in the Pecos River region.

The Cowboy Cave materials, which are dated between 100 B.C. and A.D. 500, also correlate well temporally with the Barrier Canyon Style. Comparisons of the Barrier Canyon Style with other rock art in the same general region of the Colorado Plateau suggest that the Barrier Canyon Style falls late in the Archaic sequence. It may have been, in part at least, contemporaneous with the Anasazi Basketmakers to the south, and a rough tentative dating between 500 B.C. and A.D. 500 is suggested. Evidence to support this general assignment is found in the occasional overlap in anthropomorphic types between the Barrier Canyon Style and those painted by the San Juan Basketmakers. Also, at Butler Wash, a Basketmaker site in southern Utah, certain details of torso decoration resemble those from Barrier Canyon Style art. Further, the emphasis on the depiction of the yucca fruit at Butler Wash is of interest, as a similar depiction occurs in the Maze. The absence of the bow, which may have been present in the region as early as A.D. 200 (Grant 1968:51), and the absence of Pueblo stylistic impact, which is prevalent in the

Fremont art of the same region, also suggest an early date for Barrier Canyon Style art.

One senses that the remote, awe-inspiring anthropomorphic forms of the Barrier Canyon Style are beings imbued with supernatural power. It is not unreasonable, considering the content of the paintings, to suggest that we are dealing with a shamanic art. In fact, Wellmann (1975) has described the paintings in the Maze as "the seasonal image of a harvest scene imbued with distinctly shamanistic qualities."

The presence of shamanistic symbolism in North American Indian rock art has been pointed out, and the idea that certain rock art may be the result of shamanic practices has been discussed by investigators in widely different areas: southern California (Hedges 1975), Ontario (Vastokas and Vastokas 1973), and Utah, Arizona, and Wyoming (Wellmann 1975). Shamanism is an "ecstatic technique at the disposal of a particular elite" (Eliade 1964), shamans themselves being individuals of power who have the ability to transport themselves mentally from one level of awareness to another, communicating with the supernatural by means of dreams, fasting, trance, visions, and the like. During their quest for power, aspiring shamans have to submit to an initiatory ordeal involving symbolic death and rebirth, and during ecstasy the shaman's soul is able to travel throughout this world as well as into the realms above and below.

Many shamanic practices and much of the symbolism associated with shamanism are held in common over vast areas (Furst 1974a), and the Barrier Canyon Style anthropomorphs have attributes and associations characteristic of shamans throughout the world. Horns, which are one type of headdress occurring on Barrier Canyon Style figures, are almost universally emblematic of shamanic and supernatural power. Animal spirit helpers, common to the shamanic realm (Furst 1974a:135), may explain the many tiny animals and birds that approach these figures or appear on their heads and shoulders. Birds in this context may symbolize the shamanic power of magic flight; the bird may lead the soul in flight, or the soul may actually change into a bird (Wellmann 1975). The large dog, a major figure in many Barrier Canyon Style panels, may be analogous to the jaguar, whose form New World shamans commonly are believed to assume. This belief in jaguar transformation in Central and South America has been documented from ancient times to the present (Furst 1972). In this regard, the fact that the cat does appear in a similar context in the Western Archaic paintings of the Pecos River Focus is noteworthy (P. Schaafsma 1971:131, Fig. 132; Newcomb and Kirkland 1967).

Further, according to Goldman (1963:262), among the Cubeo (a tribe of the Amazon Basin), "the *yavi* is the supreme shaman, the one who can take the form of a jaguar, who consorts with jaguars, who maintains the jaguar as a dog" —a comment that may have a certain amount of relevance here. Finally, the deathlike aspect of many of the anthropomorphs may well be significant. Skeletal motifs in rock art may in some cases relate to the shaman's initiatory journey to the Underworld.

The compositions in the Barrier Canyon Style paintings were carefully planned, and the fact that superimpositions are rare suggests that the image, not just the act of painting, was important. Further, the painting at each shelter appears to be the work of a single person, or, at the most, a limited number of people, indicating that these paintings were probably made only by a select few, probably artist-shamans. These factors, along with the powerful impact made by the paintings themselves in their impressive settings, imply that the sites where these paintings occur served as some kind of religious foci or retreats.

The Glen Canyon Linear Petroglyph Style

The Glen Canyon Linear Petroglyph Style is another early rock art style from the drainages of the Colorado and San Juan rivers. In origin, at least, it is believed to predate the Anasazi, and it is the oldest of the five styles described from the Glen Canyon by Turner (1963:12; 1971). This style was formerly referred to as Glen Canyon Style 5 by Turner, but this name has been dropped here in favor of a more descriptive terminology consistent with that used elsewhere in this volume. Although the style is best known from the Glen Canyon region, a wider distribution is suggested by its presence farther north in Utah (P. Schaafsma 1971:62–65) and to the south on the Little Colorado and its tributary drainages (Pilles 1974; Ferg 1974) (Map 3). At the present time, known distribution of the style is limited primarily to river canyons.

This petroglyph complex can be described as consisting almost exclusively of deeply dinted, rectilinear outline forms occasionally filled with horizontal or vertical hatching or both (Turner 1963) (Figs. 49, 50). Solidly pecked areas are rare. Animal representations include both mountain sheep and deer, with the former predominating. These animals, with large rectangular or oval bodies, characteristically have very small heads and tails and short, insignificant legs. Sometimes a small animal is shown within the

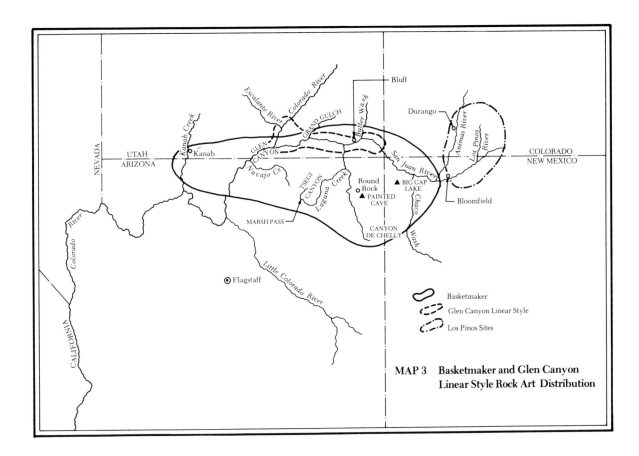

MAP 3   Basketmaker and Glen Canyon
Linear Style Rock Art Distribution

body of a large one, a type of depiction that probably represents a pregnant female. Human figures are also portrayed with disproportionately large bodies and often tend to be very schematic (Fig. 49). Arms and legs are usually minor features, but various types of headdresses may be shown. Heads themselves may be abstracted into concentric circles, a feature symbolic of shamanic power (Vastokas and Vastokas 1973:55).

A distinctive anthropomorphic figure is a small creature with facial features and headgear consisting of tall feathers or something resembling them on either side of the head, producing a "rabbit-eared" effect (Fig. 49). The shape of the body varies from a rectangular to an irregular form with rounded contours, and the interior is filled with the typical interior stripes or hatching. In the southern part of this style's range, arms, if present, tend to be long and tentaclelike (Ferg 1974). These characters often occur in pairs.

Other representational designs are animal tracks, possibly snakes consisting of long wavy lines with knobs at the end to resemble heads, and a number of simple plant motifs. Associated abstract elements include long

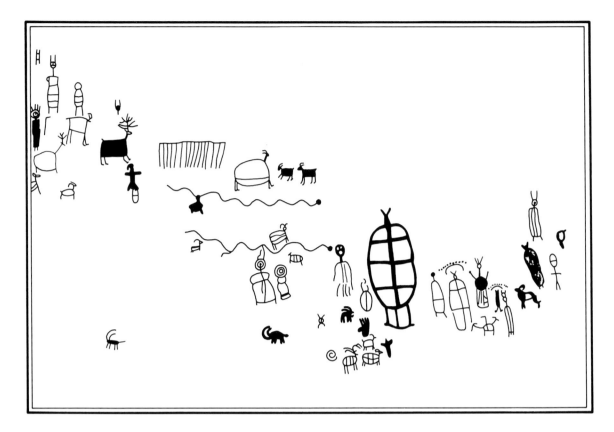

Figure 49. Glen Canyon Linear Style petroglyphs, NA 6457, West Creek Canyon, tributary of the Colorado River. (Drawing after Turner 1963, Fig. 77).

wavy lines, long lines of dots, ticked lines, rakes, zigzags, ladder motifs, connected circles, grids, and sunbursts (Turner 1963) (Figs. 49–52). The squiggle maze, "an interlocking network of lines, curvilinear and straight, that wander over a cliff wall, often for several square yards," is particularly characteristic (Turner 1963:7). As a whole, the elements of this linear style are drawn in what might be described as an uncontained or loose fashion. Many of the representational forms appear to the modern viewer to be fanciful in their interpretation, rendered with a light, imaginative touch reminiscent of the work of Paul Klee.

Patination over Glen Canyon Linear Style designs is in some cases almost complete, the blue-black patina of the original rock surface having been acquired again over the deep dints of the petroglyphs. Other figures have been nearly obliterated by weathering. These conditions are among the

Figure 50. Petroglyphs of bighorn sheep, Glen Canyon Linear Style, Grand Gulch, Utah. The designs were chalked before photographing. Scott File photograph by A. V. Kidder, courtesy of the Peabody Museum, Harvard.

evidence leading Turner to suggest that petroglyphs of this style largely predate pottery.

Direct means of dating the style, however, are still lacking. On one hand, Turner (1971) suggests that the style is of considerable antiquity, with beginning dates going back to between 6000 and 2000 B.C. On the other, he notes that in Glen Canyon these sites have pottery associations as late as A.D. 1050, centering around A.D. 800–900. These associations, however, probably represent a later reoccupation of the same sites in this long-populated region. In any event, all evidence clearly indicates that the Glen Canyon Linear Petroglyphs predate all other Glen Canyon styles. In describing the style on the Little Colorado, Pilles (1974) assigns it to the Basketmaker II occupation of that region.

On the San Juan River at Butler Wash, Glen Canyon Linear Style designs occur with the San Juan Basketmaker Anthropomorphic Style (Figs. 77, 78). Both exhibit the same amount of patination, and they are technically similar in that they are pecked in small dints and fine lines. In some cases, however, Basketmaker figures clearly superimpose the Linear Style designs. Upriver, the Sand Island site is important in demonstrating a relative dating between the two styles in the San Juan region. Here Linear style figures are located high on the cliff above the scar of an ancient sand dune. Basketmaker figures are present below and within the scar. There is one example at Butler Wash of an anthropomorph with a Linear Style body and a Basketmaker headdress; such sharing between the styles is unusual. The evidence from these sites indicates that the Glen Canyon Linear Style is the older of the two but that it was still being made just before or around A.D. 1. Prehorticultural origins are suggested for the Linear Style complex.

The distinct characters of Basketmaker rock art and Linear Style petroglyphs, along with their apparently different overall patterns of distribution (Map 3), indicate that these styles are manifestations of generally distinct ideographic and probably cultural systems. It is perhaps not amiss to point out tenuous stylistic similarities between Linear Style anthropomorphs and those from the Coso Range in the Great Basin of eastern California (Grant 1968). Depictions of bighorn sheep are also common to both, although for the most part these differ typologically. Thus the Linear Style may have historical connections outside the Colorado Plateau.

DISCUSSION

In the foregoing pages I have mentioned a number of functions that rock art sites may have served for hunter-gatherers in the Southwest. In summary, several investigators hypothesize that the Abstract Style petroglyphs in the Great Basin were made in connection with hunting magic and ritual (Heizer and Baumhoff 1962; Von Werlhof 1965; Grant 1968). In the Colorado Desert of eastern California and in the adjacent region of Arizona, petroglyphs occur near trails, campsites, and water sources, and they may have functioned in a hunting-magic context also. Likewise, they could just as well have been made in other connections associated with human activity at these spots (Hedges 1973). The large sites of abstract petroglyphs in the Chihuahuan Desert of New Mexico and West Texas also frequently occur at springs where evidence of campsites and human activity abounds. I hypothesize that the Barrier Canyon Style paintings in the shelters and alcoves of the sandstone canyons of eastern Utah served as shrines or ceremonial centers and that they reflect shamanistic activities. The shelters painted with abstract designs in southern New Mexico and in adjacent parts of Texas also may have functioned in this way.

A model from ethnology for the use of painted rock-shelters as shrines by hunting-and-gathering peoples is provided by the Australian Aborigines (Moore 1971). The Aboriginal cave paintings are divided into classes depending on specific function, of which there are several, and in connection with this, their degree of sacredness. Sites range from those in which highly sacred and esoteric representations of Dreamtime totemic species are portrayed and used in initiation ceremonies, to those of secular purpose made near campsites and seen by everyone. The first-mentioned class of sites is so sacred that the paintings bring death for those viewing them unlawfully, and painting them is a job designated to a specific man or group of men. Between these two extremes is a variety of sites differing in their degree of sacredness—sites connected with mortuary ceremonies, increase or fertility sites, sorcery sites, and sites with paintings of malicious spirits (Moore 1971:117–19). The Australian paintings serve to emphasize the fact that primitive rock art could serve a number of different functions for any one group of hunting-gathering people.

The various southwestern rock art styles discussed in this chapter have led to the definition of spheres of interaction and communication during the Archaic Period. The oldest and most widespread rock art configuration in the Southwest attributable to the Western Archaic consists of elemental abstract designs, both curvilinear and rectilinear, similar or even identical to those found in the Great Basin of western Utah, Nevada, and eastern California (Fig. 10). Its broad distribution and its relationship to the ancient substratum of Archaic art in the Great Basin are evidence for an antiquity possibly greater than that hypothesized by Heizer and Baumhoff (1962:234). I believe that this general style is the material manifestation of an interrelated ideographic system formerly shared throughout by hunting-and-gathering groups in the Archaic. In certain regions, such as the upper Rio Grande Valley and the deserts of southern New Mexico and the adjoining parts of Chihuahua, indications are that these Abstract Style petroglyphs persisted into the horticultural period.

The persistence of the Abstract Style through time and space suggests a state of cultural stability in the Archaic throughout a large area, including both the Great Basin and the Southwest. This kind of stability at this cultural level is perhaps analogous to the stable traditions of prehistoric hunter-gatherer art in Australia. Elkin (1938), in his introduction to McCarthy's work, says that the artistic designs of the Australians, "being links with the creative past, are traditional in character and comparatively unchanging in form." Among the Aborigines, songs and myths are associated with specific designs, and the art "symbolizes the very essence of the spiritual and religious beliefs of the people," art being one means of defining the mystic tenets of one's faith (Elkin 1938; McCarthy 1938:15). It is the only material record of Aborigine beliefs, and the tradition therein described restricts choice of elements and designs. Thus if the tradition does not change, the art remains constant.

The broad cultural similarity characterizing hunting-gathering groups in the Great Basin and the Southwest, as postulated on the basis of the pervasive Abstract Style of rock art, finds further substantiation in observations made by Reichard on the nature of art in culture:

> . . . in the case of art . . . most objects bear the stamp of the culture in which they were made as surely as our own paintings carry the signature of their makers, either directly or in the peculiarities of an individualized style. It is a commonplace that primitives seldom make two objects exactly alike; it is just as well known that within a given locality certain limits are set, outside of which few artists, if any, are able to go. These limits consist of broad fundamental principles of which the artists are unconscious. Some of them are, for example, choice of design elements, laying out of fields, handling of space, the use of rhythm, of symmetry, perspective, symbolism and the like. Any one of these (and other) principles may be worked out in a large number of ways and the combinations of the different methods provide infinite possibilities for the resulting style. But the number chosen within any given area is limited, just as the sounds of a language are limited, and they determine the bounds of an artist's freedom. . . . the bounds have been determined for him by tradition; the choice of designs and composition has been made by hundreds of artists preceding him in a very gradual and subtle way as little understood by them as by him. The principles which make up the sum total of any style may be isolated; the reason for the choice and combination of these particular ones can perhaps never be determined. (Reichard 1933 in McCarthy 1938:16)

Most, if not all, of the representational styles previously described probably postdate the Abstract Style. The representational styles described from eastern Utah and West Texas and adjacent parts of northern Chihuahua are highly diverse in style and content, in spite of the fact that most of them appear to reflect various types of shamanic activity. Such stylistic diversity suggests the later emergence of both ideological changes and sharply defined regionalism in the Archaic Southwest, and an approximate date for this is estimated at about 500 B.C.

How these observations based on changes and similarities in the rock art concur with the Archaic configuration described by other artifactual remains is of interest, but sufficient regional synthetic data and pattern definition are still wanting on the long period before the horticultural groups became established. Thus the difficulties in relating the art to specific Archaic configurations, most of which are based on little more than point types, are considerable.

Nevertheless, certain possible relationships of this kind have been pointed out in the preceding discussion of the various styles. The Great Basin Abstract Style of western Arizona, for example, is tentatively linked with the late Amargosa of that region, and it lies adjacent to identical petroglyphs in southern and eastern California, all encompassed in Irwin-Williams's Western Sector. The Abstract Style in southern New Mexico and adjacent areas falls within the region of the "Hueco Phase" as described by Lehmer (1948). The art, however, suggests an interrelated ideographic system underlying both.

Within the later representational group, the depiction of "Shumla-like" points in the Diablo Dam Style petroglyphs suggests affinities farther to the east, thus substantiating Wheat's observations at least for the latter part of the Archaic Period (see. p. 34 and Wheat 1955:30). Further relationships between the Pecos River and El Paso regions are indicated by the various marginal examples of paintings with likenesses to those of the Pecos River Style. The change, however, in the Archaic cultural pattern indicated by the addition of representational rock art in this region has not been identified from other archaeological remains.

Archaic archaeology in the Colorado River drainage of eastern Utah is still poorly known. Certain resemblances in the art between the Glen Canyon Linear Petroglyph Style and the late Great Basin representational styles have been mentioned. The Barrier Canyon Style, with its emphasis on the portrayal of large anthropomorphs, is a distinctive Archaic development in the western drainage of the Colorado River. Recent findings indicating possible relationships between this style and certain associated cultural material and the Pecos River region also have been discussed. The Barrier Canyon Style was part of a major early art tradition on the Colorado Plateau shared by the horticultural San Juan Basketmakers to the south and the later Fremont peoples throughout most of Utah, who also emphasized in their art large anthropomorphs in ceremonial attire. The relationships between Fremont, Basketmaker, and Barrier Canyon Style art are further discussed later.

NOTES

1. Further description of the Alamo Hueco paintings can be found in P. Schaafsma (1972:63–64) and Cosgrove (1947).

2. See Ambler (1969:111) for discussion of Basketmaker II dates north of Navajo Mountain.

3. The Texas paintings have been described in detail by Gebhard (1960) and Kirkland (1967:37–80).

4

Hohokam Rock Art
of Southern Arizona

The Hohokam were horticulturalists who lived in the river valleys and deserts of south-central Arizona between 300 B.C. and A.D. 1450. It was originally thought that the Hohokam culture was an outgrowth of the late hunter-gatherers of the San Pedro Phase of the Cochise Culture who were stimulated by a number of traits from Mexico such as knowledge of water control systems, horticulture, and ceramics. It is now believed that the Hohokam configuration made its debut in the Southwest as the result of an actual migration of people from the south, who brought with them a knowledge of village living, water management, tillage technology, and pottery making, as well as cotton and a new variety of maize (Haury 1976:351–53). In Haury's words, it was "a frontier, spacially displaced Mesoamerican society." Once in the Southwest, this group developed its own distinctive characteristics (see Table 1).

Hohokam horticulture was based on the use of extensive irrigation systems, and the ability to irrigate from living streams was probably a major factor in the expansion of the Hohokam along the river valleys of southern Arizona (Map 4). The environment of these valleys consists of a lush strip of desert riparian growth bordering the rivers, with a creosotebush, bur sage, and saltbush plant community on the flats beyond. A saguaro–palo verde community characterizes the more distant rocky hillsides. Subsistence was based on maize horticulture, which began by 300 B.C. Beans and possibly

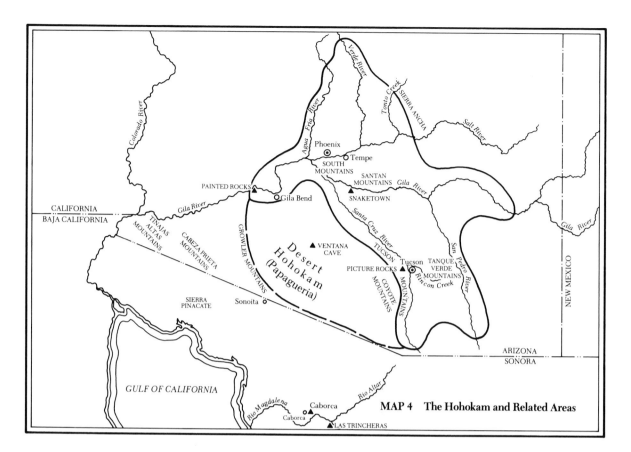

MAP 4 The Hohokam and Related Areas

squash were placed under cultivation somewhat later (Bohrer 1970). The diet was further rounded out by the local plants and animals. Edible wild plants grew prolifically in the disturbed soil of cultivated areas. Other dietary supplements included saguaro and mesquite seeds (Bohrer 1970), and rabbit, bighorn sheep, and deer were important meat sources.

Hohokam villages usually consisted of scattered clusters of houses until the Classic Period (A.D. 1100–1450). At that time settlements characterized by large adobe compounds and "great houses" began to predominate. The Classic Period is also marked by the presence of terraced hills, or *trincheras,* especially in the vicinities of Tucson and the desert Papaguería (Johnson 1963:178). These sites are northern examples of the *cerros de trincheras* ("fortified hills") of the Magdalena Basin and Altar Valley in Sonora.

A number of cultural items typical of the Hohokam have their origins in Mesoamerica. Ball courts appear early in the Colonial Period, and small earthen platform mounds that probably supported jacal temples may date as early as the Sedentary Period. Copper bells, ear plugs, mirror mosaics constructed of iron pyrites, and clay figurines of a type found in Mesoamerica are also evidence of contact with the south.

The Hohokam are also well known for their etched shell and fine work in bone and stone. Shell bracelets, slate palettes carved in the form of lizards and horned toads, and carved stone bowls are all distinctive Hohokam objects. There are several types of Hohokam pottery; the red-on-buff decorated wares are painted with numerous geometric designs and life-forms, many of which also occur in Hohokam petroglyphs (Figs. 51, 52).

THE GILA PETROGLYPH STYLE

Hohokam rock art occurs primarily in the form of petroglyphs, and sites are numerous throughout the Hohokam area (Steward 1929:161–67; Tanner and Connolly 1938; Vivian 1965:141–42; Wasley and Johnson 1965:73–74; White 1965; Snyder 1966:705–9; Kearns 1973). This petroglyph complex is referred to in this volume as the Gila Petroglyph Style.

A substantial number of both abstract and representational designs make up the element inventory of most Hohokam petroglyph sites (Figs. 53, 55). Except in those instances in which designs are obviously arranged as a planned composition, abstract and representational figures appear together on boulders or on fractured rock surfaces in a seemingly random manner. Pecking was by means of direct percussion. Technical quality shows considerable variability, from sketchy, poorly defined line drawings to beautifully carved spirals on carefully chosen boulders, the designs serving to enhance the lines and contours of the rock.

Life-forms in Hohokam art include a variety of human figures, large game animals, and perhaps dogs. Quadrupeds are pictured both as stick figures and as more solid forms. The latter are sometimes shown with a pendant half-circle in the abdominal area, perhaps signifying pregnancy (Fig. 56). As in pottery designs, the heads of Hohokam petroglyph quadrupeds have pointed noses and prominent ears, which together define a V shape. Turtles, lizards, snakes, birds, and insects are also depicted (Figs. 53, 57, 58). Occasionally animal tracks and bows also occur; the bow is found as an independent element at sites near Tucson (Fig. 59).

Figure 51. Rillito Red-on-brown plate showing water birds attacking a snake, BB 13:43. Photograph, Arizona State Museum.

Figure 52. Sacaton Red-on-buff bowl from Snaketown. Photograph, Arizona State Museum.

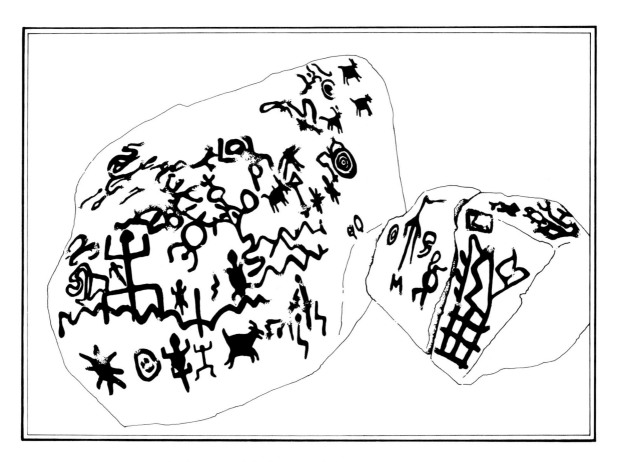

Figure 53. Petroglyph-covered boulders, Painted Rocks State Park, Gila Bend, Arizona.

Figure 54. Hohokam petroglyphs depicting bighorn sheep, deer or antelope, and a human figure, South Mountains, Arizona. The spirals and sunburst are abstract elements typical of the Hohokam Gila Petroglyph Style. Human figure is about 16 inches tall. Photograph, Ernest Snyder.

Figure 55. Gila Petroglyph Style, South Mountains, Arizona. Stick figure humans, lizards, and a snake are shown. Quadrupeds seem to represent deer, antelope, and perhaps canines. Scale measures 2 feet. Photograph, Ernest Snyder.

Figure 56. Hohokam quadrupeds: (a) Tucson Mountains; (b) Coyote Mountains.

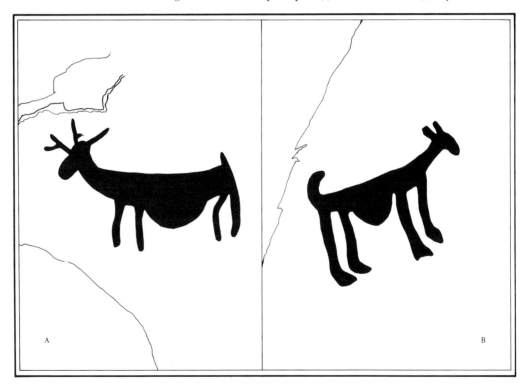

A

B

Figure 57. Gila Petroglyph Style designs: (a–b) lizard forms, Painted Rocks State Park, Gila Bend; (c) human figure and gecko, Rincon Valley, Saguaro National Monument, Tucson.

Figure 58. Santan Mountain petroglyphs, Gila Petroglyph Style. A lizard, quadruped, and centipede are depicted.

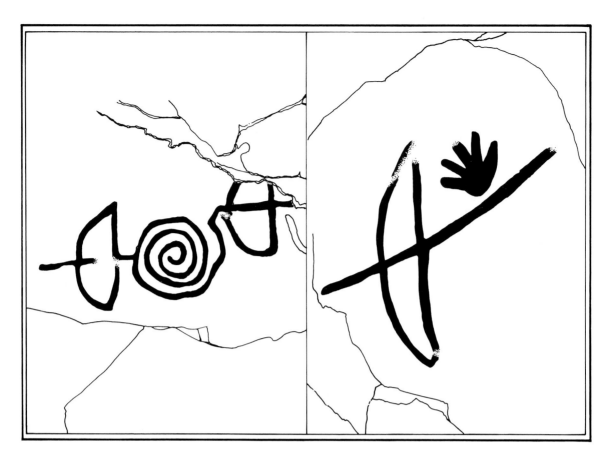

Figure 59.   Bows and arrows, Gila Petroglyph Style, Picture Rocks, Tucson.

Abstract elements are important (Figs. 60, 61). Abstract designs are primarily curvilinear, although some rectilinear elements do occur. Wavy lines, some of which represent snakes, curvilinear meanders, and mazes composed of meander segments are characteristic elements in the Gila Petroglyph Style. A few one-pole ladders (Heizer and Baumhoff 1962:83) and rectilinear grids appear at these sites. Some of the grids seem to be of Hohokam origin, while others are more heavily patinated than Hohokam work in the same group and thus seem to be older. Occasionally there are highly formalized patterns such as terraces, frets, outline crosses, diamond patterns, and large rectangular motifs, particularly in the northern Hohokam. Everywhere there are circle designs—small single circles, circles joined by lines, circle clusters, figure eights, circles with central dots, sunbursts, and concentric circles.

Figure 60. Gila Petroglyph Style elements and design complexes: (a) Tucson Mountains; (b) Rincon Valley; (c) Rincon Valley; (d) concentric circles with quadruped and snake, Santan Mountains; (e) Picture Rocks; (f) Santan Mountains; (g) Tucson Mountains.

89

Figure 61. Abstract elements and snakes, Gila Petroglyph Style, Signal Hill, Tucson Mountains. Same as in drawing, Fig. 69(a). Photograph, Helga Teiwes.

Spirals are prevalent and a hallmark of Hohokam art, in which they are more numerous than elsewhere in the Southwest. They occur in several contexts. They may appear singly, they are sometimes elaborated with ticking, and they may be incorporated into larger design complexes and abstract compositions (Fig. 60).

The meaning of the content of this art is not readily apparent. Since Mesoamerican origins for Hohokam culture have been suggested, however, some insights might be derived from Mexican ethnographic sources. In regard to the spiral, for example, the varied and complicated meanings that this has for modern Mexican Indians was summarized by Mountjoy (1974b:27–29). Following a quote from Lumholtz (1900) regarding spiral symbolism among the Huichol, Mountjoy writes, "The significant associations which tend to tie all of these representations together are rain and clouds, corn and serpents (some plumed) along with the heart and Grandfather Fire." Mountjoy quotes Weigand as saying that the Huichol associate the plain spiral with snakes and water and the ticked spiral with the internal peyote trip: "At the center of such spirals there is often a slight elaboration of the line, representing the God of Fire—originator of the peyote experience. Furthermore, according to Weigand, the pilgrimage to obtain peyote is associated with the coming of the rains" (Mountjoy 1974b:28). The spiral in western Mexico is also believed to refer to the god Quetzalcoatl, who is associated in part with agriculture and water.

Regional Variation

The Gila Petroglyph Style is remarkably consistent wherever it is found. Nevertheless, a distinction can be made between the Tucson region and the Gila-Salt sites to the north on the basis of the numbers and types of life figures represented. There is a greater emphasis on the depiction of men, animals, birds, and reptiles, especially lizards and snakes, in the Salt and Gila drainages, and the figures tend to be more carefully defined. From the Gila Basin, Tanner and Connolly (1938:15) describe mortars in the backs of lizard figures or in the centers of coiled snakes. Sites near Phoenix have birds, lizards, and men with geometric body shapes, and similar figures are present on the local pottery (Figs. 51, 52, 62, 63). Some of the human representations are very animated. They carry canes and bows and wear headdresses, and there are group compositions consisting of both humans and animals (Figs. 64, 65) (Steward 1929:Figs. 76, 77). In the Tucson region, abstract designs predominate over representational elements (Fig. 66), and the latter are less distinctive than those occurring in the Gila-Salt drainages. Although human figures sketchily drawn in stick form are found throughout the Hohokam area, this type predominates in the Tucson region. The southern anthropomorphs usually lack the imaginative gestures found in the Gila-Salt group, although figures carrying canes, sticks, flutes, bows, and balls have been recorded from the Tucson vicinity (White 1965:34–35). In a systematic survey of the petroglyphs in the Saguaro National Monument and its environs, White (1965) found only one site at which animal representations predominated over abstract elements. This site, known as Picture Rocks, is located on a small hill of granite outcrop in the eastern Tucson Mountain foothills. Among the petroglyphs here are several interesting groups: a line of hand-holding, dancing figures with tall headdresses, a group of animals, and a hunt scene (Fig. 67). In addition, there are the bows mentioned earlier; one in Figure 59 is shown with a hand print and a projectile.

Figure 62. Gila Petroglyph Style figures, South Mountains, Arizona. Note the geometric body shapes on the men, bird, and lizard. The human figure on the right with the cane is a typical Hohokam ceramic motif. Human figure at bottom is 11 inches tall. Photograph, Ernest Snyder.

Figure 63. Hohokam birds, lizards, and spiral, South Mountains, Arizona. Lower bird is approximately 18 inches long. Photograph, Ernest Snyder.

Figure 64. Line of human figures dancing or engaged in other group activity. The third figure from the right in the line carries a cane. Figures about 10 inches in height. South Mountains, Arizona. Photograph, Ernest Snyder.

Figure 65. Hohokam hunting scene, South Mountains, Arizona. Animal on left is 9 inches long. Photograph, Ernest Snyder.

Figure 66. Spirals and other circle motifs. Gila Petroglyph Style, Signal Hill, Tucson Mountains. Photograph, Helga Teiwes.

The differences described for the rock art are also observable in the ceramic decoration between the Tucson region, which has few life-forms, and the Gila Bend ceramics, on which they are more abundantly represented (White 1965:69–70). Cultural differences between the Gila-Salt region and the Santa Cruz Valley have been effectively addressed recently by Doyel (1977:93–110).

Dating the Petroglyphs

The Gila Petroglyph Style has been discussed as a whole, without divisions that correspond to the various Hohokam periods. Adequate means of dating this rock art have not been worked out, and, most important, the petroglyphs show little variation within themselves that suggest temporal change. Further, with the exception of the Classic Period *trincheras* sites, petroglyphs often occur near habitation sites occupied over a period of several hundred years, so that little precise dating is possible via this association. The Gila Plain sherds commonly present at petroglyph sites are

Figure 67.   Dancers, animals, and hunting scene, Gila Petroglyph Style, Picture Rocks, Tucson Mountains.

not temporally diagnostic. Finally, the differences in the Gila Petroglyph Style discussed previously are thought to be primarily regional as opposed to temporal in origin.

THE FUNCTION OF PETROGLYPH SITES IN HOHOKAM CULTURE

In direct association with Hohokam petroglyph sites are several commonly occurring features, including grinding slicks and pitted boulders. At Painted Rocks State Park near Gila Bend, at Picture Rocks, and at Tumamoc Hill (a fortified hill site in Tucson), shallow round pits varying from 1 inch to 7 inches across have been pecked into the horizontal surfaces of large boulders. In general, these pits are arranged in a rather irregular fashion, although on the pitted boulder at the summit of Tumamoc Hill there is one line of eight small pits about 1 inch in diameter. Also found at Hohokam petroglyph sites are shallow, smooth grinding surfaces, or "metate slicks." These occur on boulders or on bedrock surfaces, and many of them have little or no depression, suggesting limited use (Kearns 1973:279).

The function of these pits and metate slicks lies in the realm of speculation at this time. One possibility is that the designs were formerly painted, at least at certain sites, and that paint was ground either in the pits or on the slicks. Jacobo Sedelmayr, a Jesuit missionary who saw the carvings at Painted Rocks in 1749, said that they were painted (Wasley and Johnson 1965:73). The same observation was made later by nineteenth-century travelers. The Gila Bend area, however, was not occupied by the Hohokam after the mid-1400s (Wasley and Johnson 1965). Thus it seems unlikely that painting on the petroglyphs would have persisted in this exposed location, unless they were repainted in more recent times by the Pima or Papago, who may have revered the site. The Pima and Papago of today occupy the old Hohokam territory and may be the modern descendants of these prehistoric farmers. Haury (1976:353) suggests that Pima culture is a watered-down version of the Hohokam. The Pima practice of paying homage to the ancient petroglyph sites is mentioned by Fewkes (1912:148–49) and is also specifically suggested by Pima use as a trail shrine of a Hohokam petroglyph site in a Santan Mountain pass (Russell 1908:254). Alternative uses for these features are equally plausible. The grinding slicks might have been used in the preparation of foods, and the pits could have been filled with sand and thereby have supported prayer sticks, feathers, and other ceremonial paraphernalia. If so, the rocks in question would have been a ritual focus at the sites where they are present.

Other artifacts commonly associated with petroglyphs are less enigmatic. Bedrock mortars are found occasionally, and a scattering of plainware pottery and lithic debris, all of which indicate camping, is not unusual. Sometimes found among the lithic remains are battered hammerstones, which may have been used in petroglyph production.

Surveys have demonstrated that the Gila Petroglyph Style is widely distributed throughout the area of Hohokam occupation. Petroglyphs are located not only near permanent habitation and farming sites but also in the vicinities of seasonal camps, trails, and sites of other activity remote from the villages (Snyder 1966; White 1965; Kearns 1973). So far, however, attempts to correlate such variables as content and design associations with petroglyph site locations, from the point of view of geography as well as of proximity to activity sites, have produced no significant results. Still, it is possible to summarize various observations regarding site distribution.

That Hohokam rock art occurred close to permanent habitation and agricultural complexes is well established. Snyder (1966) demonstrated the proximity of petroglyph sites to irrigated fields in the South Mountains near the confluence of the Salt and Gila rivers, and Kearns (1973:274) describes petroglyphs that are part of or close to habitations, as well as within prehistoric agricultural zones near canals and irrigated fields in the lower Verde Valley. Kearns found sites both in the valley bottoms and on mesa terraces. Covered with rock cobbles, mesa terraces were most conducive to petroglyph carving and had the most sites. Nevertheless, he found that there was overall "no observable consistent placement of the sites" (Kearns 1973:279). The use of petroglyphs as a means of property identification or as boundary markers in these contexts has been suggested (Kearns 1973:93–94). Other possibilities suggested that the sites had religious or ceremonial uses or that they recorded specific events. Petroglyphs in agricultural zones may have played a role in crop propagation ritual. So far, however, the implications of these suggestions have not been adequately tested.

Trincheras sites, with which petroglyphs are consistently associated, date from the Classic Period of the Hohokam. There are two of these near Tucson in the Santa Cruz Valley (Fontana et al. 1959; Larson 1972). Long stone walls have been constructed across the hillsides at various elevations, with circular stone enclosures at the tops. Although the function of these terrace walls is not clear, some investigators believe they may have been defensive, the enclosures serving as windbreaks or sleeping circles. The petroglyphs are located on top or on the slopes or both. If these sites really were defense works, exactly why petroglyphs were made there is puzzling. Tumamoc Hill has a boulder with pits, indicating some specialized use.

Away from the irrigated river valleys, petroglyphs occur in connection with campsites and various transient activities (Kearns 1973; Bahti 1970; White 1965; Zahniser 1970). The Hohokam made substantial use of wild food resources of all types from both the riparian mesquite, saltbush, and creosote flats and the hillside saguaro–palo verde communities, especially in drought years. Analysis of seed remains from Snaketown has shown that saguaro and mesquite seeds provided foods at such times, and a multitude of other wild plants were also used (Bohrer 1970). Archaeological surveys in the Tucson Mountains indicate that this area, varying between 2 and 9 miles from permanent habitation remains in the Santa Cruz Valley to the east, was the scene of much hunting and foraging. The foothills of the Tanque Verde Mountains on the east side of the Tucson Valley were similarly exploited, and Zahniser (1970:114) feels that petroglyphs in both of these areas are related to these collecting expeditions. The sites in question vary considerably in size and occur in a variety of locations but seem to be most frequently located on low hilltops or rocky knolls. Mortars and a scattering of sherds and lithics are occasionally present.

Another kind of site associated with transient activity is the trail shrine. The Pima trail shrine at the site of Hohokam petroglyphs in a Santan Mountain pass was mentioned previously. The Pima left offerings here and tossed small pebbles at the foot of a large boulder bearing petroglyphs (Russell 1908:254). We do not know whether the Pima were continuing Hohokam use of the spot or whether they revered the place because of the petroglyphs, which may have had other significance to the Hohokam. The trail is strategically located in the landscape and has undoubtedly been in use since prehistoric times. Trail shrines consisting of rock piles on which stones or artifacts were placed as offerings, usually without petroglyphs, have an ancient tradition of use in the Sonoran Desert (Hayden 1967:339).

Also relevant to this discussion are the numerous petroglyphs at Painted Rocks, west of Gila Bend. This site consists of thousands of carvings on an isolated boulder outcrop. Projecting above the flat desert terrain, the spot was a conspicuous landmark, and an Indian trail passed close by. There are no village sites in the immediate vicinity. The petroglyphs belong to the Gila

Petroglyph Style; the boulder with pits found here was mentioned earlier. The site is unusual in its very great number of figures and in the numerous superimpositions, both indicating long and extensive use. There are two significant factors relating to the location of the site: (1) the Gila Bend district is on the western fringe of Hohokam occupation (Vivian 1965:140); and (2) Gila Bend is believed to have been situated along or at the termination of shell and possibly also salt transport routes from the Gulf of California (Hayden 1972:78–79). Hohokam Indians traveling out of their own riverine domain, either west into foreign Yuman territory or south on a shell or salt expedition to the Gulf, might have paid homage at such a spot as this. This hypothesis finds support in ethnographic analogy with the Papago and the Hopi. Both groups sustain a large body of myth and ritual surrounding salt-gathering expeditions (Underhill 1946:211–42; Talayesva 1942), and Hopi, en route to their salt source in the Grand Canyon, carve clan symbols at a site on the way as records of their trip. The petroglyphs at Painted Rocks are not arranged in countable sequences, as the Hopi clan symbols are, and thus do not appear to be tallies; but some other type of record might have been involved.

Furthermore, Hayden (1972) proposes that Hohokam petroglyphs located at several sites on trails in the Papaguería were made in connection with shell expeditions to the Gulf of California. Most of these are along trails thought to connect with Gila Bend. Elements at these sites are limited in variety and number and consist primarily of stick-figure anthropomorphs, zigzags, and circle motifs.

RELATED AREAS

Contemporaneous with the Hohokam of the river valleys of southern and central Arizona were pottery-making cultures adapted to the desert province of the Papaguería of southern Arizona and northern Sonora. A distinctive complex known as the Trincheras Culture was centered in the Magdalena and Altar valleys of northern Sonora, the name *trincheras* being derived from the terraced hillsides or "fortified" hills that are the most obvious architectural features of these sites (Johnson 1963:178). These desert groups probably had roots in the Cochise, and their cultural systems reflect different adaptive responses to the local environment. Subsistence in the dry Papaguería was based primarily on hunting and gathering. Trincheras subsistence patterns are

Figure 68. Cerro las Trincheras in the Magdalena River Valley, Sonora. Photograph, Harry Crosby.

poorly defined, but there seems to have been a varied adaptation that included adjustments to riverine, desert, and even coastal conditions (Bowen 1974).

The nature of the relationships between the Trincheras and Papaguerían cultures and the Hohokam has been dealt with at length by various investigators. Opinions range from those that regard the Papaguerían and Trincheras cultures as manifestations of a "Desert Hohokam" complex, which shared traits with the River Hohokam and were thereby incorporated into the general Hohokam picture (Johnson 1963; Haury 1950), to the view that no correlation exists between the Papaguería and the Hohokam (Schroeder 1964:104–6). The last view, however, is not borne out by the rock art. Shared petroglyph elements and stylistic traits throughout the entire area suggest that all the various populations in question, including the Hohokam, were in communication and participated in shared ideas. One of the prime mechanisms for this interaction may have been the shell trade from the Gulf of California. The Trincheras people themselves were the major suppliers of shell for the more northerly Hohokam (Johnson 1963:181), and such a trade would have been an important means of facilitating direct commuínciation with the north.

The rock art of the Trincheras Culture is less well known than that of the Hohokam. Nevertheless, petroglyphs are fairly common in the Magdalena-Altar riverine region (Bowen 1972:62; Hinton 1955:8–9). Many of these are associated with the rock *trincheras*, southern counterparts of the "fortified hills" in Arizona. Design elements consist of anthropomorphic, zoomorphic, and geometric figures in the Hohokam style. On Cerro las Trincheras (Fig. 68), the first of these sites to be so named (Johnson 1963:178), are representations of quadrupeds, spirals, and other abstract designs, both curvilinear and rectilinear (Figs. 69, 70). From Caborca and a Trincheras site near La Nariz east of Sonoita. Lumholtz (1912) illusrates further Hohokam-like designs—again spirals, a set of frets, lizards with the typical central bulge, and a pattern of interlocking scrolls. He mentions that these are similar to other designs in the region. He describes a rock with pits, also at La Nariz: "small artificial excavations in a row, each looking like the inside of a cup, only more shallow." Similar pits are found at Hohokam petroglyph sites, including Tumamoc Hill, an Arizona *trincheras* site.

Differences between the Trincheras petroglyphs of Sonora and the Arizona Hohokam lie primarily in the degree of refinement in design and in technical matters, the Sonoran figures generally excelling in these aspects. Hayden has concluded that the style found at Sonoran Trincheras sites is distinctive, although very closely related to the Hohokam (1972:82).

OBSERVATIONS ON THE HOHOKAM SUGGESTED BY ROCK ART

The rock art of the Hohokam offers certain insights into the nature of Hohokam culture, with regard to both its internal development and its external origins. The artistic tradition that is so unmistakably Hohokam, along with other archaeological remains, suggests that the Hohokam Culture finds its origins to the south in western Mexico. Vague cultural similarities seem to

Figure 69. Spirals and curvilinear motifs, Cerro las Trincheras, Sonora. Photograph, Harry Crosby.

Figure 70. Quadrupeds, Cerro las Trincheras, Sonora. Photograph, Harry Crosby.

exist between the San Blas complex of Nayarit and the Pioneer Period of the Hohokam (Mountjoy 1974a:117). Haury (1976:352) states that these similarities increase as one moves south into Michoacán, and it is his proposal that the Hohokam arrived in the Southwest as the result of a migration of peoples from this area up the west Mexican coast. Among the evidence he cites in support of this hypothesis is that similar but stylistically distinct life-forms exist in Hohokam designs and on Chupicuaro and Chalchihuites pottery. These life-forms appear early in Hohokam art and they are also present in the petroglyphs.

The spiral, a dominant motif in both Hohokam rock art and pottery decoration, is frequently present in the petroglyphs of Sinaloa and Nayarit (Mountjoy 1974b), where it occurs as single elements and in composite designs such as those found in the Hohokam. Although Mountjoy (1974b:30) suggests that the spiral arrived in the Southwest from Mexico via the West Coast, his estimated dating for this event (post–A.D. 1100) is much too late, as the spiral occurs in the Southwest, and specifically in the Hohokam, several hundred years earlier. Haury (1976:251) notes that it peaks in use as a pottery design in the Santa Cruz Phase, between A.D. 700 and A.D. 900. If the distinctive spiral complex present in Hohokam art did derive from western Mexico, as seems likely, it is earlier in its occurrence there than Mountjoy estimates.

The consistent character of their art suggests that the Hohokam were not subject to rapid changes in ideas that would have led to radical modifications of their ideographic structure. Shifts that do occur in the rock art are changes of emphasis that probably grew out of gradual internal developments or spread from one region to another. This idea is supported by evidence provided by other media, such as ceramic decoration and jewelry design (Jernigan 1978), which can be dated with considerably more precision than the rock art. In these, one finds the persistence of certain forms throughout most of Hohokam history, along with slow, step-by-step development of one form from preceding ones.

5

The Anasazi

Contemporaneous with the development of the Hohokam in southern Arizona was the emergence of yet another major tradition, to the north in the Colorado Plateau country and the Rio Grande Valley. From the Pecos River of New Mexico to the Muddy River in eastern Nevada, people were sharing in a broadly uniform culture today known as the Anasazi, a Navajo term meaning "the ancient ones."

The land of the Anasazi is colorful and rugged, an arid terrain of mesas, buttes, and broad tablelands dissected by deep canyons sculptured through layers of bright sandstone by wind and rain (Fig. 71). Canyons and arroyos that flow with streams after flood-producing summer rains characterize the landscape. The primary river systems are confined to the upper Rio Grande on the east side of the Continental Divide, and the Colorado with its major tributaries, the Little Colorado and the San Juan, on the west. Mountain ranges with alpine forests and high plateaus with ponderosa pine rise out of the mesa country. The average elevation of the region is around 6,000 feet. At this altitude, low, open forests of piñon and juniper interspersed with sage flats cover the plateaus and mesa tops. As altitude decreases, grassland steppes become prevalent, finally giving way to sparse vegetation and true desert conditions in the lower river regions.

The Anasazi ranged widely in the course of their activities, but they were primarily farmers. Their remains are concentrated in those zones in

Figure 71.   Canyon del Muerto from Antelope House Overlook, Arizona. Photograph, Karl Kernberger.

which rainfall provided the necessary moisture for crops to grow. The archaeological record indicates that the Anasazi developed from a hunting-and-gathering Western Archaic base to which horticulture was gradually added (Irwin-Williams 1973). Corn, beans, and squash were the primary domesticates, and cotton was cultivated in the hotter regions.

There was significant regional variation within Anasazi culture (Map 5), undoubtedly fostered by varied cultural responses to regional environments, different outside contacts, and geographically determined areas of communication and interaction. So far this type of variation within the Anasazi culture has been identified primarily on the basis of pottery types and architectural styles. Indications are that variation within Anasazi rock art corresponds with regional variation defined on the basis of other archaeological remains.

One means of ordering Anasazi chronology is the Pecos Classification, first proposed at the Pecos Conference by A. V. Kidder (1927). Any single chronological scheme designed to embrace developments over such a large area is of necessity arbitrary, failing to recognize minor temporal differences in the developmental sequence between regions or even subregions. Thus the dates presented here should be regarded not as fixed but as convenient reference points for cultural stages, subject to fluctuation from place to place. The Pecos Classification divides the Anasazi into the following time periods (Willey 1966:187):

Period	Dates (A.D.)
Basketmaker II	1–400
Basketmaker III	400–700
Pueblo I	700–900
Pueblo II	900–1100
Pueblo III	1100–1300
Pueblo IV	1300–1700
Pueblo V	1700–present

Basketmaker I does not exist as a formal period within Anasazi culture history; it was originally only a hypothetical construct to account for developments believed to have preceded Basketmaker II, the first clearly recognizable period in the Anasazi sequence. Cultural developments immediately prior to Basketmaker II are currently viewed as late manifestations of the Western Archaic (Irwin-Williams 1973).

In this chapter only the rock art through Pueblo III will be considered. After this time, throughout the Anasazi area major changes took place in

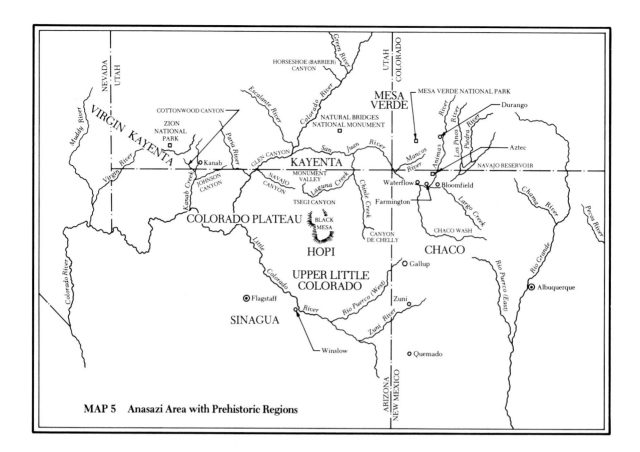

MAP 5   Anasazi Area with Prehistoric Regions

settlement pattern, in social organization, and seemingly also in religious structure. Associated with the last was the adoption by the Pueblos of a new art tradition. All of these changes mark the beginning of Pueblo IV, and the art of this and the following period will be discussed in Chapter 8.

THE FIRST ANASAZI ROCK ART: THE BASKETMAKER II PERIOD

The oldest rock art of the Anasazi is that of the Basketmaker II Period. The Basketmakers were the first horticulturalists of the area, dependent upon the cultivation of corn and squash as a part of their subsistence. Their culture is probably best known from the canyons of the Colorado Plateau, where dry caves have preserved cultural remains that would have perished long ago in open sites. Within these canyons these part-time farmers practiced flood-water and spring-water farming. They sometimes lived in semipermanent houses in the open and at other times occupied shelters in the canyon walls, which also served as places to store food and material goods and bury the dead. It is in these shelters that most Basketmaker rock art is found.

The population during this period is thought to have been small, and such shelters were probably occupied by not more than two or three nuclear family groups, perhaps including members of three generations (Lipe 1970:99). These groups are believed to have traveled into the highlands in the quest for wild food such as game, seeds, and piñon nuts, which supplemented their cultivated canyon crops. They hunted with atlatls and curved throwing sticks, the latter similar to the so-called rabbitsticks still used by the Hopi.

The Basketmakers were not only painters but also skilled craftsmen, as testified by their baskets, sandals, woven string bags, robes, and dog-hair sashes. Personal adornment was a major concern for these people. Varied and complex hair styles and head ornaments, necklaces, pendants, and earrings of seeds, seashells, and ground and polished stone have all been recovered from excavations in the dry caves, and many of these items are illustrated in the rock art of the period.

Possibly two distinct art styles can be attributed to the first Anasazi inhabitants of this region. One is the long-enduring petroglyph tradition of the Glen Canyon Linear Style, with origins in the Archaic, described in Chapter 3. Late examples of the Linear Style may have been done by the early Anasazi in some of the riverine districts of the Basketmaker region. The second, referred to here as the San Juan Anthropomorphic Style, includes both paintings and petroglyphs and is dominated by the depiction of large anthropomorphic figures. This style, associated with Basketmaker II remains, is concentrated in the drainage of the San Juan River (Map 3).

I mentioned earlier that the Basketmakers on the lower and central San Juan were participants, along with the painters of the Barrier Canyon Style and the later Fremonters, in a regional tradition involving the portrayal of large human figures with supernatural attributes. I suggest that the art styles involved were underlain by a related ideographic system or religious structure based on shamanic practices.

The San Juan Anthropomorphic Style

The diagnostic element of this style is the large, broad-shouldered anthropomorphic figure depicted in rows, in pairs, or scattered across a cliff surface (Plates 9, 10; Fig. 72). This Basketmaker anthropomorph is sometimes

Figure 72. Basketmaker II paintings in red and white, San Juan Anthropomorphic Style, Painted Cave, Buttress Canyon, Arizona. Small human figures in yellow (below) are later in origin. Figure on upper right is approximately 2 feet tall. Photograph, Karl Kernberger.

very elaborate. Two colors were frequently used in the painted renditions, and several types of headgear, necklaces, earrings, and sashes are portrayed. Some figures have eyes and other facial features. Hands and feet with fingers and toes are typical, usually in a drooping position that emphasizes the immobility and static frontal attitude in which these anthropomorphs are always shown.

San Juan Anthropomorphic Style paintings seem to outnumber petroglyphs. Possibly this is because they so commonly were made on protected sandstone surfaces within the deep alcoves typical of the plateau cliffs. These pale walls provide excellent surfaces for painting and, because of their lack of patina, are less suitable for the making of petroglyphs. Frequently, in the same shelters where paintings occur, there are other Basketmaker remains such as habitation debris and slab-lined cists containing burials and stored items.

A functional correlation may have existed between the paintings and the other activities taking place there. The earliest correlations between the paintings of the broad-shouldered beings and Basketmaker II remains were made by Kidder and Guernsey (1919) in their exploration of sites in the vicinity of Marsh Pass on Laguna Creek. They reported full-front figures between 1 foot and 5 feet in height, solidly painted in chalky white. These anthropomorphs have long arms and legs and small heads, and some wear headdresses and have zigzag designs in red and yellow across the torso. Painted hand prints are the only other motif commonly found in association. Nearby in Tsegi Canyon, however, there is an occasional stirrup-shaped object near the Basketmaker figures. This may represent a ceremonial pouch such as those depicted in the hands of Basketmaker figures at Butler Wash. Figures of the type described here also occur in the highlands south of Glen Canyon, where other Basketmaker remains show a specific affinity with those from Tsegi Canyon and Marsh Pass (Long 1966:62–64).

Haury (1945b), in association with Basketmaker II remains in Buttress Canyon in the Chinle drainage, describes hand prints and large broad-shouldered anthropomorphs painted in several colors (Plates 2, 9; Fig. 72). Some are outlined in red and have dotted or striped decoration on their torsos. Headgear is helmet-shaped.

Canyon de Chelly and Canyon del Muerto (hereafter referred to collectively as Canyon de Chelly, for the sake of simplicity), at the upper reaches of the Chinle drainage, are notable for their wealth of Anasazi art, which was recorded in detail by De Harport (1959) and Grant (1978). These red canyons are veritable outdoor art galleries, the shelters and smooth walls of the canyons having been decorated with drawings for nearly two thousand years, beginning with the Basketmakers and extending through the modern Navajo. Most of the rock-shelters contain a Basketmaker II occupation and were reoccupied by subsequent Anasazi groups (De Harport 1951). Variety and excellence characterize the representations of the human figure of the Basketmaker Period.

Many of the simpler figures are painted in a single solid color, usually white, and resemble those just described from the Marsh Pass–Tsegi district. Others are painted in outline only and have interior decoration. The finest paintings are those solidly painted in one color and outlined with a contrasting one (Fig. 73 and Plate 10). Belts, necklaces of small beads or with large pendants, and a variety of headgear adorn these Canyon de Chelly anthropomorphs. Some have hand prints stamped in the torso area. A number of figures in the canyons are depicted with eyes, which are frequently indicated as vertical ovals, usually placed close together.

An odd type of headgear found on a number of figures in one Canyon del Muerto shelter consists of two projecting devices, one from the left side of the head, usually from the ear region, and the other rising from the top (Plates 10,

Figure 73. San Juan Anthropomorphic Style paintings superimposed by smaller human figures and birds in the Chinle Representational Style, Canyon del Muerto. Photograph, Karl Kernberger.

11; Fig. 74). In one instance these objects are clearly feathers, as indicated by the detail in the painting, but in others the series of arcs or similar shapes at the end of the "feathers" are enigmatic. This type of headgear occurs also in Basketmaker petroglyphs at Butler Wash on the San Juan River (Fig. 75).

As elsewhere, hand prints accompany Basketmaker anthropomorphs in Canyon de Chelly, and Grant (1978) suggests that painted figures of atlatls in Canyon del Muerto are Basketmaker II in date. What else is contemporaneous with the large anthropomorphs here is uncertain. Because of the large number of paintings in these shelters and their continuous occupation, it is sometimes hard to distinguish between Basketmaker II work and that which immediately followed, particularly since some of the older forms seem to have persisted into post–Basketmaker II times. Nevertheless, a comparison of the Canyon de Chelly sites with Basketmaker II sites elsewhere (Haury 1945a; Kidder and Guernsey 1919) strongly suggests that the many small solid

Figure 74. Paired Basketmaker anthropomorphs with distinctive headgear, Canyon del Muerto. Figures are about 3 feet tall. Photograph, Karl Kernberger.

Figure 75. San Juan Anthropomorphic Style petroglyphs, San Juan River at Butler Wash, Utah. Largest figure is between 4 and 5 feet tall. Photograph, Philip Hobler.

elements appearing along with the large Basketmaker anthropomorphs in Canyon de Chelly date from a later period.

One of the most spectacular displays of the San Juan Anthropomorphic Style occurs at the mouth of Butler Wash on the San Juan River (Figs. 75–78), where Glen Canyon Linear Style designs are present along with Basketmaker figures (see Chapter 3). The figures here are petroglyphs pecked into the exposed faces of red rock cliffs blackened by patination. The dinting of the figures is fine and carefully controlled, suggesting indirect percussion. Long rows of heroic trapezoidal anthropomorphs, commanding in appearance, dominate the scene. They typically wear necklaces consisting of several narrow strands of beads, and many figures wear fringed belts. Torsos are further decorated with sets of wavy lines reminiscent of torso decoration in

Figure 76. Detail of anthropomorphs on San Juan River at Butler Wash. Photograph, Curtis Schaafsma.

the Barrier Canyon Style. Some figures are phallic and others, probably female, have small anthropomorphic figures depicted within.

There is an interesting array of spectacular headdresses. Some consist of a series of vertically arranged arcs or crescents. There are also, as mentioned earlier, figures with left "ear" devices and matching pieces on the tops of their heads, as at Canyon del Muerto. A third type of headgear possibly characteristic of this locality consists of an elongate inverse trapezoidal device (Fig. 75). This is usually solidly pecked with linear extensions past the solid portion. Some of these, in addition to the crescent series, are pictured alone as well as in an anthropomorphic context, suggesting that these adornments in themselves may have been emblematic. The crescents also occur in the chest portion of one figure.

Other elements and attributes occur here, some of which are not common in the San Juan Anthropomorphic Style elsewhere. There are figures of mountain sheep and thick snakes. Hand prints are pecked alone or in pairs.

Figure 77.   San Juan Anthropomorphic Style petroglyphs, Butler Wash on the San Juan River. Small Glen Canyon Linear Style anthropomorph with face and antennae appears at upper left.

Figure 78.   San Juan Anthropomorphic Style with yucca plant and later Anasazi petroglyphs, San Juan River at Butler Wash. Basketmaker figures are between 3 and 4 feet tall. Glen Canyon Linear Style animal at upper right.

Atlatls and wavy lines with loose end spirals are depicted, and dots extend in horizontal rows between the anthropomorphs. Large doughnut-like elements with tabs resemble a wooden pendant from a Basketmaker III Cave. The pendant is thought to have originally been decorated with tesserae (Jernigan 1978:187, Fig. 91). Some figures carry bags or pouches; pouches are also depicted alone. In addition to the pairs of vertical wavy lines down the torso, the animal in the chest region and the figures of snakes are other details reminiscent of Barrier Canyon Style work. Yucca plants and stalks heavy with fruit (Fig. 78) have also been found in the Barrier Canyon Style. Nearby, in Butler Wash itself and elsewhere in southern Utah, masks with hair occur occasionally in these sites.

On the western edge of the distribution of the Basketmaker anthropomorph is an interesting focus: south of Kanab, Utah, in Snake Gulch, a tributary of Kanab Creek, are a number of spectacular figures, rather crudely painted in two colors, with oversized heads and tapered bodies (Fig. 79). The figures have their own regional characteristics distinct from those so far discussed from the San Juan drainage. Some appear to be wearing masks, the features of which are indicated with straight lines. A few feathers rising from the central part of the head represent headgear. Heavy "hairbobs" or "shoulder bobs" (P. Schaafsma 1971:41) occur at either side of the head, and necklaces and sashes are prominent. The Snake Gulch anthropomorphs are notable in their detailed likeness to the anthropomorphs in the Fremont rock art (see Chapter 6). They have not been dated other than on a stylistic basis, and associated cultural remains, if any, have yet to be described.

Basketmaker anthropomorphs at the eastern end of their distribution on the San Juan near Bloomfield, New Mexico, are in petroglyph form and solidly pecked, although some show evidence of having once been painted (Fig. 80). All share the slightly tapered trapezoidal body shape and drooping hands and feet characteristic of Basketmaker figures elsewhere, but elaboration outside of simple headgear is generally lacking. Further details may have been supplied by the painting.

Considering their elaborate headgear and other paraphernalia and the occasional depiction of masks, I feel that the Basketmaker anthropomorphs not only had ceremonial import but that they exceeded the realm of the ordinary; they were probably representations either of supernatural beings themselves or of shamans. Images such as these may have been thought to contain the soul force of the beings they represent. The many hand prints around or in the torso area of some of the figures support this possibility; they

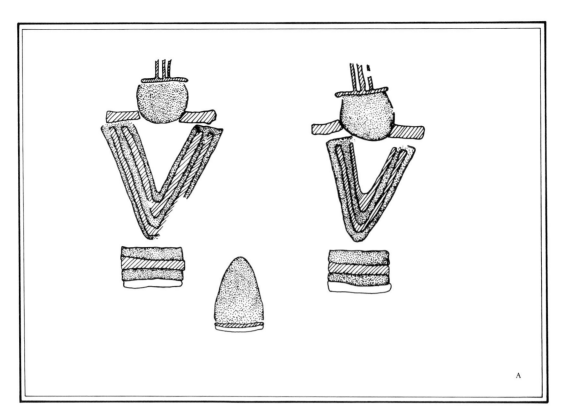

Figure 79. Paired anthropomorphs painted in ceremonial attire, Snake Gulch, Arizona.

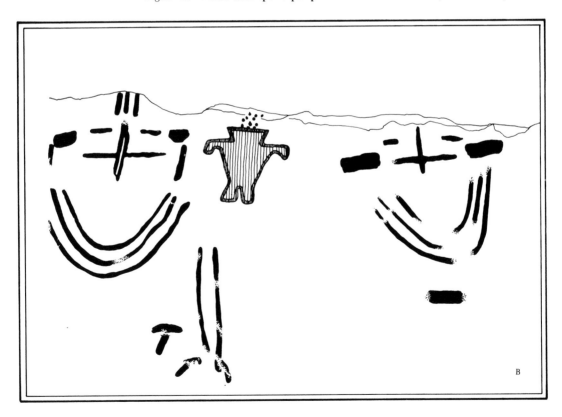

C   D

probably were so placed in order to identify the supplicant who had offered prayers to, or through, the beings portrayed.

The hand print, a universal symbol in primitive art and an important motif in Pueblo paintings even today, has persisted from these earliest beginnings. Many Basketmaker caves are filled with solid or patterned prints in several colors (Plate 2). The idea that these prints, usually made by pressing a paint-covered hand against the rock, served as a means of identification is supported by ethnographic information. Modern Pueblo Indians are reported to leave hand prints at sacred places where they have prayed in order that the supernatural engaged will be able to identify the supplicant (Ellis and Hammack 1968:36). Hand prints randomly placed in these shelters, as well as those associated with the large and elaborate anthropomorphs, were probably made by the Basketmakers for similar reasons.

Basketmaker II Rock Art outside the Central San Juan Drainage

The modest Bloomfield anthropomorphs mark the edge of the Basketmaker world in which the large human figure played a major role in the

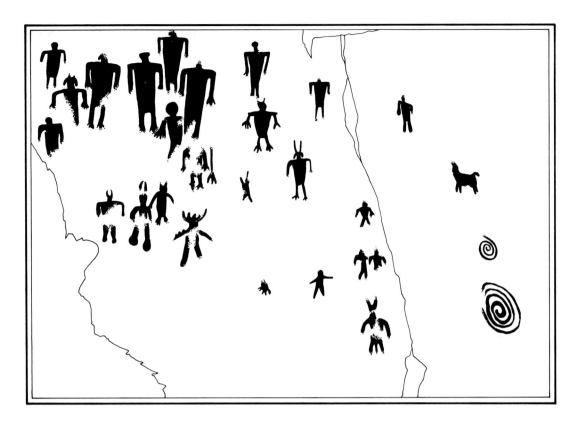

Figure 80. Anthropomorphic petroglyphs, San Juan Anthropomorphic Style, Bloomfield, New Mexico. Larger figures about 2 feet tall.

graphic art. The absence of the San Juan Anthropomorphic Style to the east in the Navajo Reservoir district (Map 3) is notable, particularly since a Basketmaker II occupation was well established there. This configuration, known as Los Pinos Phase, has been studied in considerable depth (Eddy 1961). The absence of the San Juan Anthropomorphic Style in the Reservoir area indicates that Los Pinos Basketmakers were not participants in the ideographic system that fostered its production immediately to the west on the San Juan. In fact, none of the rock art in the Navajo Reservoir district could be attributed to Los Pinos occupation (P. Schaafsma 1963). That Los Pinos Basketmakers were distinct from those in the central and lower San Juan is suggested also on the basis of other archaeological data.

Rock art characteristic of the Basketmaker II period has not been identified from other parts of the Anasazi domain, although this may be due to the failure of observers to recognize Basketmaker art rather than to an absence of such material. On the Rio Grande at this time, however, we are still dealing with a completely different artistic tradition having to do primarily with petroglyphs in the Great Basin Abstract Style on talus boulders. Elements present in the early rock art along the Rio Grande include sunbursts, wavy lines, wandering lines, concentric circles, rakes, bird tracks, dot designs, and stick-figure humans, some of which have oversized hands and feet. It is evident that this art reflects an ideographic system separate from that of the early Anasazi on the plateau.

In contrast, the art of the Basketmaker III through Pueblo III periods seems to be more uniform throughout the entire Anasazi area from Nevada to the Rio Grande, indicating that by then a greater amount of interchange was taking place within the Anasazi realm.

LATER DEVELOPMENTS: BASKETMAKER III– EARLY PUEBLO II

Early in the Anasazi sequence, there is a transition from the San Juan Anthropomorphic Style to styles and figure types more typical of the Anasazi tradition as it continued until around A.D. 1300. Probably gradual, this transition nevertheless led to a distinctive break with the past.

Exactly when and how fast this occurred is somewhat ambiguous because of the lack of refined dating. At roughly the same time, however, significant changes were taking place in Anasazi culture, and to judge from the proliferation of settlements from this period in many parts of the plateau, the new mode of existence was extremely successful. Pottery was introduced, increasing domestic efficiency, and the atlatl was replaced by the bow and arrow. Other, more fundamental developments seem to have been associated at least in part with an increasing dependence on horticulture. New and more productive varieties of corn were being grown, and beans were also placed under cultivation. The increasing importance of domestic crops fostered a more stable settlement pattern, with the construction of permanent houses concentrated in small year-round villages. These changes were basic and must have produced accompanying shifts in social and religious organization. For instance, in these early villages we find kivas—religious structures that imply the development of a formal religious organization.

Concomitant changes in Anasazi rock art included a gradual reduction in size and importance of the large, stylized anthropomorphic figures that had dominated early Basketmaker art, while a whole complex of new elements came into play. As the subject matter of rock art was greatly expanded, new figure types creating different directions in aesthetic expression began to emerge. It seems clear that the old ideographic system from which the large anthropomorphs derived was giving way to new thought systems, provoking the use of many new designs. Along with these changes in content, there is a marked increase in the number of petroglyph panels. The field research necessary to determine the reason for this has not been done, although it may relate in part to a difference in rock art functions and hence a wider choice of site locations. A few distinct style complexes can be described from the period, and again these are best known from the San Juan drainage, although there is some evidence that related styles were present as far east as the Rio Grande (Lang 1976).

The Chinle Representational Style

This style, described as "Modified Basketmaker–Developmental Pueblo" rock art by Grant (1978), is best known from Canyon de Chelly where it occurs sometimes in petroglyph form but is more often found in rock-shelters as paintings. The style, however, has a wide distribution in the canyons of the lower central San Juan drainage. In Canyon de Chelly during the years following the early Basketmakers, the rock art was highly diversified. Many of the anthropomorphic figures believed to date from this period show typological continuity with earlier forms, but new elements are also numerous. The more traditional anthropomorphs, in addition to being smaller, are often painted in a single solid color and outlined in another. Others are vertically divided into two colors (Plate 12). The torso configuration tends away from the strictly trapezoidal toward the triangular. Arms, hands, heads, and legs may be omitted. When feet are depicted they turn out to the side. Some human representations tend to have pointed shoulders, and exaggeratedly long necks come into vogue. Triangular-bodied figures may be arranged in long rows, and frequently they are shown holding hands (Figs. 81, 82, 83).

Small stick-figure humans appear about this time. They may be engaged in a variety of seemingly ordinary activities—walking, running, sitting in groups, and so on (Plates 13, 14; Fig. 84). They are a long step removed from the immobile and remote anthropomorphs of the San Juan Anthropomorphic Style. The earliest flute players are believed to be Basketmaker III in date and are stick-figure depictions; they are often seated and sometimes occur in pairs (Plate 15 and Fig. 85). They usually lack the hump and the phallus

Figure 81. A variety of small human figures, Chinle Representational Style, Ceremonial Cave, Canyon del Muerto. Photograph, Karl Kernberger.

Figure 82. Human figures and birds painted in white, Chinle Representational Style, Canyon de Chelly.

123

Figure 83. Red and white painting of anthropomorphic figure with headdress and spear, Chinle Representational Style, Pictograph Cave, Canyon de Chelly. Figure is approximately 1 foot tall. Photograph, Karl Kernberger.

Figure 84. Red and white seated stick figures, Chinle Representational Style. Ceremonial Cave, Canyon del Muerto. Figures are about 5 inches tall. Photograph, Karl Kernberger.

Figure 85. Seated fluteplayer under rainbow and other figures, Chinle Representational Style, Pictograph Cave, Canyon de Chelly. Faded Basketmaker hand prints (above) provide scale. Photograph, Karl Kernberger.

commonly found in later representations of Kokopelli (Grant 1974; Smith 1974; see pp. 132–33).

Headdresses depicted as vertical lines of dots are widely diagnostic, and "rabbit-eared" headgear consisting of two lines, possibly representing feathers at either side of the head, is also common. Red figures in Plate 14 and Figure 84 wear white headbands. Birds, specifically ducks and turkeys, as headgear or as devices replacing the entire head of the human figure are typical of this period (Figs. 73, 86).

Birds as independent elements are also a major theme in the Chinle Representational Style (Figs. 73, 87, 88). Like some of the human figures, they are solidly painted with an outline in a contrasting color. They are often represented rather realistically. Turkeys, ducks, and cranes, or other long-legged wading birds are recognizable. Most have crescent-shaped or semicircular bodies, and the heads and necks of many were painted with a fugitive, or impermanent, red pigment that has since flaked away while the body shape remains (Fig. 88). As pointed out by Grant (1978), this phenomenon has led to the misinterpretation of these designs as "baskets," especially when the birds occur on the heads of anthropomorphs. A sense

Figure 86. Paintings in red and white of small human figures with birds on their heads, Chinle Representational Style, Pictograph Cave, Canyon de Chelly. Photograph, Karl Kernberger.

of flight is often conveyed by the legs, which are swept back at an angle. Wings, however, are not depicted.

In contrast, representations of quadrupeds during this period are not of major importance in Canyon de Chelly, although there are some painted mountain sheep and some highly stylized animal outlines in white. Grant (1978:182–83) discusses the presence of pecked sheep distinguished by gaping mouths and extended hooves. The body configuration of these sheep is not highly formalized. Grant notes that the human figures occurring with the sheep resemble the painted ones of this period.

Rainbow arcs in two colors painted above human figures, feathered darts, and the ubiquitous hand print are also found. Hand prints may be solid, patterned, or rendered as negative designs, an effect achieved by holding a hand to the cliff and spraying pigment or clay around it. Abstract elements are few, the zigzag being the most common.

Grant (1978) places a terminal date for this complex in Canyon de Chelly around A.D. 1000, after which he describes a degenerate period during which fewer elements were represented and painting technique declined in quality.

Figure 87. Small birds and row of human figures in white, Chinle Representational Style, Ceremonial Cave, Canyon del Muerto. Human figures between 3 and 4 inches tall. Photograph, Karl Kernberger.

Figure 88. Red and white painting of birds in flight. Heads, now absent, were painted in fugitive pigment. Chinle Representational Style, Ceremonial Cave, Canyon del Muerto. Large birds about 10 inches long. Photograph, Karl Kernberger.

127

Hidden Valley

In the Animas Valley of southwestern Colorado, miniature designs painted on the walls of rock-shelters in Hidden Valley are ascribable to this stage. The caves in question were lived in by both Basketmaker II and Basketmaker III Indians, the occupation ending with the latter around A.D. 700 (Morris and Burgh 1954). The paintings are very small, most between 3 and 8 inches high. Black, white, green, yellow, and red pigments were used. Outside of a few zigzags and circle motifs, most of the elements are life-forms. Lines of ducks, with from two to twenty in a group, are painted here, and deer and mountain sheep are represented individually. Stick-figure humans, including flute players, are also depicted (Daniels 1954:87–88).

Of special interest are the several series of tiny masks ranging in number from one to nine in a group (Fig. 89). These small red faces lack outlines and consist of eyes and nose or mouth over which may be a feather or a heavy cap similar to those depicted on certain anthropomorphs from Kanab and Canyon de Chelly. These interesting little masks have not been found outside the Hidden Valley caves, although rock art investigations in culturally related regions have been intensive (P. Schaafsma 1963; Smith 1974).

The Rosa Representational Style

One of the best-known rock art styles of this period is the Rosa Representational Style from the upper San Juan drainage in northwestern New Mexico (P. Schaafsma 1963:7–35; 1972:5–6). Its distribution includes the San Juan and Los Pinos rivers within the Navajo Reservoir district and the Largo Canyon drainage to the south. Rosa Style figures are also found along the San Juan River itself as far west as Waterflow. This entire region has been designated part of the Mesa Verde culture of the Anasazi (Eddy 1966:390).

Within the Navajo Reservoir district, it was originally estimated that the style dated primarily from the Rosa Phase occupation, A.D. 700–850, and it was believed to be roughly equivalent to early Pueblo I in terms of cultural attainment (P. Schaafsma 1963; Eddy 1966:471–84). It is possible, however, that the style may also be associated with the preceding Sambrito Phase and the following Piedra Phase; if so, the dating of the style would thus be expanded to include the period between A.D. 400 and A.D. 950 (Eddy 1966:470, Table 6). In no case could it have lasted beyond A.D. 1050, at the end of the Arboles Phase, when the district was abandoned.

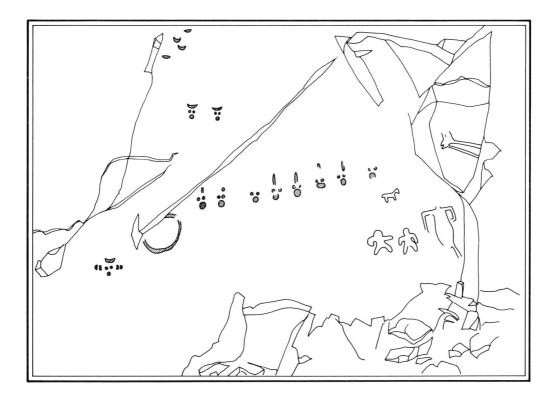

Figure 89. Line of tiny red masks and anthropomorphs, Hidden Valley, Colorado.

Rosa Style petroglyph makers usually selected exposed, darkly patinated sandstone surfaces for their work. As with the Cave Valley Style (see p. 122) and rock art in Canyon de Chelly following the early Basketmakers, broad-shouldered human forms varying from trapezoidal to triangular are a dominant motif (Figs. 7 and 90). There are also a few basically rectangular figures with small heads and exaggerated necks. Arms and legs are thin and often very short. Hands and feet are usually absent; if present, they are poorly drawn. Occasionally chest ornaments, perhaps representing pendants, are depicted on the larger figures. Head ornamentation is fairly standardized and consists of two feathers on either side of the head, creating the rabbit-eared effect, or of a single feather projecting at an angle. The bird headdress is absent here. Rosa figures are arranged in rows of hand-holding people, are depicted singly, or are shown occasionally in family groups (Fig. 91 and P. Schaafsma 1972:Fig. 4).

As in the Chinle Representational Style, there is a typological gradation between the solid broad-shouldered forms and the stick figures, all of which appear to be contemporaneous. The stick figures are smaller and are rather

Figure 90. Anthropomorphs, Rosa Representational Style, Carrizo Canyon drainage, New Mexico. Largest figure about a foot tall. New Mexico State Planning Office; photograph, Karl Kernberger.

Figure 91. Family group, Rosa Representational Style, San Juan River, Navajo Reservoir. (After Schaafsma 1963: Fig. 12).

poorly pecked, probably by direct percussion with a hammerstone, but they often assume active stances, getting away from the flat frontal perspective that characterizes the larger anthropomorphs. Arms of these figures are invariably held down, never up. Flute players occur, and there are lively bowmen in action-packed hunt scenes.

Animals, comparable in form and technique, are rendered simply and species are only rarely identifiable. Mountain sheep are very rare, but antlers sometimes indicate a deer. A single animal is sometimes shown enclosed in a circle of dots that appears to represent a corral or trap, an interesting adjunct to the hunt scene. Birds are rare; when they do occur, they are usually long-legged wading birds. Ducks and turkeys, so frequent in the Canyon de Chelly work, are virtually unknown. As is the case elsewhere during this time period, abstract designs are few; they include small spirals, wandering lines, and other basic motifs.

West and north of the Rosa region, within the immediate area of Mesa Verde, stylistically related petroglyphs from Mancos Canyon show broad-shouldered, triangular-bodied men holding bows and staffs and others with bird headdresses. Cranes and miscellaneous, poorly defined quadrupeds typical of the period are also present (Fig. 92).

The Cave Valley Representational Style

To the west, in the drainage of the Colorado River, this same basic configuration is found in the Cave Valley Style (P. Schaafsma 1971:116–17) from the central Virgin Kayenta region in southwestern Utah and the adjoining areas of northern Arizona. The style occurs in the rock-shelters of the region (Wauer 1965; Steward 1941:Fig 61; Judd 1926:Pl. 60) with early Anasazi remains loosely referred to by early investigators as generalized Basketmaker (as opposed to cliff dwellers) (Judd 1926:92–93). It was tentatively assigned in previous study to an early period in the Anasazi sequence; now, on the basis of comparisons with Anasazi rock art of Basketmaker III and Pueblo I periods elsewhere, this temporal placement seems to be further substantiated.

Cave Valley Style rock drawings occur most often as paintings in black, red, yellow, green, pink, and white. The style is characterized by human figures in frontal view with tapered bodies and broad, flat-topped, bucket-shaped heads. They are usually painted with short arms and legs, which are sometimes also triangular in form and echo the larger triangles and trapezoids

Figure 92.   Petroglyphs, Mancos Canyon, Mesa Verde, Colorado. Photograph, Milwaukee Public Museum.

used in the body. Headgear is usually a crown of vertically or horizontally aligned dots. Variations on this type are also present in Figure 108.

There are, in addition, small, thick stick figures in profile; as in the Canyon de Chelly paintings, these are sometimes shown running or sitting with arms outstretched. In Figure 93, a recumbent flute player is depicted with a small hump and pointed cap, next to a typical Cave Valley Style anthropomorph. Small amorphous and unidentifiable quadrupeds and birds, and a few abstract designs such as dot rows, wavy lines, and concentric circles, also occur.

In sum, following the San Juan Anthropomorphic Style of the Basket-maker II Period, there is a gradual reduction in the size and importance of the human figure, along with a multiplication of different human figure types. These figures, instead of maintaining a static frontal rigidity and invoking an air of otherworldliness, are often busily engaged in a variety of activities. The earliest appearance of the flute player occurs before A.D. 700, as evidenced by the presence of this figure in the Hidden Valley shelters. Other life-forms

Figure 93. Cave Valley Style anthropomorph and fluteplayer, Snake Gulch, Arizona.

present in these panels are birds and animals, the species depicted varying somewhat from region to region. Cranes, ducks, and turkeys, possibly with ceremonial implications, are among the birds that can be identified, the last two concentrated in Canyon de Chelly and elsewhere in the lower central San Juan drainage. Hunt scenes with bowmen and deer and traps or corrals are typical in the Rosa Style. The number of abstract elements in the early Anasazi work described here is small, and these consist largely of simple designs such as wavy lines, concentric circles, and simple spirals and dots. Grant (1978) has suggested that this change from early Basketmaker work may reflect a certain degree of secularization in the rock art, with a concern for daily affairs becoming more evident.

On the other hand, the importance of the bird, which undoubtedly has ritual significance, in the art of this period and in particular in the Chinle Style cannot be overemphasized. Some of these bird representations may relate to shamanic practices of the period and the properties of magic flight, as described previously. In many parts of the world shamans claim to be able to engage in flights in which the soul, leaving the body, assumes the form of a bird. The duck-headed figures may represent shamans with this ability (Wellmann 1975; Grant 1978).

The duck, a figure widely associated with shamanism, has a long history of ritual significance in both the Southwest and Mexico. In Mexico it is a prominent figure in the prehistoric art of the west coast, and it plays a major mythological and ritual role among the Cora-Huichol (Furst 1974a:139). In the Southwest it is important in Anasazi art during the period currently under discussion, as well as in some of the mural paintings and petroglyphs of Rio Grande Style art of the later Pueblo peoples (Dutton 1963). Its significance may be interpreted through ethnographic comparisons (Furst 1974a, 1974b; Parsons 1939). Among both the Huichols and the Pueblos, gods may assume the form of a duck, especially when they are traveling between sacred mountains and the sea. In the Pueblo world, ducks serve as messengers to the rain clouds of the four sacred directions, as seed bearers, and as messengers of the gods. At Zuni they may even be the kachina dead or the gods themselves transformed. The leader of the Zuni kachinas, Pautiwa, may on occasion take the form of a duck. The duck is also associated with supernatural curing.

A recently described Colima figurine from Jalisco, Mexico, is a noteworthy parallel to the Anasazi representations. The head of the figure is covered by a duck effigy. In one hand he holds a spear thrower, in the other a bundle of darts. The figurine dates from between 200 B.C. and A.D. 400–500 (Von Winning 1974:72–73), thus just preceding or even somewhat overlapping the Anasazi examples. In sum, the bird-headed figure, along with the smaller and simplified renditions of the broad-shouldered anthropomorphs, is evidence for the persistence of shamanism. Although shamanism may have been less important at this time, as suggested by the reduced and simplified broad-shouldered figures, those with birds as, or on, their heads suggest that a new dimension may have been added to shamanic thought and practice.

LATE PUEBLO II AND PUEBLO III ROCK ART

During late Pueblo II and Pueblo III times, population shifts and developments in Anasazi culture led to larger village concentrations, climaxing in the large towns of Chaco Canyon between A.D. 1050 and A.D. 1150 and in the cliff villages of Mesa Verde and the Kayenta region in the 1200s. At this time, before the withdrawal from the north and west began, the

Anasazi rock art tradition reached its greatest point of territorial expansion. The middle and late 1100s, however, were a time of major changes in settlement patterns during which the northern and western regions, including the Virgin Kayenta and the Kayenta area north of the San Juan, were abandoned. Increasing aridity as a period of alluviation ended and the beginning of sheet erosion, possibly brought about by the decrease in available moisture and by overuse of farmed areas, were probably instrumental in bringing about the social changes that occurred (Dean 1970:151). Dean points out that at the same time the Anasazi also would have felt the first pressures from the north and west, as the southern Paiutes began to penetrate Anasazi territory in northwestern Arizona and southern Utah. Whatever the causes, the pattern of small villages spread out over a wide area began to change, and in general, a period of population aggregation began.

Studies of community patterning in villages during this period have suggested that among the results of population consolidation was the coming together of hitherto separate groups of people or lineages and consequently the development of multiclan villages (Dean 1970:164–70). Dean proposes that mechanisms were developed for maintaining clan identity during this period of increasing social complexity. These mechanisms may have some bearing on the interpretation of some of the rock art associated with the late cliff dwellings in the Kayenta region and in Canyon de Chelly.

In spite of, or possibly in response to, the general pressures of the time, this period in Pueblo history was highly creative. Trends evident from early Anasazi days culminated just before A.D. 1300. Peaks were attained in architectural construction and design and in ceramic form and decoration. Geometric pottery motifs became highly structured and intricate, as the technical aspects of their execution reached new standards of excellence. A similar direction prevailed in the rock art, which also followed with unbroken continuity in the tradition established earlier. The proliferation and variety of forms described for the preceding period were maintained for a while. As Turner (1963:7) aptly phrases it in describing Glen Canyon Style 4 (A.D. 1050–1250), "Design elaboration is rampant."

Petroglyphs on cliff faces and talus boulders dating from this period are exceedingly common, while paintings are prevalent in inhabited rockshelters. The representation of the human hand print persists unabated throughout Pueblo II and III. It occurs as a petroglyph motif as well as a print stamped in paint, the latter being found on the walls of shelters housing late Pueblo III cliff dwellings (Fig. 5). During this time, the human figure is reduced to a size comparable to all other elements, and new figure types emerge alongside older ones. The highly formalized rectilinear stick figure with arms held up as well as down is a characteristic anthropomorphic type late in the Anasazi tradition (Plate 11; Figs. 94, 95).

The rigid stylization seen in the rectilinear stick figures indicates a general interest in formal patterns, and, to this end, a tightening of form. In the rock art this is accomplished by an increase in the number of geometric designs resembling those from pottery and textiles. There is also a greater number of abstract designs such as rectilinear scrolls, spirals, and concentric circles. These elements, along with the rectilinear shapes of men and lizards, could be said to be diagnostic of the rock art of the period. Representational elements are rendered with an effort to produce pleasing visual patterns. The carefully delineated patterns of sandal tracks, both the plain solid types (Fig. 96) and those in outline with decorative interior patterning, indicate an interest in aesthetic effect. By the same token, the better drawings of mountain sheep, particularly in the Kayenta region, are done with finesse and with attention to horns and body shape in order to create an elegant, almost abstract design.

Lizards, rare in earlier work, emerge as an important element in late Anasazi art, often being almost indistinguishable from anthropomorphs; hence the term "lizard-man" for those figures that are ambiguous (Fig. 97, upper left). The ambiguity may have been intentional. The recent excavation of a lizard-woman effigy from a kiva at Salmon Ruins, a Pueblo III site on the north bank of the San Juan near Bloomfield, New Mexico, indicates that the anthropomorphic lizard may have been a supernatural of ceremonial importance.

Another personage appearing in the rock art of this period is the humpbacked flute player (Figs. 98–100). Known by the name of his modern Pueblo kachina counterpart, Kokopelli, this figure is one of the few that has survived in recognizable form from the ancient days of the Anasazi into modern times. The date at which he first appears is not certain, but he is definitely present with hump and flute in Anasazi rock drawings, ceramic decoration, and kiva wall paintings after A.D. 1000. On the other hand, flute playing figures are present in the rock art of the Anasazi from Basketmaker III on, but because the diagnostic hump (humpbacked figures being almost universally associated with supernatural qualities; Furst 1974a:137) and phallus are usually lacking on these earlier depictions, it is not clear whether ordinary people or mythical personages are being represented. I am inclined

Figure 94. Eroded bedrock petroglyphs of stick figure and sandal tracks, late Anasazi, Canyon de Chelly. Sandal tracks provide scale. Photograph, Karl Kernberger.

Figure 95. Late Anasazi petroglyphs, Pictograph Point, Mesa Verde National Park. Photograph, Scott Files, Peabody Museum, Harvard University.

Figure 96. Kayenta Representational Style and earlier Anasazi work, Smith Fork Bar, Glen Canyon. Photograph, Scott Files, Peabody Museum, Harvard University.

Figure 97. Late Anasazi Petroglyphs, Chaco Canyon. Photograph, Mary Whittemore, Scott Files, Peabody Museum, Harvard University.

Figure 98. Late Anasazi petroglyphs with dancing humpbacked flute player, lizard men, and long-tailed quadrupeds, Chaco Canyon. New Mexico State Planning Office; photograph, Karl Kernberger.

Figure 99. White painting of reclining humpbacked flute player, Canyon de Chelly. Photograph, Karl Kernberger.

Figure 100. Petroglyphs of reclining humpbacked fluteplayers with insect attributes, Long House Valley, Kayenta region.

to feel that the latter is the case, and that the earlier depictions are the same figure in an earlier conceptual form.

Kokopelli was and is a character with multiple but interrelated attributes. He is usually an ithyphallic being with a hump, and in many representations he lies on his back or is shown dancing while he plays his flute. Some depictions show him with antennae and other insect features (Fig. 100). Kokopelli in his many aspects is well summarized in an article by Wellmann (1970), and much of the following derives from Wellmann's discussion.

One interpretation of this figure is that he is a rain priest who calls the clouds and moisture with his flute. At Hopi the flute is played over springs to attract the rain, and gourds for carrying drinking water are sometimes attached to the end of the flute. Kokopelli is also associated with certain insects, the locust in particular. Locust is a patron for the Hopi Flute Society and for those that cure arrow wounds and is an important figure in the emergence myth. As he was sent to look for an entrance into the Upper World, the Clouds shot lightning bolts through him, but he just continued to play his flute. Locust also plays the flute to melt the snow when appealed to by the sun-loving snakes (Parsons 1938:337–38). This tale may help explain the frequent association in the rock art of the humpbacked flute player with a snake (Wellmann 1970:1680). Petroglyphs also depict Kokopelli with a flute or a bow in mountain sheep hunting scenes, and one painting from a wall in Fire Temple, a modified Great Kiva on Mesa Verde, shows phallic humpbacked hunters, one of whom is wearing a headdress of mountain sheep horns (Fig. 101). In these instances Kokopelli appears to be a hunting priest and perhaps also serves to promote the fertility of the game animals.

Fewkes, on the other hand, has a very different view of these phallic horned figures painted on the walls of Fire Temple. On the basis of his interpretation that this structure was used for the performance of the New Fire Ceremony, he points out (1921:88) that these are probably Horned Priests such as those who participate in the New Fire Ceremony at Hopi. Their phallic aspect also has a modern Hopi counterpart in this ceremony, since one aspect of fire is life itself—thus the use of fertility symbolism. Fewkes cites these paintings as one piece of evidence that the kiva was used for New Fire rites by the ancient Mesa Verde people. This is an interesting view, but his interpretation is not conclusive for either the function of the site or the meaning of the paintings.

The modern kachina counterpart of the Kokopelli figure in the old Anasazi art lacks a flute, but Hawley (1937) suggests that this may have been replaced by the long snout. The Kokopelli kachina is primarily concerned with increase and fertility, hence his connection with rainmaking necessary for the maturing of corn and other crops (Lambert 1967:400). His favorite pastime, however, is seducing maidens, and his hump is said to be filled with babies, blankets, or seeds, some of which he gives to each girl he seduces (Wellmann 1970:1681).

In sum, Wellmann (1970) has pointed out that in his more universal role, Kokopelli, "may be compared with the Universal Trickster archetype, who, in spite of his unrestrained sexuality, in his roles as hunting magician and rain priest changes from an unprincipled amoral force into a creator who brings order and security into the chaos of the world."

As mentioned previously in the case of Fire Temple, the graphic art of the late Anasazi has also been preserved on the walls of kivas and other rooms of cliff dwellings, both as paintings and as crude designs scratched into the plaster. Wall paintings of this period consist of geometric designs that commonly take the form of decorative bands (Fig. 102) and small life-forms.

Figure 101.   Phallic hunters, painted on wall of Fire Temple, Mesa Verde National Park. Scott Files, Peabody Museum, Harvard University.

Figure 102.   Abstract wall painting, Spruce Tree House, Mesa Verde National Park. Photograph, Milwaukee Public Museum.

The latter resemble rock art elements in type, and like the rock art they are small and rather scattered in arrangement. The painting of integrated murals decorating an entire wall surface was not yet being practiced. Textile and pottery motifs were sometimes carved on the building stones of Pueblo III structures as exterior decoration (Woodbury 1954:162–63, Fig. 34b–f). These occurrences are invaluable aids in dating late Anasazi rock art by means of stylistic and element comparisons.

The Kayenta Region

There are a number of regional variations within the late Anasazi rock art. The rock art of the Kayenta, specifically that from Glen Canyon, Tsegi Canyon, and Monument Valley and environs, is probably best known, having been studied in more detail than that from any other single Anasazi region (Kidder and Guernsey 1919; Foster 1954; Turner 1963; P. Schaafsma 1966b and 1974). Undoubtedly the early investigators were attracted to the Kayenta rock art at least in part because of its pleasing aesthetic qualities and excellent workmanship.

Kayenta rock art is usually associated with habitation remains by which it can be dated. The peak of the Anasazi rock art tradition in the Kayenta region dates between A.D. 1050 and A.D. 1250 and is characterized by petroglyphs, although rock paintings are also found. This distinctive complex is described from Glen Canyon as Glen Canyon Style 4 (Turner 1963:6–7). In keeping with the terminology used in this volume, the name has been changed here to the Kayenta Representational Style. The style is typified by large numbers of mountain sheep. The best sheep are shown with elegant long horns and cloven hooves (Fig. 103). Body shape varies from rectangular to crescent- or bird-shaped. In addition to mountain sheep, Turner lists birds, flute players, hunting scenes, anthropomorphs with enlarged appendages and genitals, concentric circles, and watch-spring scrolls (spirals) as being diagnostic designs in this phase of Anasazi art in Glen Canyon (Fig. 104). There are also lizards, snakes, bird tracks, sandal designs, and complex blanket and pottery motifs. Human types include stick figures and triangular-bodied figures with headdresses. The triangular-bodied anthropomorphs in Figure 96 are probably earlier, however, than the A.D. 1050–1250 period embraced by the Kayenta Representational Style. According to Turner (1963:7), anthropomorphs with birds as heads or headdresses still seem to be part of this later inventory, found at sites with Mesa Verde pottery

Figure 103.   Bighorn sheep, Kayenta Representational Style, Betatakin, Tsegi Canyon, Arizona. Photograph, Karl Kernberger.

Figure 104.   Rectangular scrolls or spirals, Kayenta Representational Style, Glen Canyon. Photograph, Martin D. Koehler, Scott Files, Peabody Museum, Harvard University.

Figure 105.   Clay paintings, Tsegi Painted Style, Canyon de Chelly. Photograph, David de Harport, Scott Files, Peabody Museum, Harvard University.

associations in Glen Canyon. Shields are a new feature, appearing in the Glen Canyon art before A.D. 1250 and in the Tsegi at the end of Pueblo III (A.D. 1250–1300).

During the following phase of Anasazi occupation in Glen Canyon, between A.D. 1250 and A.D. 1300, a period of degeneration occurred in which the variety of subject matter declined and designs were poorly executed (Turner 1963:6). Elements include sheep, lizard-men, stick figures, concentric circles, and negative designs. A degeneration in form is also noticeable throughout other areas of the northern Kayenta region, and technique tends to be sloppy, particularly among the paintings associated with the Tsegi Phase cliff dwellings (A.D. 1250–1300). I refer to these paintings, which can be described as a distinctive unit within the late Kayenta rock art complex and can be dated around A.D. 1250–1300, as the Tsegi Painted Style. They are common in the rock-shelters of Tsegi and Navajo canyons, and their distribution ranges from Grand Gulch, north of the San Juan, south down the Chinle drainage to Canyon de Chelly.

These paintings consist largely of designs casually painted and in some cases smeared on with thick clay mixtures (Fig. 105). They are most commonly done in white, although tans and various shades of pink and purple clays were also used. The work of this final period is characterized by a wealth of hand prints and scattered renderings of stick-figure men, lizards, concentric circles, and, along with these, splotches of paint thrown or sprayed against the cliff seemingly at random. In the Tsegi, mud balls were thrown at the walls, some aimed specifically at the painted designs.

Some of the most complex clay paintings are those from Scaffold House and Flute Player Cave in Tsegi Canyon (Plate 16, Figs. 106, 107; P. Schaafsma 1966b). The latter contains a spectacular mural of clay paintings spanning a distance of between 50 and 60 feet across the back wall of the alcove. The paintings occur in various shades of rose, red, deep brown and tan clays, and white. Probably because the clays were easily obtainable, the figures here are unusually large. They include mountain sheep, lizards, centipedes, and numerous geometric motifs. Beneath the Pueblo work the faint forms in tan clay of two Basketmaker anthropomorphs can be seen (Fig. 107). A reclining flute player loosely painted in thick white clay is superimposed on other paintings. This figure measures an astounding 5 feet in length. A giant lizard (10 feet long) and a large centipede are similarly painted in white on the rocks below and appear to be the work of the same hand.

Most Tsegi Painted Style sites cannot boast such a wealth of color and design, and with their scattered hand prints and other modest paintings they are considerably more prosaic. If they lack value on aesthetic grounds, however, they may have other significance for archaeology. At Inscription House in the Navajo Canyon drainage, most of the paintings occurred above the rooftops of Tsegi Phase houses. These rooftops and the adjacent space on the cliff wall, where the paintings occur and holes were drilled for the purpose of anchoring looms and hanging things, were used as work and utility spaces by the occupants of the rooms of the pueblo. Dean (1970) demonstrates that the rooms of the pueblo were organized into clusters, each occupied by a household that usually consisted of an extended family. Thus it was suggested that the paintings above each room cluster were done by the household occupants and served, intentionally or incidentally, as a means of territorial demarcation within the crowded confines of the dwelling (P. Schaafsma 1974). Subsequent analysis of the paintings at Inscription House in relation to room clusters indicated that such a functional relationship is possible in this ruin and that it should be tested further elsewhere. At Inscription

Plate 9. Basketmaker II San Juan anthropomorphic Style paintings, Painted Cave, Buttress Canyon, Arizona. Green figure approximately 2.5 feet tall. Photograph, Karl Kernberger.

Plate 10. Pair of Basketmaker anthropomorphs in white, outlined in red, Canyon del Muerto, Arizona. Headgear with the element extending from the side of the head is distinctive. Figures about 3 feet tall. Photograph, Karl Kernberger.

Plate 11. Anasazi paintings from Basketmaker II (A.D. 1–400) through Pueblo III (A.D. 1300), Canyon del Muerto. Photograph, Karl Kernberger.

Plate 12. Anthropomorphs, Chinle Representational Style, Ceremonial Cave, Canyon del Muerto. Photograph, Karl Kernberger.

Plate 13. Walking couple, Chinle Representational Style, Ceremonial Cave, Canyon del Muerto. Figures 6–8 inches tall. Photograph, Karl Kernberger.

Plate 14. Rows of human figures, Chinle Representational Style, Ceremonial Cave, Canyon del Muerto. Figures are about 5 inches tall. Photograph, Karl Kernberger.

Plate 15. Fluteplayers under rainbows with birds, Chinle Representational Style, Pictograph Cave, Canyon de Chelly. Flute players are about 8 inches tall. Photograph, Karl Kernberger.

Plate 16. Clay paintings, Tsegi Painted Style, Fluteplayer Cave, Tsegi Canyon, Arizona. Large sheep is over 4 feet in length. Photograph, Karl Kernberger.

Figure 106. Clay paintings, Tsegi Painted Style, Flute Player Cave, Tsegi Canyon, Arizona. Photograph, Karl Kernberger.

Figure 107. Five-foot-long flute player of Tsegi Painted Style superimposing earlier Anasazi work, Flute Player Cave, Tsegi Canyon, Arizona. Photograph, Karl Kernberger.

House, the paintings consist largely of hand prints, a symbol often used for purposes of identification in the Pueblo world today. The hands in Figure 5 occur above a wall dividing room clusters, and the hands may have served to emphasize this boundary.

Also of significance in the Tsegi Painted Style are the large white circular paintings occurring with cliff dwellings. They tend to be situated on the right-hand side of the village alcove and are visible from some distance (Figs. 108–11). Anderson (1971) suggested that these paintings may have served as integrative symbols standing for certain socioreligious institutions or affiliations. As such they would have served a social function at a time when such devices were helpful in furnishing a means of group solidarity. Ethnographic support for this type of interpretation has been offered by Hopi elders who feel that the large circular painting with an interior anthropomorphic design at Betatakin is a Fire Clan symbol representing Masauwu (Fig. 109).

The large number of bighorn sheep represented in the rock art of the Kayenta region deserves further comment. The importance of this figure in Kayenta rock art sites throughout the prehistory of the region, beginning with the Glen Canyon Linear Style, indicates that this animal was highly significant in the lives of these Anasazi. A brief search through the literature in regard to animal bones recovered from excavations in a number of different Anasazi regions tends to substantiate this view (Table 2).

In the rugged canyon terrain of the Kayenta region, where sheep representations are very common, the bone counts from a large number of sites indicate that this animal predominated as a source of food. It may also be significant that faunal analysis from sites on Black Mesa (Douglas 1972) revealed more deer than sheep. This district, although culturally within the Kayenta region, is south of the major canyon areas where bighorn sheep seem to have been more common.

To the south and east of the Kayenta, the representation of bighorn sheep decreases significantly. In sites outside the Kayenta, sheep bones occur in varying quantities, but they are usually superseded in numbers by bones of deer and sometimes antelope. Badger House Community on Mesa Verde (Hayes and Lancaster 1975:190), at which bighorn sheep bones outnumbered deer bones, is an exception. Thus preliminary analysis indicates that the numbers of bighorn sheep represented in the rock art do seem to correspond with variation in the use of this animal by the Anasazi. One may then ask whether differential use between regions reflected differences in preference or in the availability of this animal. Woodbury (1965) observes that within

Figure 108. A shield figure, popularly known as Bat Woman, one of several large white circle designs, Tsegi Painted Style, Bat Woman House, Tsegi Canyon drainage. Photograph, Curtis Schaafsma.

Figure 109. Negative image of anthropomorphic figure within large white circle, Tsegi Painted Style, Betatakin, Tsegi Canyon drainage. Hand prints provide scale. Photograph, Karl Kernberger.

TABLE 2.

Bone Counts for Bighorn Sheep and Deer from Excavations in Anasazi Regions or Districts

Region or District	Data on Big Game Animals
KAYENTA	Mountain sheep, cottontail, jackrabbit common; deer and pronghorn occur sparingly (Kidder and Guernsey 1919: 99–100).
	Glen Canyon—sites of all ages—994 unworked bones; 12 deer, 104 mountain sheep; 354 deer or sheep and small mammals (Sharrock et al. 1963).
	Basketmaker sites: sheep common, deer and antelope rare (Guernsey and Kidder 1921).
	Glen Canyon—of larger game animals, bighorn predominates, 31% of bone total; deer, 4.3%; but notes that 16 sheep and 13 deer could have provided these percentages (Lipe et al. 1960:218).
	Glen Canyon—bighorn most common at all sites (Lipe 1960).
	Mountain sheep bones predominate at NA 7456 (A.D. 1200–1225), NA 7486 (ca. A.D. 1225), and NA 7478 (A.D. 1100–1225), though 32 sheep bones from NA 7486 may be misleading as all may be from same individual (Ambler et al. 1964).
	Glen Canyon—bones of mule deer and sheep in nearly all excavations and in surveyed sites. Bighorn more common in lower elevations. Expect propinquity determines take (Woodbury 1965:46).
	Black Mesa—bones from 14 sites; deer and rabbits most numerous P I-III and a few mountain sheep bones (Douglas 1972).
	Glen Canyon—bighorn predominates, 300 out of 496 bones; deer, 59 (Sharrock et al. 1961: 265).
MESA VERDE	Mesa Verde sites 1644, 1676, and Badger House, Bighorn sheep 360 bones, mule deer 295 (Hayes and Lancaster 1975:190).
	Mesa Verde Mug House—deer primary food animal, 85 individuals; bighorn, minor food animal, 32 individuals (Rohn 1971:104–5).
	MV Site 499 (late P II, early P III). Turkey and deer chief meat sources (Lister 1964). Site 499 had 3 sheep bones representing 1 individual (Lister 1966).
	General discussion of bone in BM III-P III sites in La Plata District, no numbers given but lists bone of deer, elk, mountain sheep (Morris 1939).

Region or District	Data on Big Game Animals
AZTEC	Deer and rabbit most common, followed closely by bighorn sheep and turkey: no exact numbers given; also notes, "While artifacts of horn and core are not plentiful, those made from sheep bone are nearly as frequent as those from deer" (Richert 1964:30–31).
CHACO	Mention of elk and deer only, no sheep (Kluckhohn 1939:147–59).
	Tseh So—antelope and mule deer mentioned as favorite food animals among big game; horns, jaw, and teeth of sheep recovered from two sites (Brand et al. 1937:63–65).
	Kin Kletso—data on faunal remains as tools; 53 deer bone vs. 24 of sheep (Table 10); percentages of total animals represented in the artifacts: among percentages of known bones, 22.3% deer; 12.8% bighorn. On whole, twice as many deer as sheep. Bighorn "a frequent contributor to the Kin Kletso artifacts," while appearing only as a single instance among the 375 awls at Pueblo Bonito (see Judd 1954); did not appear among the implements at Bc-51 or Bc-50; is represented in ninth place among the unworked bone at Bc-50; does not appear among artifacts or as unworked bone at Bc-192, 236, or Leyit Kin (Vivian and Mathews 1964).
UPPER LITTLE COLORADO	Broken K Pueblo—deer outnumber sheep in bone counts: deer, 138; sheep, 36 (Hill 1970:111–12).

Figure 110. White circle motifs, Tsegi Painted Style, Navajo Canyon, Arizona. Photograph, Milwaukee Public Museum.

Figure 111. Concentric circles and anthropomorphs, Tsegi Painted Style, Standing Cow Ruin, Canyon del Muerto. Photograph, Karl Kernberger.

Glen Canyon itself, propinquity determined take, judging from the increased number of sheep bones from sites in the lower (and more rugged) elevations. This was probably true on a regional basis.

Reasons for depicting game animals such as the bighorn sheep and deer were probably related to general interest in and the importance of the hunt, but a certain amount of ceremonial significance was undoubtedly attached to the game depictions. Studies of hunting methods of contemporary southwestern Indians reveal that a great deal of social and ceremonial organization still goes into the procuring of animals for food and other uses (Kluckhohn 1939:149; Beaglehole 1936). Further, ethnographic data show that the horned sheep has supernatural significance and that horns in themselves indicate shamanic and godly power (see pp. 239, 317). Thus it is not surprising to find that religious connotations are indicated in the art by depictions of humpbacked hunters and flute players in association with the bighorn sheep and their tracks.

The Virgin Kayenta

Immediately to the west, the Virgin Kayenta petroglyphs of the Pueblo periods, before the abandonment of the region in 1150, resemble the work of the Kayenta Representational Style as it appears within the Kayenta region proper. Farther west, petroglyphs in the southwestern corner of Utah and in eastern Nevada show less variation in subject matter, and stylistically shapes become rounded, moving away from the crisp forms of central Kayenta petroglyph elements. Stick-figure lizards and flute players are less common, as are pottery and textile motifs. Mountain sheep continue to be represented in large numbers, and deer with very elaborate antlers are depicted (Fig. 112). Hooked ladder motifs increase, and unformalized abstract designs, perhaps borrowed from the Great Basin Abstract Style, appear to be contemporaneous with the Pueblo designs (P. Schaafsma 1971:117–24). This complex, formerly described as the Western Virgin Kayenta Style (P. Schaafsma 1971:117), is referred to here as the Virgin Representational Style.

Rock art from other Anasazi regions during this period has not been studied in detail and information for organizing the material into styles is insufficient. Certain observations, however, can be made.

Mesa Verde

On the Mesa Verde Wetherill Mesa survey, rock art was recorded at twenty-seven sites (Hayes 1964:120). Hand prints predominated, with bird

Figure 112. Petroglyphs of deer and bighorn sheep, Virgin Representational Style, Harrisburg Creek, Utah.

tracks next in number. Animal representations and human figures followed. Horned quadrupeds, probably mountain sheep, were found at only three sites out of the twenty-seven.

The well-known petroglyph panel at Pictograph Point on Chapin Mesa is illustrated in Figure 95. Rectilinear anthropomorphs, lizards, spirals, and hand prints characterize the group. A pair of stylized birds and a sheep are present near the top.

Most of the Wetherill Mesa rock art was found at cliff dwellings, although on the whole these dwellings are less elaborately decorated with graphic designs than those of the Kayenta region. Perhaps the rough sandstone at Mesa Verde sites was less conducive to this kind of treatment than the smooth expanses of cliff surfaces to the west. On the other hand, several large, well-done wall paintings of geometric patterns have been preserved in Mesa Verde ruins.

The Little Colorado

A notable region in the late Pueblo II–Pueblo III stages of Anasazi rock art is the upper and middle Little Colorado River drainage in eastern Arizona. The distinctiveness of this art is another piece of archaeological evidence of the regional development, referred to as the Winslow tradition (Pilles 1974:2), that occurred here after A.D. 1075. The rock art consists primarily of petroglyphs. Workmanship is well controlled and the panels are rich in content. The beautifully conceived and delineated abstract patterns are outstanding (Figs. 113, 114). Some incorporate what appear to be original motifs, while others are strictly traditional and consist largely of bold frets and circular scrolls. Spirals and rectangular scrolls are also characteristic. The variety and elaboration in life-forms rival that of the Kayenta (Figs. 114–18).

Although the idea has not been investigated, the complexity and interconnectedness of some of the scenes in petroglyph panels from Petrified Forest suggest that events from myths are being illustrated. Human figures usually have prominent hands and feet, and the genitalia are often exaggerated. Sexual symbolism is more common here than in other Anasazi rock art. Elegant lizards with rectilinear configurations frequently have torsos accentuated by a central bulge or circle, a feature found in Hohokam art. Most of the quadrupeds from these sites defy identification, although some are recognizable as mountain sheep and deer, and Pilles (1974) lists antelope as the animal most commonly portrayed in panels of late Pueblo III and early

Figure 113. Maze and other rectilinear design petroglyphs in Petrified Forest National Monument.

Figure 114. Abstract elements, tadpoles, lizard man, and other petroglyphs, Petrified Forest National Monument, Arizona.

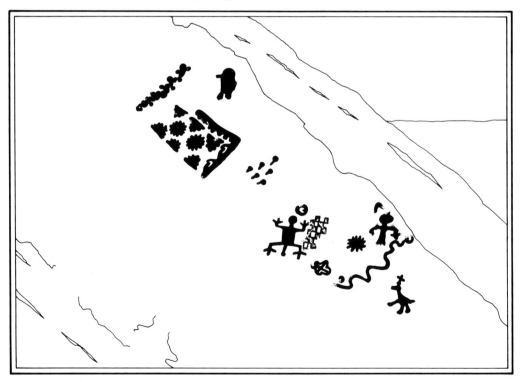

Figure 115.   Petroglyphs, Petrified Forest National Monument, Arizona.

Figure 116.   Petroglyphs of anthropomorph, footprints, and elk, Petrified Forest National Monument, Arizona.

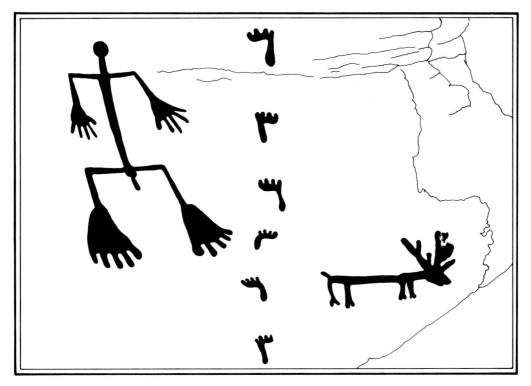

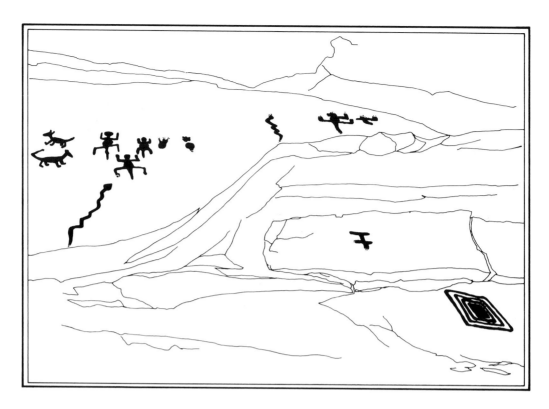

Figure 117.   Snake, lizards, and quadrupeds, Petrified Forest National Monument, Arizona.

Pueblo IV date. Long-tailed creatures may represent carnivores. There are centipedes and scorpions. The tracks of bear, badger, cat, deer, sheep, and antelope appear, as well as numerous human hand and foot prints. Other unusual depictions show an abstract version of the prints of bare feet, arranged as a set of tracks in linear sequence.

Unlike other Anasazi regions so far considered, the upper and middle Little Colorado River drainage was not abandoned by the Pueblos at the end of the 1200s. It continued to be occupied, albeit with the population finally concentrated in the vicinities of the modern villages at Hopi and Zuni, into the ethnohistoric present. As a result, there is temporal continuity in the rock art, through the Anasazi tradition being discussed here, into the Rio Grande Style (Chapter 8). This style, which derives from the Jornada Style of the Mogollon (Chapter 7), appeared in the early 1300s. Certain differences in stylistic features and in the element inventory between the pre–A.D. 1300 sites in the Upper Little Colorado and those farther north, however, suggest that certain Mogollon artistic impulses and mythological views were shared with

Figure 118.   Petroglyphs, Cave of Life, Petrified Forest National Monument, Arizona.

the former region even before this date. Among these southern features are the heavy emphasis given animal tracks and footprints, the occasional depiction of faces on humans and even animals, the presence of long-tailed quadrupeds probably representing cats, and animals with bent legs. The outlined cross is also probably part of this complex.

The Rio Grande Region

On the eastern edge of the Anasazi world in the valley and tributary drainages of the Rio Grande in northern New Mexico, the rock art before A.D. 1300 is overshadowed by the proliferation of petroglyphs of the Rio Grande Style. This style complex replaced the old Anasazi tradition and dates between A.D. 1325 and the present (P. Schaafsma 1972:129–63). The older rock art is poorly known. As described previously, certain petroglyphs prior to this time are part of an abstract style that probably dates from the Archaic into the Basketmaker II period. In addition, there are petroglyphs estimated to date between A.D. 1000 and A.D. 1300 that are characterized by solidly pecked life-forms similar to those from the Anasazi tradition on the Colorado Plateau: quadrupeds, including deer and on occasion mountain sheep, rectilinear stick figures, lizards, and flute players. Birds are common in this art and fish, some of which are clearly catfish, also occur. Tracks, including animal, human, and sandal prints, are common. Abstract designs consist of spirals, concentric circles, zigzags, and wandering lines that act to unify or join the elements in the panels in which they occur. As elsewhere, textile and pottery motifs with frets appear in the petroglyphs of the period (Durham 1955; P. Schaafsma 1968, 1972).

SUMMARY

A number of interrelated, major changes took place in the Pueblo world around A.D. 1300. The abandonment of vast areas of Anasazi territory and the aggregation of the population into increasingly larger pueblos continued, resulting in the ultimate concentration of the Pueblo people in the Hopi and Zuni regions of the Little Colorado drainage and in even greater numbers on the Rio Grande to the east. New sociocultural integrative devices were necessary to the organization and survival of the large villages developed at this time, and when these were finally adopted they furthered the growth of large pueblos, some of which numbered well over a thousand inhabitants and are more properly viewed as towns. The Rio Grande art style, with a new symbolic content and pantheon of figures, replaced the Anasazi tradition, and it is believed to be one manifestation of socioreligious institutions that functioned to integrate these large pueblos. This art complex, to be considered later in this volume (Chapter 8), as well as its associated religious institutions, derived from the Jornada Mogollon immediately to the south (Schaafsma and Schaafsma 1974).

The enduring and prolific Anasazi rock art tradition of the Colorado Plateau embraces about 1,300 years of southwestern prehistory. In its final stages it bears little resemblance to the first Basketmaker art, but from its beginnings there is an ongoing continuity between the various styles and changes. The biggest differences to be found, perhaps, are those between art of the early Basketmakers and that which followed. From its beginning in the San Juan drainage, the Anasazi tradition finally reached a distribution from Nevada to the Rio Grande just before its final developments. Soon after A.D. 1300 it was essentially replaced by the Rio Grande Style.

Changes occurring in Anasazi rock art through time and space were dynamic, not static, shifts that reflected changes within the thought systems and concerns of the people. Hypotheses concerning the content of the rock art and its relationships to Pueblo ideology have been suggested for further study. How these sites are situated and what figures or figure complexes occur in connection with habitation areas, storage sites, points along trails, water sources, and so forth are all significant factors. Surveys on Mesa Verde (Hayes 1964) and in Tsegi Canyon (P. Schaafsma 1966b) have demonstrated that rock art is most commonly associated with cliff dwellings during the late period and was thus intimately connected with the daily lives of the people. Perhaps it was primarily decorative; yet there is evidence to suggest that it served a social function as well.

No tradition operates in a vacuum, and the surrounding areas were clearly in communication with, and thus influenced to various degrees by, the dynamic Anasazi socioreligious and art complex. The rock carvings of the Sinagua area around Flagstaff are related to late Kayenta work, although the Sinagua, like the Little Colorado Anasazi, showed an even stronger preference for formal abstract design (Colton 1946a:8).

Some of the paintings made in conjunction with the enigmatic, early fourteenth-century cliff dwellings of the Sierra Ancha in south-central Arizona bear a resemblance to thirteenth-century Pueblo designs to the north.

The Sierra Ancha paintings consist of hand prints as well as involved, abstract textile designs and large circular motifs (Haury 1934). Numerous colors were used in painting these figures—white, red, green, yellow, brown, black—and the colored pigments were commonly employed in conjunction with a white background. Conventionalized life-forms are also depicted. In regard to the latter, however, Haury (1934:142) mentioned that the animals and human figures usually found in northern Arizona have few or no equivalents in the Sierra Ancha.

How the two areas may be related, if at all, is not clear. Trade relationships did seem to exist between the so-called Salado Indians of the Sierra Ancha and the Pueblos of the Little Colorado, and Little Colorado pottery types are thought to have provided inspiration for Salado Polychrome (Steen 1966:4). Possibly the abstract paintings also derived from the north.

Early in the Anasazi tradition is the unquestioned connection between it and the Fremont of Utah, one of the more spectacular developments in southwestern art. The Fremont seems to have borrowed heavily from Basketmaker rock art and presumably also participated in a related ideology, with its emphasis on the production of large and elaborate anthropomorphic figures. From this point the Fremont developed further elaborations in its own direction, maintaining the theme of large anthropomorphic representations after it had been abandoned to the south, while incorporating other motifs, often Pueblo in origin.

6

The Fremont of Utah

On the northern periphery of the Southwest and beyond, the archaeo-logical complex labeled Fremont embraces a separate but Southwest-related development that paralleled the Anasazi. Ambler (1966:273) proposed that this cultural configuration be given equal taxonomic status with the Anasazi, Hohokam, and Mogollon.

Fremont archaeological remains fall into two physiographic provinces, the Great Basin in western Utah and the Colorado Plateau to its east, the two being divided by the high Wasatch Plateau in central Utah (Map 6). Regional divisions of the Fremont Culture within these provinces (Ambler 1966; Marwitt 1970) include the Parowan, Sevier, and Great Salt Lake Fremont in the western or Great Basin province and the Uinta and San Rafael Fremont on the Colorado Plateau. Variation in Fremont rock art corresponds to these cultural divisions. Ambler further divides the San Rafael Fremont into northern and southern zones, divisions that I have retained because they denote important style shifts in the rock art.

The Fremont Indians combined horticulture and wild-food gathering as a means of subsistence, with a heavier emphasis than their Anasazi neighbors on the latter. In addition to cultivating corn, beans, and squash, for a major portion of their diet they gathered grass seeds, bulbs, and nuts and hunted mountain sheep, deer, bison, and small animals and birds.

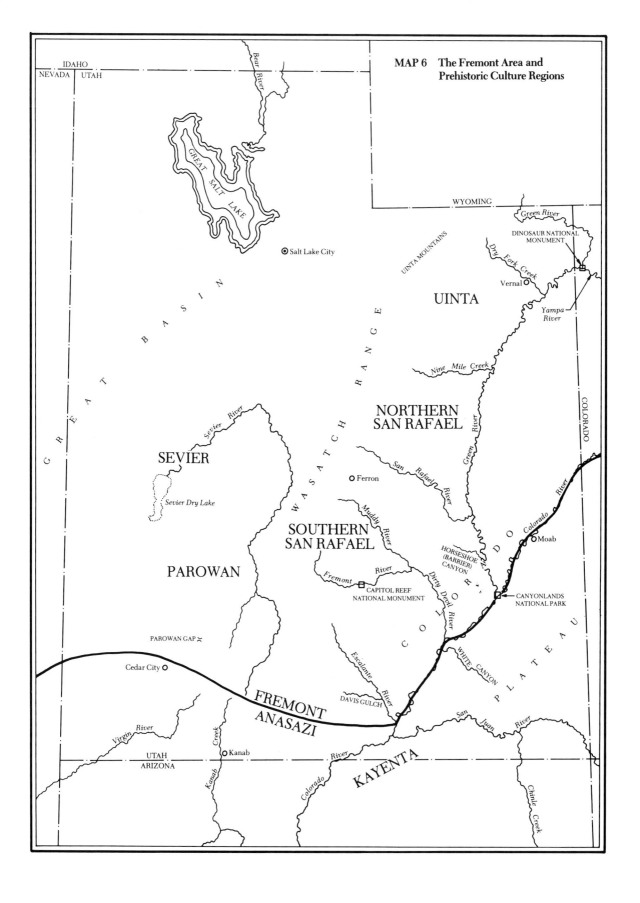

MAP 6   The Fremont Area and
Prehistoric Culture Regions

IDAHO
NEVADA   UTAH

Bear River

GREAT SALT LAKE

⊙ Salt Lake City

WYOMING

Green River

DINOSAUR NATIONAL
MONUMENT

Dry Fork Creek

UINTA MOUNTAINS

Vernal ○

UINTA

Yampa River

G
R
E
A
T

B
A
S
I
N

Nine Mile Creek

W
A
S
A
T
C
H

R
A
N
G
E

Green River

San Rafael River

NORTHERN
SAN RAFAEL

COLORADO

Sevier River

SEVIER

Ferron ○

Colorado River

Sevier Dry Lake

Muddy River

SOUTHERN
SAN RAFAEL

○ Moab

PAROWAN

Fremont   River

HORSESHOE
(BARRIER)
CANYON

CANYONLANDS
NATIONAL PARK

Dirty Devil River

CAPITOL REEF
NATIONAL MONUMENT

C
O
L
O
R
A
D
O

PAROWAN GAP ⋈

Escalante River

WHITE CANYON

P
L
A
T
E
A
U

Cedar City ○

FREMONT

DAVIS GULCH

ANASAZI

Virgin River

Creek

San Juan River

UTAH
ARIZONA

○ Kanab

Kanab Creek

River

Colorado River

KAYENTA

Chinle Creek

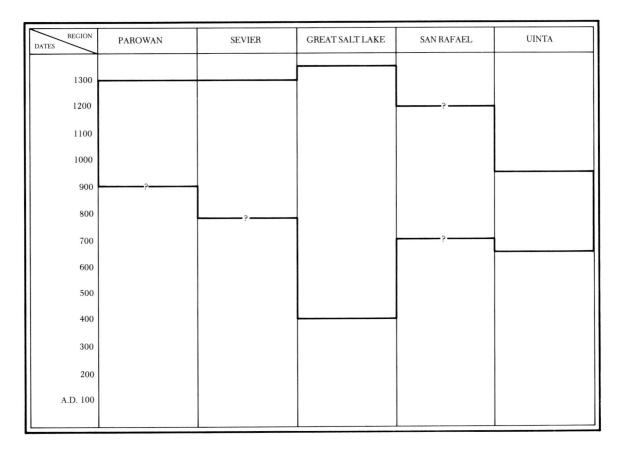

REGION / DATES	PAROWAN	SEVIER	GREAT SALT LAKE	SAN RAFAEL	UINTA
1300					
1200				?	
1100					
1000					
900	?				
800		?			
700				?	
600					
500					
400					
300					
200					
A.D. 100					

Figure 119.   Fremont dates by region (Marwitt 1970:137–45).

Horticulture promoted a certain degree of sedentary life. The Fremont people made a plain grayware pottery and elaborate figurines. Settlements were small and usually consisted of a few houses that probably accommodated the members of one extended family. The absence of kivas in these sites suggests that Fremont religious structure differed from that of the Anasazi.

Dating the Fremont Culture has been a point of controversy. In a recent review of all available data Marwitt (1970:151) says carbon-14 dates strongly indicate that the Fremont emerged as a recognizable entity about A.D. 500 or before and ended around A.D. 1300. Suggested dates for regional developments within the Fremont culture also vary; Marwitt (1970:137–45) has proposed the dates given in Figure 119 for the various Fremont regions. Ambler (1969, 1970) and Gunnerson (1969) have offered a more restricted overall dating: A.D. 1000–1200 and A.D. 900–1200, respectively. Basketmaker themes in Fremont art suggest a beginning date in agreement with Marwitt.

Throughout the twentieth century, the rock paintings and petroglyphs of Utah have been the subject of articles and have been mentioned in archaeological reports. Early articles by Albert Reagan (1931, 1933, 1935) and Frank Beckwith (1931) appeared in various publications, and in the 1920s Reagan and Jesse Nusbaum made a distinctive photographic collection of the petroglyphs from Dry Fork Valley and Nine Mile Canyon in northeastern Utah. These records are now on file in the Donald Scott collection of the Harvard Peabody Museum and at the Museum of New Mexico in Santa Fe. In 1931 Morss published a report that for the first time defined the Fremont Culture and included the most thorough consideration of the rock art associated with it to that time. Wormington (1955), Gunnerson (1957, 1969), and Aikens (1967) have discussed rock art in connection with Fremont archaeology in general. Using the Donald Scott photographic files as a data base, I described the Fremont rock art from throughout Utah within its archaeological context (P. Schaafsma 1971). This has been followed by another study of Utah rock art by Kenneth Castleton (1978).

REGIONAL STYLES

The hallmark of Fremont rock art everywhere is the broad-shouldered human figure in ceremonial regalia. Typically it has a tapering torso and horned or other elaborate headgear. Adornment varies from region to region, but common embellishments are heavy necklaces represented with dots or as solid yokes, very large ornamental earrings or "hairbobs," and sashes. Facial features, especially eyes, may be depicted. Feet usually point out to either side, and fingers are splayed. Many figures hold small shields.

These figures dominate the Southern San Rafael Style, both in number and in size (Figs. 120, 121). Three methods were used to define the petroglyph figure: (1) solid pecking, often used for small figures; (2) outline, which allowed for a considerable amount of ornamental detail; and (3) the depiction of facial features and attire like necklaces, belts, and bandoleers, outlines being absent. The anthropomorphs on the Fremont River in Capitol Reef National Monument are excellent regional examples. Some painted or pecked anthropomorphs in the Southern San Rafael Style lack appendages and resemble the distinctive Fremont figurines (Morss 1954) (Fig. 122). Eyes are drawn as slits near the top of the head and chins are full and rounded; these may be drawings of masks (see also P. Schaafsma 1971:Fig. 52 and Plate

Figure 120. Fremont anthropomorphs and animals, Southern San Rafael Style, Fremont River, Capitol Reef National Monument, Utah. Largest figure approximately 3 feet tall. Photograph, Curtis Schaafsma.

Figure 121. Elaborate anthropomorphic figures, Southern San Rafael Style, Fremont River, Capitol Reef National Monument, Utah. Figures are approximately two feet tall. The panel has been defaced by bullets. Photograph, Curtis Schaafsma.

167

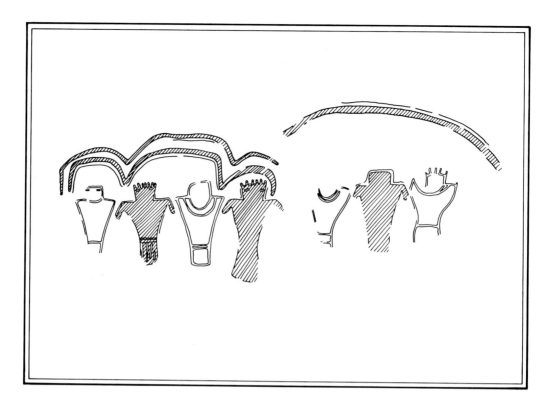

Figure 122. Alternating pecked and incised Fremont anthropomorphs, Southern San Rafael Style, Horseshoe (Barrier) Canyon. Figures are about 8 inches tall.

27). Rainbow arcs occur above the heads of human figures in Horseshoe (Barrier) Canyon (Fig. 122) and the vicinity of Ferron (P. Schaafsma 1971:Fig. 42).

Mountain sheep are another very important element in Southern San Rafael petroglyph sites; some examples are more than 3 feet long (Fig. 123). With their thin horns, cloven hooves, and square or crescent-shaped bodies, they are typologically like those of the Anasazi. Other elements may accompany human figures as subsidiary designs. Snakes and centipedes and insects are some of the life-forms occurring in these panels. Animal tracks, including those of bear and badger, wavy lines, and zigzags may be present.

Striking paintings of shields and anthropomorphs have been recorded from Davis Gulch in the Escalante drainage (Fig. 124). Two different types of paint seem to have been used in these paintings, one of which has subsequently flaked off, leaving the panel looking rather abstract. Nevertheless, the remaining heavy white pigment well defines a variety of striking and original body designs and shield patterns distinguished by imaginative use

Figure 123. Mountain sheep, Southern San Rafael Style, Capitol Reef National Monument. Sheep between 2 and 3 feet long. Photograph, Curtis Schaafsma.

Figure 124. White paintings of shields and anthropomorphic figures, Southern San Rafael Style, Davis Gulch. Photograph, University of Utah, Scott Files, Peabody Museum, Harvard.

Figure 125. Horned anthropomorphs holding shields, Southern San Rafael Style, Moab, Utah. Large figures approximately a foot tall. Photograph, Karl Kernberger.

Figure 126. Horned shield bearers and bighorn sheep, Southern San Rafael Style, Moab, Utah. Large figures approximately a foot tall. Photograph, Karl Kernberger.

of stripes, chevrons, dots, and spirals. The one representational element appearing on these shields is the negative image of a horned Fremont anthropomorph, an unusual figure made by painting solidly the surrounding circular shield and leaving the enclosed anthropomorphic silhouette blank.

In Davis Gulch and elsewhere, figures hold shields in their hands and at arm's length; but some Fremont anthropomorphs have their torsos totally covered by large shields. Especially fine, large, decorative shields and shield bearers of this type have been documented in southeastern Utah (Wormington 1955:Figs. 64–65a-1). Figures 125 and 126 show shield bearers of both types from near Moab; these figures are relatively small, and the broadly curved horns are typical of the Moab locality.

The Fremont shield may have been the model for shield designs appearing in late Anasazi work, a motif (and possible artifact as well) introduced to the Anasazi during the period of Kayenta expansion northward across the Colorado in late Pueblo II and early Pueblo III times. This could account for the presence of shield bearers and the popularity of the large shieldlike circular paintings in late Pueblo III sites in the Kayenta region (P. Schaafsma 1971:139).

In northeastern Utah, the Fremont anthropomorph is very similar to that of the Southern San Rafael zone, but in the Classic Vernal Style petroglyphs in Uinta sites (P. Schaafsma 1971:8–25) this figure becomes even more forceful and imposing as it assumes life-size proportions and increased decorative complexity (Figs. 127–33). There is a major emphasis on clarity of form and a nice use of contrast between line, textural effects, and solid areas. Bold use of both angular and curved elements adds further impressiveness to these panels. As in the Southern San Rafael Style, solid, outline, and nonoutline figures occur, the last two variants being most common. On the basis of his research in Dinosaur National Monument, Burton (1971) proposes that these different methods represent changes through time, and that an evolution or progression is evident from the smaller solidly pecked types (Fig. 134) to those lacking outlines (Figs. 129, 131), in which figure definition is minimal.

Some of the finest Classic Vernal Style petroglyphs are in the Dry Fork Valley north of Vernal (P. Schaafsma 1971:8–27). Anthropomorphic figures here occur in clustered groups or in lines along the cliff. They have facial features and precisely defined ornamental detail. Headgear is highly variable (Figs. 127–32 and P. Schaafsma 1971:Fig. 8). Horns appear only occasionally; elaborate crowns of dots arranged in various patterns are more usual, and helmet-type headgear is also pictured. Earrings and hairbobs are common,

Figure 127.   Anthropomorphic figures, Classic Vernal Style, Dry Fork Valley, Utah. Figures approximately life-size. Photograph, Reagan-Nusbaum.

Figure 128.   Anthropomorphic figures in ceremonial attire, Classic Vernal Style, Dry Fork Valley, Utah. Photograph, Reagan-Nusbaum.

Figure 129. Large anthropomorphic figures, Classic Vernal Style, Dry Fork Valley. Photograph, Reagan-Nusbaum.

Figure 130. Horned human figures, Classic Vernal Style, Dry Fork Valley. Photograph, Reagan-Nusbaum.

Figure 131. Anthropomorph, Classic Vernal Style, Dry Fork Valley, Utah. Photograph, Reagan-Nusbaum.

Figure 132. Shield figures and other anthropomorphs, Classic Vernal Style, Dry Fork Valley, Utah. Large figure approximates life-size. Photograph, Reagan-Nusbaum.

Figure 133. Abstract shield figure, Classic Vernal Style, Dry Fork Valley. Photograph, Reagan-Nusbaum.

174

Figure 134. Fremont petroglyphs, Dinosaur National Monument, Utah. Small solidly pecked figures are about a foot in height. Photograph, Scott Files, Peabody Museum, Harvard University.

and multistrand necklaces of tiny beads or of large stones, as well as yoke neckpieces, are shown. Fringed aprons or breechcloths, arm bands, belts or sashes, and torso decoration or attire are pecked in detail. Arrows are pictured in association with some of these anthropomorphs. Figures are sometimes shown holding shields, but in the Classic Vernal Style they more commonly carry what may be interpreted as either human heads or masks (P. Schaafsma 1971:Figs. 4, 5, Plate 1). Tear streaks, a device also known as the "weeping eye" motif, appear on the faces of the head masks or heads as well as on the full figures. As in the Southern San Rafael Style, there are full-fledged shield figures (Figs. 132, 133).

Material counterparts to the ornamentation of the Fremont figure have been recovered from excavations. Remains of masks have been found in sites from Dinosaur National Monument (Burton 1971:65). Headgear of feathers and of deerskin occur in the archaeological record, as well as a large variety of ornaments—pendants of cordage and rabbit fur and round, trapezoidal, or crescent-shaped pendants of sandstone, alabaster, turquoise, bone, tooth, and shell (Gunnerson 1969:155; Wormington 1955:174).

Additional elements in the Classic Vernal Style are the numerous large spirals and other circular motifs. Mazes, small spirals, scorpions or centipedes, and one-pole ladders are minor elements occurring in context with the large anthropomorphs. Small and large quadrupeds, including bison, bear, deer, and elk, are depicted. Bear tracks occur in these petroglyphs and lizards make an unexpected appearance in sites in Dinosaur National Monument (P. Schaafsma 1971:Fig. 18). The latter are highly realistic portrayals, unlike the stylized rectilinear Anasazi renditions. Flute players, both upright and reclining, appear occasionally both in the Dry Fork Valley and in Dinosaur sites (P. Schaafsma 1971:Plate 10, Fig. 16).

In the intervening Northern San Rafael region, the emphasis in the rock art differs significantly from that in the Uinta and Southern San Rafael. The human figure is less important in both size and number, and animal representations and abstract elements predominate (P. Schaafsma 1971:Table 3). As in the Uinta and Southern San Rafael regions, petroglyphs outnumber paintings. Although some of the work is carefully executed, on the whole craftsmanship is poorer in Northern San Rafael petroglyphs than in those from other eastern regions. Figures tend to be more crudely pecked and less attention was paid to the effects of figure definition and design. Rock art sites of this region are best known from Nine Mile Canyon, a western tributary of the Green River (Figs. 135–38). The Fremont anthropomorph in these panels is solidly pecked and characteristically horned. He often has a fringed horn headdress, resembling elk antlers (Fig. 135). Shields or bows and arrows may be part of his apparel, but elaborations beyond this are rare. He is nearly always accompanied by abstract elements and game animals, including deer, mountain sheep, elk, and sometimes bison. Hunting scenes with bowmen are sometimes present (Figs. 135, 136). Serpents with head plumes and rattles and long-necked wading birds also appear. Abstract elements include wavy lines, reticulate patterns, spirals, concentric circles, and dot patterns (for a complete listing see P. Schaafsma 1971:Table 3).

West of the Wasatch Plateau in the rock art of the mountain foothills and the Great Basin itself, discrete Fremont styles are less easily identified, although two styles, Sevier Style A and the western Utah Painted Style, were described earlier (P. Schaafsma 1971:85–89). The human figure with horns, hairbobs, and occasionally shield in hand denotes Fremont workmanship. The western Fremont anthropomorph, however, seldom attains the numbers, the heroic proportions, or the elaboration of the eastern examples. In the Sevier region and in eastern Nevada, typological connections in anthropomorphic

Figure 135. Hunt scene and antlered anthropomorphs, Northern San Rafael Style, Nine Mile Canyon. Photograph, Reagan-Nusbaum.

Figure 136. Hunting scene, Northern San Rafael Style, Nine Mile Canyon. Photograph, Frank Beckwith, Scott Files, Peabody Museum, Harvard University.

177

Figure 137. Bighorn sheep, anthropomorphs, and abstract elements, Northern San Rafael Style, Nine Mile Canyon, Utah. Photograph, Reagan-Nusbaum.

Figure 138. Petroglyphs, Northern San Rafael Style, Nine Mile Canyon. Photograph, Reagan-Nusbaum.

forms can be seen between the Fremont representations, frequently triangular, and the Anasazi Cave Valley Representational Style figures to the south. In the Great Salt Lake region and in the northern part of the Sevier drainage, triangular and trapezoidal human figures, painted in red, make up the western Utah Painted Style (P. Schaafsma 1971:85, Figs. 81, 82).

Quadrupeds, more than half of which are identifiable as mountain sheep, outnumber human representations in Sevier sites. Birds, snakes, tracks, and hand prints or footprints constitute the remainder of the representational designs. The abstract elements of the Great Basin Abstract Style dominate the western Utah sites, making up more than half the total inventory (P. Schaafsma 1971:87). Formal pottery designs derived from Pueblo prototypes also appear in these sites. Petroglyphs at Parowan Gap include both types of abstract designs as well as Fremont anthropomorphs (P. Schaafsma 1971:Fig. 105, Plate 50).

Explanations for the regional variation in Fremont rock art must be sought within each regional subculture. Regional variation within the Fremont pattern seems to have appeared early, and investigators have proposed that Fremont variation grew out of regionally differentiated Archaic patterns (Aikens 1972:61) that were in part related to differences in environment. These factors undoubtedly had some effect on the development of the rock art and its associated ideographic system within each Fremont region. In addition, different outside contacts would have contributed further to regional patterns in the rock art.

SHAMANS OF THE NORTH

The shields, arrows, and animals in Fremont work suggest warfare and hunting. Actual hunting scenes occur in the Northern San Rafael Style; the headdresses of the Fremont anthropomorphs in this region are nearly always in the form of horns or antlers. The panel from Nine Mile Canyon in Figure 136 may represent a hunt shaman with a herd of bighorn sheep. It has been suggested that the lines joining the sheep and the anthropomorph illustrate consanguinity (Ritter and Ritter 1976:161). In many parts of the Southwest, however, horns may represent special power without being associated with the hunt. In the Uinta region, heroic human figures are shown carrying either human heads or masks, depictions that suggest warfare or ritual or both. A word of caution is in order, as the apparel of war can signify symbolic or ceremonial conflicts rather than strife between human groups. Nevertheless, Wormington describes an unusually large number of arrow points from the Turner-Look sites, which she thinks indicate a greater emphasis on either hunting or warfare than is evident elsewhere in the Southwest (1955:86). This observation does seem to corroborate what appear to be war and hunt themes in the rock art. The large Fremont figures do not seem to be in any way connected with the development of horticulture, since these figures are most highly developed in the Uinta district, where gardening was less important than in any other Fremont region except around Great Salt Lake.

I suggested earlier that the Fremonters were participants, along with the Basketmakers and the Barrier Canyon Style artists who preceded them, in an ideographic system that fostered the representation of heroic and elaborate, possibly shamanic, human figures. This artistic tradition in the Fremont reached a climax in the Uinta and Southern San Rafael regions, the latter bordering on the Anasazi and overlapping the Barrier Canyon Style paintings in areal distribution. The tapered, horned human form, however, occurs in all Fremont contexts in both eastern and western Utah, indicating that this figure was a pan-Fremont one, more important in some regions than in others.

The hypothesis that the art of all three groups is connected with historically related shamanistic practices on the Colorado Plateau needs to be explored further. First of all, such practices may be related to the general level of sociocultural integration of the groups in question. Although little is known about the painters of the Barrier Canyon Style art, we believe they were hunter-gatherers lacking a high degree of social organization. Both the Basketmakers and the Fremont practiced horticulture, which, because of the need to tend the crops, promoted increased sedentariness. Neither culture, however, had large organized villages. Basketmaker II settlements, which were limited to two to four nuclear families, may have been only seasonally occupied. Fremont settlements with five to perhaps a dozen nuclear families in residence were slightly larger and probably more permanent; but the settlement pattern was not structured, and a loose political organization is probable (Gunnerson 1969:61). Pan-village, specialized religious units such as kivas are absent, although Wormington (1955:166) mentions circular structures with low walls of dry-laid masonry in Fremont contexts, which she suggests "may have been used for some purpose connected with religious rites." In any case, judging from ethnographic examples, the social structure would have been such that religious activities would have rested in the hands of specialized religious practitioners like shamans, and not in an organized priesthood of the kind that exists among the Pueblos.

Second, stylistic and typological similarities between Fremont and Basketmaker figures are obvious both in basic body shape and decorative detail, signifying a cultural continuity of some sort. Likenesses in necklace forms and torso decoration and the sharing of such features as hairbobs and arm bands demonstrate a close connection between the two, although stylistic nuances and the specific forms employed in headgear, for example, are mutually exclusive. The Fremont and the Barrier Canyon Style also share a preoccupation with large, tapered human figures. In both, the heads of anthropomorphs are large and usually rectangular or bucket shaped; in many cases only the heads and torsos are portrayed. However, decoration and ornamentation in these two kinds of rock art diverge widely.

Also, despite certain outward similarities, different themes are emphasized in the Barrier Canyon Style, in the San Juan Anthropomorphic Style of the Basketmakers, and in the Fremont. Warfare motifs, for example, are absent in the earlier Barrier Canyon and San Juan Anthropomorphic styles, and the ghostly, ancestral-spirit overtones of the Barrier Canyon Style anthropomorphs are not present in the Fremont. Nevertheless, in all three style groups the human figures are so elaborately attired that they suggest beings of special significance, and the horns on the Barrier Canyon Style and Fremont figures are thought to indicate their shamanic or supernatural powers. We seem to be dealing with a single tradition encompassing three related but different art styles in which the anthropomorphic figure receives special emphasis. These styles, in turn, are undoubtedly underlain by a single tradition of religious ideology that existed in this area over many centuries.

7

The Mogollon

The Mogollon Culture of southern New Mexico, southeastern Arizona, and adjacent parts of Texas and northern Mexico (Map 7) comprised a complex series of cultural developments and a period of major changes that affected southwestern history for centuries afterward. No single description will circumscribe what is meant by "Mogollon," and the rock art of this region also varies considerably, both geographically and temporally.

The geographic character of the Mogollon area is highly diverse. In the west it encompasses the rugged, well-watered wooded highlands of southeastern Arizona and southwestern New Mexico and adjacent parts of the Sierra Madre Occidental of northern Chihuahua and Sonora. To the east is grassland steppe and the arid basin-and-range country stretching to the Guadalupe and Sacramento mountains and the Sierra Blanca Range, which separate the southern desert from the high plains of eastern New Mexico (Fig. 139). The Chihuahuan Desert is characteristic of the lower elevations, particularly in the Rio Grande Valley of southern New Mexico and Texas.

The Mogollon Culture developed out of the late eastern Cochise in the highland provinces. This particular transition from a hunting-gathering level of existence to farming is most adequately documented in the archaeological record of the Southwest (Martin, Rinaldo, and Antevs 1949). Maize, beans, and squash were known very early in this region. Excavation in Bat Cave, an important Western Archaic site in the Plains of San Agustin, demonstrated that corn was present in the region as far back as 2000 or 3000 B.C. (Dick 1965;

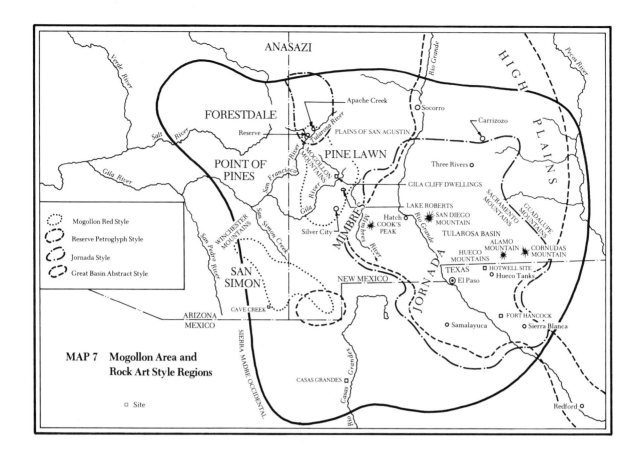

MAP 7 Mogollon Area and
Rock Art Style Regions

Mogollon Red Style

Reserve Petroglyph Style

Jornada Style

Great Basin Abstract Style

□ Site

Martin and Plog 1973:277). It was not until around 300 B.C., however, that cultural shifts resulting from an increasing dependence on farming as a way of life began to take place, with village living and the use of pottery. Village life has been documented at its earliest in the San Simon region, from an open site location on Cave Creek (Sayles 1945). The actual transition from foraging to sedentary existence has been preserved in great detail in the prehistoric remains in the dry deposits of Tularosa and Cordova caves in the Pine Lawn region (Martin et al. 1952).

Regional variations within the Mogollon are viewed slightly differently by various investigators (Wheat 1955:11, Table 1; Martin and Plog 1973:90; Willey 1966:Fig. 4–1). Horizontally crosscutting the regional temporal sequences or phases are general time sequences—Mogollon 1, 2, 3, 4, 5—the differences between which are based primarily on pithouse shape and ceramics (Wheat 1955). These time periods serve as guidelines by which the regional phases can be integrated (Fig. 140).

Figure 139.   Cooks Peak, southern New Mexico. Photograph, Karl Kernberger.

The Mogollon Culture is best known from the western highland regions where it was first identified (Haury 1936; Martin, Rinaldo, and Kelley 1940; Martin 1943; Martin, Rinaldo, and Antevs 1949; Martin et al. 1952; Wheat 1955). In this highland or mountain area the culture dates from 300 B.C. to A.D. 1350. Pithouse settlements prevailed during Mogollon periods 1 through 4. Sites consisted of from one to fifty houses, fifteen to twenty-five being the average number. Houses were randomly distributed throughout, and their features are so variable that a typically Mogollon pattern cannot be described (Martin and Plog 1973:92). A single large pithouse, thought to have been a ceremonial structure, is present in most of these sites. Subsistence practices combined farming with hunting and gathering of wild plant foods. Corn, beans, squash, and gourds were raised, and yucca pods, black walnuts, cacti, acorns, grass seeds, and sunflower seeds, all found in the late Cochise and

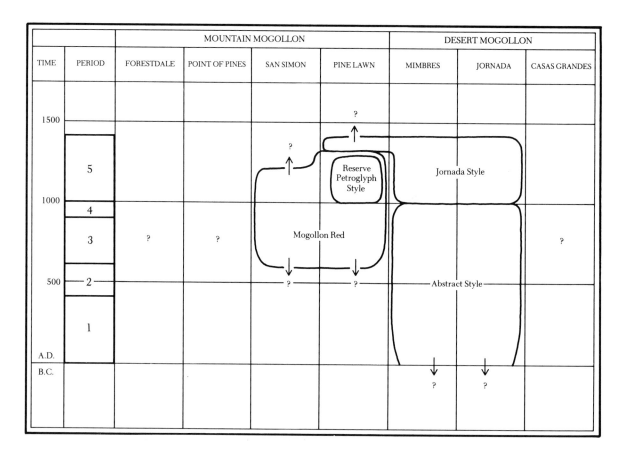

TIME	PERIOD	MOUNTAIN MOGOLLON				DESERT MOGOLLON		
		FORESTDALE	POINT OF PINES	SAN SIMON	PINE LAWN	MIMBRES	JORNADA	CASAS GRANDES
1500					?			
	5			?	Reserve Petroglyph Style		Jornada Style	
1000	4							
	3	?	?	Mogollon Red				?
500	2			?	?	Abstract Style		
	1							
A.D.								
B.C.						?	?	

Figure 140. Schematic chart showing estimated time periods and regional distributions of rock art styles in the Mogollon area.

early Pine Lawn phases in Tularosa and Cordova caves, give us some idea of the variety within the Mogollon diet.

After A.D. 1000 there was a shift away from the pithouse settlements to villages consisting of above-ground dwellings of the pueblo type. In the north around Tularosa and Reserve, changes in village form as well as in ceramics (which involved the addition of the black-on-white pottery tradition of the Anasazi to the old Mogollon brown wares), indicate that the indigenous Mogollon development was at that time interrupted by contact with the adjacent Anasazi. In the Reserve vicinity, contemporaneous changes in the rock art also reflect the influence of the southern Anasazi, although occasional elements and certain stylistic features are more akin to those of the Mimbres region to the south and east.

The eastern, or what is herein referred to as the Desert, Mogollon is divisible into the Mimbres and Jornada regions (Map 7; Lehmer 1948;

P. Schaafsma 1972:90ff.; Marshall 1973). In the Jornada region the Mogollon pattern of horticulture, pithouses, and pottery does not appear until A.D. 800 or 900 (C. Schaafsma 1974:55; Lehmer 1948:89), but following this there is a continuous Mogollon occupation until the end of the San Andres and El Paso phases around A.D. 1400, when the region was abandoned. The Desert Mogollon also experienced a change from pithouse villages to above-ground pueblos after A.D. 1000. Developments in the Mimbres Valley involved villages like the Swarts Ruin, with 125 rooms around a main plaza area.

As we shall see in this and the following chapters, the later rock art of the Jornada and Mimbres regions, collectively referred to as the Jornada Style (P. Schaafsma 1972:95–119), may be regarded in its historical sense as the progenitor of modern ceremonial art throughout much of the Southwest. Jornada iconography, art styles, and figure types were adopted by the Pueblos, who have maintained the tradition, albeit with certain distinct changes, until the present day. In turn, many of the forms and associated concepts in Pueblo art were within the last two or three hundred years adopted by the Athabaskan latecomers to the area, the Navajo and Apache (Fig. 198).

Before discussing the Jornada Style and its interesting ramifications, we must examine the older indigenous graphic art developments within the Mogollon. The various rock art styles within the Mogollon area correspond only in a most general way to the regional sequences outlined in Figure 140. From the beginning, the major distinctions were between those of the western highlands, or the Mountain Mogollon, and those of the Desert Mogollon regions, differences that seem to suggest different ideologies in these geographic provinces.

THE MOUNTAIN MOGOLLON: MOGOLLON RED PAINTINGS AND THE RESERVE PETROGLYPH STYLE

Small elements painted in red are the predominant type of rock drawing in the highland Mogollon regions where field research has been conducted (P. Schaafsma 1972:71–74) (Figs. 141–44). Mogollon Red sites are common in the San Francisco drainage and along the Gila and its tributaries in the Mogollon Mountain complex. Other regions such as Forestdale, Point of Pines, and San Simon have had little or no investigation. Although these paintings do seem to

Figure 141. Mogollon Red Style paintings on the San Francisco River near Reserve, New Mexico. The terraced element in the upper right is atypical and is believed to derive from the Jornada Style where it occurs commonly. New Mexico State Planning Office; photograph, Karl Kernberger.

Figure 142. Simple stick figure a few inches tall and zigzag design, Mogollon Red Style, San Francisco River near Reserve, New Mexico. New Mexico State Planning Office; photograph, Karl Kernberger.

Figure 143. Mogollon Red zigzag and set of parallel lines only a few inches tall, San Francisco River near Reserve. Note the tiny surfaces used for painting. New Mexico State Planning Office; photograph, Karl Kernberger.

Figure 144. Small Mogollon Red designs on underside of rock overhang, Middle Fork of the Gila River. A long-necked bird in flight is depicted at the extreme left. New Mexico State Planning Office; photograph, Karl Kernberger.

189

concentrate in the highlands, the distribution of the style is not strictly limited to this geographic region, as evidenced by a few such paintings in the desert ranges to the south and east.

Mogollon Red sites are not large, usually being limited to a single small shelter or protected area of a cliff. The paintings themselves consist of small elements in red; sometimes white paint was also used. Each design seems to have been conceived as a separate entity, and its isolated effect is often heightened by broken rock surfaces. Most frequently depicted are sketchy stick-figure humans, wavy lines or zigzags, and simple concentric circles (Figs. 141–43). Other popular elements are human figures with thickened torsos, often vaguely triangular, one-pole ladders, and bird tracks. Ovals, sunbursts, dot motifs, parallel zigzags, and series of short lines occur a little less frequently but are widely distributed geographically (P. Schaafsma 1972:72, Table 1). Small paintings of fish are rare but distinctive, and birds and animals are sometimes represented (Fig. 144).

Two human figure types appear to represent specific personages. One of these, distinguished by a one-horned headdress, also appears in the petroglyphic art of the region. The other is a figure in profile holding a staff or similar object (P. Schaafsma 1972:78). The latter finds a more elaborate counterpart in the Jornada Style and may be late in the Mogollon Red time sequence. Overpaintings or superimpositions are very rare, and one has the impression that for the most part these sites are single statements and saw limited use. A major exception is a heavily decorated rock-shelter by the San Francisco River near Reserve. At this site, paintings continue throughout the rock-shelter for about 100 feet, and the paintings are superimposed by petroglyphs in the Reserve Style, indicating that the site received long and sustained use. Pits 1 or 2 inches deep in rocks below the paintings may have served a ceremonial function.

The distribution of Mogollon Red sites has not been systematically plotted in any locale to see how the paintings correlate with other remains, but in the drainages of the San Francisco and the upper Gila, paintings are fairly numerous, and habitation sites, although not often directly associated, are usually not far away. In a rock-shelter in the Winchester Mountains of the San Simon region, however, bedrock mortars, lithics, and Alma Plain sherds occur along with the paintings. Other paintings associated with habitation are those within the large occupied cave at Gila Cliff Dwellings.

A number of other red paintings in the Mogollon Mountain region differ from the Mogollon Red Style but do not constitute a large enough sample to enable us to classify them into other stylistic groupings. These include the heavy zigzags (44 inches tall) and large circle motifs on the lower Middle Fork of the Gila (Fig. 145 and P. Schaafsma 1972:Fig. 65), and the human figures with two horns or tripartite headdresses and other designs in Pictograph Canyon at Lake Roberts (P. Schaafsma 1972:Fig. 66). Although the anthropomorphs at Lake Roberts are not grossly different from some human representations in the Mogollon Red Style, they measure up to 24 inches high and have unusual headgear. The abstract designs characteristic of Mogollon Red are absent. At still another site west of Silver City, paintings resemble Hohokam pottery motifs (P. Schaafsma 1972:Fig. 68).

Mogollon Red paintings have not been dated by objective means, but several lines of evidence suggest that the style was an enduring one in highland Mogollon prehistory. Possibly derived from the more complex Polychrome Paintings attributed to the Western Archaic horizon, they may date from early in the Mogollon sequence. That they were being done, however, after the sophisticated Jornada Style art had made its appearance in the Desert Mogollon provinces to the east after A.D. 1050 is indicated by the rare Jornada-derived element that appears among the simple Mogollon Red designs. The cloud terrace in a site near Reserve is a case in point (Fig. 141). At Gila Cliff Dwellings, the location of Mogollon Red designs suggests that they were made from rooftops of the pueblo dwelling, which dates from the end of the Mogollon between A.D. 1270 and A.D. 1350. On the other hand, in the Reserve district where both Mogollon Red paintings and petroglyphs occur, the paintings are superimposed by the petroglyphs, which probably date after A.D. 1000 and eventually may have replaced the paintings in the northern part of their range.

By comparison, the Reserve Petroglyph Style, found largely in the San Francisco–Tularosa river drainages near Reserve and Apache Creek, comprises a rather heterogeneous group of designs (Figs. 146–50). Tracks of bear, deer, raccoons, and humans, along with depictions of animals, lizards, frogs, and stick-figure anthropomorphs with both rectilinear and curvilinear appendages, are typical. The legs of the lizards and/or stick-figure men often point forward or up rather than down. There are flute players, both upright and reclining, and interlocking frets, sunbursts, spirals, concentric circles, reticulate designs or grids, wavy lines, and barred elements. Many of these motifs are found in the rock art of the adjacent Anasazi region. Work is often crudely done and sometimes tends to be cluttered (Fig. 146). Elements may be joined and panels integrated with long meandering lines. The one-horned personage

Figure 145. Large red circular element, Middle Fork of the Gila River. New Mexico State Planning Office; photograph, Karl Kernberger.

described previously for the Mogollon Red Style also occurs in these petroglyphs (P. Schaafsma 1972:Fig. 74). Visually, the most pleasing figures are the large quadrupeds often found in isolated situations or high on cliff faces (Fig. 148); they are rather elegant and usually technically superior to the other petroglyphs. Some have long tails and seem to represent mountain lions or coyotes. Large heads and eyes and long snouts indicate their affiliation with Jornada Style work rather than with the Anasazi. Other carved figures include the outlined cross (Fig. 149), also very common to the south in the Mimbres region, and fringed-winged birds, possibly representing eagles (P. Schaafsma 1972:Fig. 72).

Bear tracks are common to the point of being almost diagnostic of the style (Fig. 150), and some insight into the possible significance of this element for the prehistoric occupants of New Mexico is available by a comparison with its place in modern Pueblo iconography. In the Pueblo world, the bear track stands for the curing power of the bear, and the paw is equal in power to the mask of other deities. When Keresan shamans put on their bear paws,

Figure 146. The Reserve Petroglyph Style, Tularosa Canyon, near Reserve, New Mexico. The panel is very cluttered and many lines have been deeply abraded in the soft rock. New Mexico State Planning Office; photograph, Karl Kernberger.

Figure 147. Elements of the Reserve Petroglyph Style, Tularosa Canyon. The stick-figure lizard with all legs pointing forward is typical. Lizard approximately a foot tall. New Mexico State Planning Office; photograph, Karl Kernberger.

Figure 148. Large Mogollon quadrupeds on cliff above petroglyphs of Apache origin, San Francisco River, Reserve. New Mexico State Planning Office; photograph, Karl Kernberger.

Figure 149. Outlined cross, zigzag, and spiral element, Reserve Petroglyph Style, Tularosa Box, Reserve. Cross approximately 10 inches across. New Mexico State Planning Office; photograph, Karl Kernberger.

Figure 150. Bear track petro-
glyph, Apache Creek. New Mexico
State Planning Office; photograph,
Karl Kernberger.

they "become bears" (Parson 1939:170). Bear paw effigies from Tularosa Cave
dated A.D. 700–900 (Martin and Plog 1973:186, Plate 35) affirm the ancient
significance of this element in the ceremonial life of the Indians of the
Southwest.

Exactly how the Reserve petroglyphs functioned within their cultural
context is not known, although a ceremonial purpose is indicated by the
designs themselves. Hough (1907:71) noted that on top of the cliff above a
large petroglyph site in the Tularosa Box Canyon below Apache Creek were
several round enclosures or shrines at which pottery had been broken in large
quantities.

The shift from Mogollon Red paintings to the Reserve Style petroglyphs
in the north has certain sociocultural implications. Judging from other
archaeological data, this was a time of change. After A.D. 1000, the culture in
the northern part of the highland Mogollon region became, functionally and
structurally, more and more similar to the neighboring Anasazi. This trend is
attributed to the Anasazi ability to adapt to this neighboring zone at a time
when expansion was beneficial for them (Martin and Plog 1973:194). A shift in

settlement pattern from pithouse villages to contiguous-roomed pueblo structures and the appearance of black-on-white Anasazi-like pottery testify to an increasing Anasazi impact on the region. A change in social and religious organization is implicit in the appearance of the so-called Great Kivas (Martin and Plog 1973:193–94) and in the new settlement pattern. The content of the rock art indicates something about the concurrent change in ideology, which involved the incorporation of Anasazi ideas and, to a lesser degree, symbolism from the Mimbres region.

THE DESERT MOGOLLON

The Mogollon of the arid lands to the south and east of the highlands occupied a vast area of what is now south-central New Mexico and adjacent parts of Chihuahua and Texas. This is typically basin-and-range topography with north-south–oriented mountain ranges separated by wide valleys or basins (Lehmer 1948:Fig. 1). The dominant life zone of the region is that of the Chihuahuan Desert, with creosote, mesquite, and ocotillo in the lower elevations, and grasslands, mesquite, and yucca in the upper portions. Somewhat more restricted in area are the Upper Sonoran and Transition life zones found in the foothills and mountains up to 8,000 feet. Through the middle of this country flows the Rio Grande.

''Desert Mogollon'' is an inclusive term embracing both the Mimbres and the Jornada Mogollon regions, which are united throughout their cultural history by participation in common art traditions. It was here that the Jornada Style flourished after A.D. 1050. This graphic art complex, however, was preceded by the Mogollon Red Style, which is found occasionally in this region, and the prolifically occurring, abstract petroglyphs discussed in Chapter 3, which are essentially a Chihuahuan Desert component of the Great Basin Abstract Style. The latter are largely attributed to the hunter-gatherer population of the region. As explained earlier, on the basis of evidence provided by patination and the superimpositions of designs, it is proposed that this rock art style continued to be made by the early Mogollon following the hunter-gatherer period that ended around A.D. 800, if not earlier (C. Schaafsma 1974:54). Continuity in the art is not surprising, as Lehmer (1948) described other continuities in cultural artifacts between the early Mogollon phases and the preceding period.

Mogollon additions to the Abstract Style consist of the depiction of a number of representational elements, including small reptiles, quadrupeds, stick-figure anthropomorphs, and animal tracks; the last are distinctive though not identifiable by species. They often have a narrow heel, and toes vary from four to seven in number and may be exaggerated in length (P. Schaafsma 1972:Fig. 81).

Eventually this ancient complex of abstract designs and simple representational figures was replaced by the striking elements of the Jornada Style. Datable from its appearance on decorated wares from Mimbres sites, the Jornada Style is believed to have appeared first in the Mimbres region sometime around A.D. 1050.

Concurrent with the appearance of Jornada Style art in the Desert Mogollon region were other significant changes (Lehmer 1948; C. Schaafsma 1974; Le Blanc 1975, 1976). Le Blanc's recent research in the Mimbres Valley has led him to hypothesize a sharp rise in population, which he dates around A.D. 1000, and at the same time a rapid shift in subsistence strategy and settlement pattern. The former involved a probable shift from dry farming and collecting to intensive irrigation agriculture (Le Blanc 1975, 1976). In the archaeological record we see a change from haphazardly arranged pithouses to above-ground pueblo structures of stone and mud masonry or coursed adobe. These pueblo units were arranged in a linear fashion with an east-west orientation or as a complex around courtyards and a central plaza. Villages of the latter type in the Mimbres River Valley and the Tularosa Basin consisted of more than a hundred rooms.

Whereas in the pithouse villages a single slightly larger house or one with specialized features is thought to have served a ceremonial function, in the pueblo houseblocks this type of communal activity may have taken place in a large room within the block. Wall or mural painting was also practiced in these sites (Kelley 1951:118; Brook 1971:74; Davis 1968:27–28). Unfortunately, the plaster in every case so far encountered (except at Redford, Texas, where painted bands were distinguishable, and at the Hot Well site near El Paso, from which a piece of plaster was recovered with a portion of a design intact) has been so fragmented that the nature of the decoration has been lost. It is not clear whether these rooms have other features that might indicate use for ceremonial purposes, unless the "altar" (Kelley 1951:118) or "step" (Brook 1971:74) in the Redford example is such an indication.

Stone balls, animal effigies, among which are bear and lion fetishes (Di Peso 1974:308), stone palettes, fish-form pendants, and shell tinklers are among the new ceremonial objects appearing at this time. Copper bells and reel-shaped objects are also found in El Paso Phase sites.

In terms of temporal factors, the distribution of pottery types, and architectural changes, it is reasonable to relate events in the Jornada and the Mimbres regions to those at Casas Grandes immediately to the south in Chihuahua. The indigenous culture in the Casas Grandes region was Mogollon or Mogollon-like, with pithouse villages and brown-ware pottery resembling those of the Mogollon (Lister 1958). As summarized by Di Peso (1966), at the end of the Viejo Period, the settlement pattern changed to small clusters of above-ground pueblolike houses linked by walls around small plazas, and trade pottery from the Mimbres and Jornada regions indicates that there was contact with the Desert Mogollon at this time, a shift away from an earlier western upland Mogollon affiliation. In the following Medio Period, rapid changes in architecture led to massive construction and large house clusters with such features as stairs and stairwells. Domestic water systems that included village water supplies, canals, and subterranean drains were also introduced. The plumed serpent motif appears in the art during this period. El Paso Polychrome is a major pottery type in the Casas Grandes region, and Chupadero Black-on-white and Little Colorado wares also appear. These developments are followed by further growth toward urbanization, accompanied by the presence of Mesoamerican platform mounds and ball courts, which ended when Casas Grandes collapsed about A.D. 1340.

Di Peso (personal communication) has noted that a Mexican art style and iconography is suddenly evident at Casas Grandes around A.D. 1060, at about the time the region came under the domination of the south (Di Peso 1968). These changes at Casas Grandes are attributed to the arrival of merchant or *pochteca* groups from West Mexico, heavily under Toltec influence. In turn, these economic endeavors on the northern frontier of Mexico were associated with missionary activities of certain Mesoamerican cults of the gods, Tezcatlipoca, Quetzalcoatl, and Huitzilopochtli successively, each cult with its own identifiable trait cluster (Di Peso 1974:292). Tlaloc and Xipe Totec are among other Mesoamerican deities whose symbolism was manifest at Casas Grandes (Di Peso 1974:565). In a summary statement Di Peso suggests that Casas Grandes's "power over the district and its influence on the culture of the Southwest may have been tremendous" (1966:21).

Although the complex urban system of Casas Grandes was not present in the Jornada and Mimbres regions, there was nevertheless a network of communication and exchange between the two that was sufficient to reorganize Desert Mogollon culture after A.D. 1050 and result in a new ideology reflected in the art.

THE JORNADA STYLE

Masks and faces with almond eyes and abstract decoration, horns, feathers, and pointed caps; mythical beings with round staring eyes; large blanket designs; animals with bent legs and formal decorative patterns on their bodies; horned serpents; flying birds and spread-winged eagles; turtles, tadpoles, fish, and insects; corn, cloud terraces, and rainbows—these startling figures of the Jornada Style replaced the repetitious, simple figures of the earlier rock art of this region (Figs. 151–96; Plates 17–23).

Clearly this is the tradition that produced the decorative art of Mimbres ceramics, so well known for its exquisite design qualities and ingenious interpretive approach (Cosgrove and Cosgrove 1932; Brody 1977). Comparisons with Mimbres pottery decoration show that the rock-cut figures are less detailed (differences in the media involved would account for this), and on the whole the rock art has a slightly narrower life-form inventory. On the other hand, the goggle-eyed beings and the abstract masks and faces, the latter characteristic of the eastern Jornada province, are only occasionally represented on the ceramics. Compositions involving action scenes or more than one figure are less imaginative than those found within the confines of Mimbres bowls in spite of the fact that the rock surfaces gave the Mimbres artists a larger field in which to work. More often than not, however, figures on the rocks are petroglyphs isolated on boulders and small outcrops, although sometimes a number of masks will be placed together on separate but neighboring rocks or rock faces, and one senses that they were meant to be encountered as a group. Superimpositions are not usual, and this factor, along with the decorative aspects of the figures and their occasional placement in strategic locations for dramatic effect, suggests that part of their function was in the viewing after their manufacture.

In an earlier study (P. Schaafsma 1972), I divided the Jornada Style rock art into eastern and western phases on the basis of differences between sites in the Mimbres Valley to the west and the Jornada region to the east. The two regions were distinguished primarily by the presence of the more elaborate decorative aspects of the art in the east and, along with this qualitative

Figure 151. Seated Mimbres figure and a mountain sheep near Cooks Peak, New Mexico. Human figure approximately 20 inches long. New Mexico State Planning Office; photograph, Curtis Schaafsma.

Figure 152. Face or mask, slightly under life-size, Cooks Peak. New Mexico State Planning Office; photograph, Curtis Schaafsma.

Figure 153. Tlaloc blanket design near Cooks Peak. New Mexico State Planning Office; photograph, Curtis Schaafsma.

difference, a richer element inventory, including significantly larger numbers of masks. Also, rock paintings as well as petroglyphs are an important medium of expression in the Jornada region, and from an aesthetic point of view some of the finest designs in the entire style are the mask paintings in the rock-shelters at Hueco Tanks near El Paso, Texas. Since the Mimbres occupation to the west is believed to have terminated possibly as much as 150 years before the Jornada region to the east was abandoned, it is possible that the numerous masks and the Hueco Tanks paintings postdate the Mimbres petroglyphs and are assignable to the El Paso Phase of the final Jornada Period.

Knowledge of the western phase of Jornada Style work is limited to three petroglyph sites on boulders and rock outcrops in the Mimbres Valley and below Cooks Peak. Some of the more complete anthropomorphic representations from these sites have counterparts on Mimbres ceramics (Fig. 151). Masks or faces, relatively crudely executed, are present in very limited numbers. They are round and have oval or round eyes and facial streaks but not noses (Fig. 152). Several mythical personages appear. The goggle-eyed

Figure 154. Large ogrelike being, Cooks Peak. New Mexico State Planning Office; photograph, Curtis Schaafsma.

Figure 155. Bearded anthropomorphic figure with phallus and snake's body, Cooks Peak. New Mexico State Planning Office; photograph, Curtis Schaafsma.

202

figure, so prevalent in the rock art of the Jornada region, is depicted in abbreviated form at the Mimbres sites. His presence is signified by the eyes alone or eyes attached to striking blanket motifs (Fig. 153). This figure is believed to be a northern version of the Mesoamerican Rain God, Tlaloc (see pp. 235–237) and henceforth in this discussion will be referred to by that name. Other mythic beings are illustrated in Figures 154 and 155. One is an ogrelike figure, and the bearded phallic anthropomorph with tall cap or horn and serpent's body appears to be a Mimbres version of Quetzalcoatl, the Mesoamerican Feathered Serpent.

Balanced, static figures of animals with bent legs and big heads with eyes and teeth are typical of the Jornada Style everywhere. Mountain sheep, turtles, rattlesnakes, and lizards create decorative and contained solid patterns (Figs. 8, 155–57). Large tadpoles in outline are shown with faces (Fig. 158), and fish depictions are highly realistic (Fig. 159). Both tadpoles and fish were found pecked on bedrock surfaces near potholes in which water collects during rainstorms.

Cloud terraces with rainbows in the base, burden baskets, and human and animal tracks are other noteworthy designs (Figs. 160–62). The animal tracks in particular are abstract and decorative, consistent with the Mimbres aesthetic mode, although as a subject they are one of the elements in the Jornada Style inventory that has a continuity with older Mogollon art. The outlined cross, present at an earlier date in association with the Abstract Style, also occurs in the Mimbres petroglyphs.

It is within the region of the Jornada Mogollon and the eastern Mimbreños, from the Rio Grande Valley to the mountain ranges east of the Tularosa Basin (Map 7), that the Jornada Style rock art developed to its fullest. Masks and ceremonial figures are among the most diagnostic and striking designs found here. They are highly individual and diversified, no two figures being exactly alike. A few personages can be isolated and tentatively identified. Among these the goggle-eyed Tlaloc figure is the most distinctive as well as the most frequently represented; depicted in a limited number of standardized forms, it appears in nearly every Jornada Style site or site grouping thoughout the Desert Mogollon region.

What can be called "classic" Tlaloc or Rain God types in the eastern Jornada Style are abstracted anthropomorphic designs consisting of a trapezoidal or rectangular head above a similarly shaped, larger block representing the body (Plate 17; Fig. 163). Their outstanding feature, in addition to their shape, is the large round or square eyes that occupy the top half of the

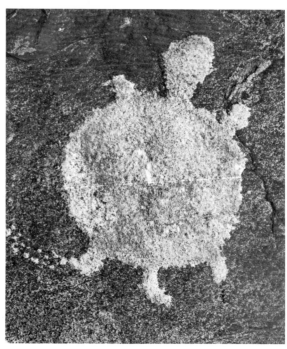

Figure 156. Turtles 8 to 12 inches long, Cooks Peak. New Mexico State Planning Office; photograph, Curtis Schaafsma.

Figure 157. Rattlesnake, Cooks Peak. Snake approximately 16 inches long. New Mexico State Planning Office; photograph, Curtis Schaafsma.

204

Figure 158. Tadpoles carved in bedrock, Cooks Peak. New Mexico State Planning Office; photograph, Curtis Schaafsma.

Figure 159. Mimbres fish, Cooks Peak. New Mexico State Planning Office; photograph, Curtis Schaafsma.

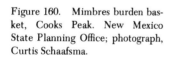

Figure 160. Mimbres burden basket, Cooks Peak. New Mexico State Planning Office; photograph, Curtis Schaafsma.

Figure 161. Human footprints carved in sequence across bedrock at a Mimbres petroglyph site near Cooks Peak. New Mexico State Planning Office; photograph, Curtis Schaafsma.

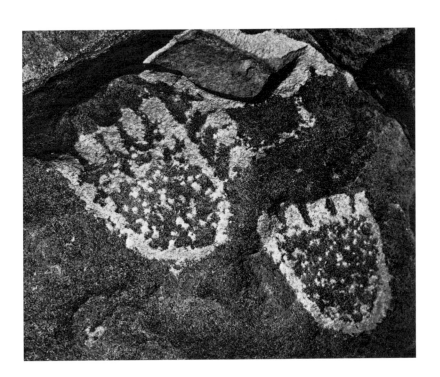

Figure 162. Decorative bear tracks, Cooks Peak. New Mexico State Planning Office; photograph, Curtis Schaafsma.

Figure 163. Classic Tlaloc painted in black and white on roof of cavate shelter at Hueco Tanks, Texas. Badly faded cloud terraces are part of this figure's headgear. This Tlaloc is one of 7 that occur in the shelter; a second figure is visible on the lower left. Photograph, Karl Kernberger.

head. The lower half may be solid or filled with vertical hachuring or geometric designs. The appendageless torso is commonly covered with decorative geometric motifs incorporating opposed stepped elements and angular blanket motifs characteristic of the style. These figures occur in groups as well as singly. Some petroglyph figures of the trapezoidal type are pecked on rock faces that naturally conform to the shape of the figure (Plate 17), and it is likely that such faces were deliberately selected.

A second and less usual type of Tlaloc is a further abstraction of the figure just described. In these instances Tlaloc is represented by eyes placed above a free blanket design without a bounding outline (Fig. 164; see also Fig. 153). As described previously, a still further abbreviation of the Tlaloc motif is one in which eyes alone are represented. Perhaps these are Tlaloc masks. More complete Tlaloc-like anthropomorphs have narrow rectangular torsos with geometric decoration and arms and legs; these are common at Cornudas Mountain. Finally, a single distinctive Tlaloc at Alamo Mountain carrying a staff and wearing a rain kilt is a complicated design with Mexican stylistic affinities (Fig. 165). This figure, as will be discussed later, was important in identifying the Tlaloc throughout the Jornada Style.

To date, no other class of figure in the Jornada Style is as readily identifiable or as common as Tlaloc. Masks and faces exhibit a bewildering number of attributes, most of which do not appear to occur in consistent

Figure 164. Large Mimbres-like blanket design above which occurs a pair of square Tlaloc eyes, Hatch, New Mexico. New Mexico State Planning Office; photograph, Karl Kernberger.

Figure 165. A petroglyph depiction of Tlaloc with Mesoamerican stylistic affinities, Alamo Mountain, New Mexico. The rock has turned since the figure was made. The fringed kilt signifies rain. The figure is about 3 feet tall.

Figure 166. Masks and faces at Three Rivers, New Mexico. Masks approximate life-size. New Mexico State Planning Office; photograph, Karl Kernberger.

Plate 17. Classic Tlaloc, or Rain God figure, filling trapezoidal boulder face, near Vado, New Mexico. Figure is between 2 and 3 feet tall. Photograph, Karl Kernberger.

Plate 18. Red and green mask with star or cross symbolism, Hueco Tanks, Texas. Photograph, Karl Kernberger.

Plate 19. Pair of solid type masks with tall conical caps, Hueco Tanks. The negative pattern in the mouth region of the right-hand figure resembles two superimposed fish. Photograph, Karl Kernberger.

Plate 20. Solid type masks, Cave Kiva, Hueco Tanks. Photograph, Karl Kernberger.

Plate 21. Solid type mask in red and orange, Hueco Tanks. Photograph, Karl Kernberger.

Plate 22. Red mask with earrings and elaborate headgear, Hueco Tanks. Photograph, Karl Kernberger.

Plate 23. Red and yellow "long" mask from open shelter near top of granite outcrop, Hueco Tanks. Photograph, Karl Kernberger.

Plate 24. Fifteenth-century mural painting from Pottery Mound, New Mexico, kiva 9, layer 2. Photograph, University of New Mexico.

76.70.774

clusters (Figs. 166–71). As petroglyphs, the typical masks have rounded outline forms varying in shape from vaguely rectangular to more nearly circular. In many cases the top of the head is flat. In general, features consist of eyes, nose, and mouth; ears and earrings occur occasionally. The eyes are typically almond shaped, although square and round eyes are also depicted. A central dot or vertical line designates the pupil in most instances, but at San Diego Mountain two dots were used (Fig. 168). Eyebrows are common. The triangular nose is usually placed high in the face and may drop from the top of the head or be a linear extension of the eyebrows. Treatment of the mouth varies and, along with headgear and facial decoration, may have been a diagnostic feature for purposes of identification. Facial designs are varied; horizontal facial division and chin and cheek markings are perhaps the most typical.

Interesting variations in masks include those lacking outlines (Fig. 171) or carved on rock corners so that the angle of the rock serves as a profile (Figs. 166 lower left; 167 f, g). At Three Rivers there is a cluster of masks pecked at the top of upright basalt columns; of this group, three are corner types. Their position at the top of the column serves to anthropomorphize the entire column, which is perhaps the effect intended.

The painted masks at Hueco Tanks deserve separate consideration because of their distinctiveness within the style and the degree of sophistication they exhibit. Painted masks are not unique to Hueco Tanks; others have been recorded from the nearby Hueco Mountains (John V. Davis, personal communication), from the Sacramento Mountains, and elsewhere to the north. At these sites they occur in small numbers but are basically like the Hueco Tanks paintings. The latter fall into two major typological categories (Newcomb and Kirkland 1967:196–97), the outline or linear mask and the solid mask. Both are usually smaller than life size.

The linear mask is the more common of the two. Most are painted in red or black or a combination of the two, although white, gray, and yellow are also used. This type is similar to the petroglyph representations. Outlines are usually present, and features and decoration tend to be linear. Shape varies from a modified rectangle to the flat-topped but otherwise oval or rounded form. Some of the simpler masks or faces are very expressive and seem to portray individual personalities almost like caricatures (Newcomb and Kirkland 1967:Plates 131, 236 H-K). Others are more formal and have ceremonial decoration (Fig. 172).

The solid mask paintings, beautifully handled, are technically superior to

Figure 167. A variety of Jornada Style faces and masks (a-g), Three Rivers; (h-i), Alamo Mountain, New Mexico. Figures (f) and (g) are on rock corners.

F

G

H

I

Figure 168. Horned ceremonial masks and bird, San Diego Mountain, New Mexico. Faces approximately life-size. New Mexico State Planning Office; photograph, Karl Kernberger.

Figure 169. Jornada Style mask and other designs, San Diego Mountain. New Mexico State Planning Office; photograph, Karl Kernberger.

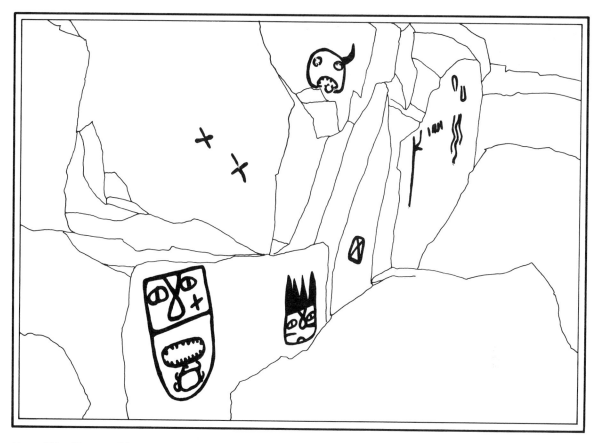

Figure 170.   "Long mask" and other Jornada Style petroglyphs, Three Rivers.

Figure 171.   Face lacking outline, Three Rivers, New Mexico. New Mexico State Planning Office; photograph, Karl Kernberger.

215

Figure 172. Black outline mask or face with ceremonial decoration, Hueco Tanks. Figure smaller than life-size. Photograph, Karl Kernberger.

Figure 173. Solid type mask from Cave Kiva, Hueco Tanks. Slightly smaller than life-size. Photograph, Karl Kernberger.

the outline masks. They are usually done in thin washes of red, although black, white, brown, yellow, red and yellow, red and blue, and red and green masks also occur (Newcomb and Kirkland 1967:197). These usually lack an outline and consist of carefully painted solid areas that may define meaningful negative space such as the eyes and facial decoration (Plates 18–22; Fig. 173). The use of solid patterning establishes a new aesthetic mode: heavy horizontal bands, variously divided, turning the mask into a pleasing abstract pattern. There are examples of bearded faces and masks with protruding tongues (Figs. 173, 174). In at least one instance the tongue is divided. Cloud-terrace facial decoration and fish motifs in conjunction with the masks are notable (Plate 19).

Hueco Tanks, a complex of three massive granite outcrops rising several hundred feet above the desert floor, has numerous water traps, rock-shelters, and overhangs where paintings occur. One of these (Toness and Hill 1972) containing eight fine masks is illustrated in Figure 175. Extensive exploration of the area indicates that the solidly painted masks are in more remote and hidden locations than the linear ones, thus suggesting that the solid masks may have served a more esoteric function (John V. Davis, personal communication).

Among the varieties of masks in the Jornada Style, a few more personages or classes of figures can be distinguished. Among them, the symbolism of the Mexican-derived Quetzalcoatl indicates that this deity or variations thereof are present in anthropomorphic form. We have seen the composite human-serpent representation of this figure from the Mimbres region (Fig. 155), and horned and plumed serpents are a part of the Jornada iconography (Fig. 176). There is evidence to suggest that the forward-reaching horns or the conical caps are distinguishing features of this personage in the Jornada Style. Three masks from Hueco Tanks with conical caps are illustrated in Figures 177 and Plate 19. The one in Figure 177 has a horned and plumed head on top of the cap. Below the paired conical cap masks is a small spotted feline, also wearing such a cap (Davis and Toness 1974:81). The significance of this figure is not clear, although it has Mesoamerican overtones. Other masks with forward-reaching horns may represent special facets of this deity. The petroglyph of a death's-head with such a horn (Fig. 178) suggests the Mexican portrayals of Quetzalcoatl with the Death God, Mictlantecuhtil, as his twin (Anton 1969:70). Figure 167a may depict Quetzalcoatl in his alternate form as Ehecatl, the Wind God, identifiable by his projecting mask, which may take the form of a bird's beak (Caso 1958:22).

Figure 174. Red mask combining both solid and linear painting, Hueco Tanks. Note the divided protruding tongue. Photograph, Karl Kernberger.

Figure 175. View of Cave Kiva showing eroded rock forms and some of the painted masks, Hueco Tanks. Photograph, Karl Kernberger.

218

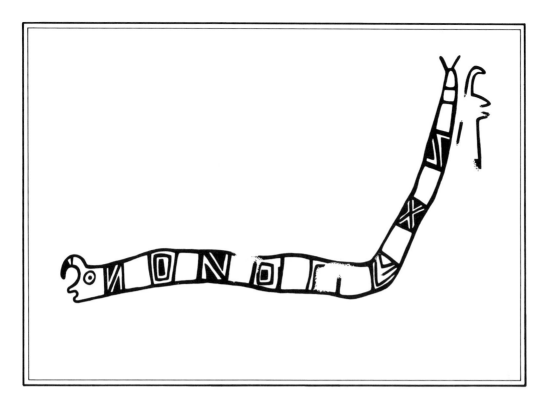

Figure 176. Horned serpent painted in red with decorated body, Hueco Mountains, Texas.

Another class of figures, less readily identified as specific supernaturals, is that of the two-horned beings. These may be divided into two categories on the basis of consistent differences in the way the horns are depicted. The horns of one group are those of the bighorn sheep, broad at the base and curving out from the center of the head. (P. Schaafsma 1972:Fig. 97). The horns of the other tend to be slightly longer and straighter and are farther apart (Fig. 167b and Plate 20).

There are other masks or faces with deer antlers or antelope horns (Fig. 168), and "helmet masks" with animal heads above a human face are depicted at San Diego Mountain and Hueco Tanks (Newcomb and Kirkland 1967:Plate 145; P. Schaafsma 1972:Fig. 99). Masks with crooked mouths (Fig. 167) occur in several instances. In later Pueblo iconography this irregular feature signifies a particular personage. There is also what might be referred to as the "long mask," extended in length and divided horizontally. Three masks of this type have a cross or star on the cheek (Plate 23 and Fig. 170), and some are depicted with an open mouth and teeth. The paw print on two

Figure 177.   Elaborate mask with abstract decoration and conical cap, Hueco Tanks. The cap is topped with a horned and plumed head, probably that of a serpent. The figure is 23 inches tall.

Figure 178. Profile head with forward reaching horn and macabre aspects, Three Rivers, New Mexico. New Mexico State Planning Office; photograph, Karl Kernberger.

Three Rivers examples is notable. Whether a single personage is depicted here is not clear. The paw print and star, judging from parallel iconography among the Pueblos, could signify warrior associations. There are stars on the rock above the mask in Figure 170, which has a paw print on the chin and a nose in the shape of an hourglass. The hourglass has warrior associations for present-day Indians in the Southwest (see pp. 312, 315).

Finally, naturalistic heads sometimes appear (Fig. 179). Other human forms are shown with head and torso or in full figure (Figs. 180, 181, 182; P. Schaafsma 1972:Fig. 87). The humpbacked phallic anthropomorph in Figure 180 has a macabre aspect, but comparison with a very similar figure in an Awatovi painting (Smith 1952:Fig. 53b) suggests it may represent Kokopelli. The Awatovi figure is shown with a piece of corn stuck in his belt, analogous to the bump in the rock in the torso area of the petroglyph. Other distinctive personages are those in Figure 182. Above is a stylized phallic man in profile holding a cloud terrace on a staff. A similar figure was observed earlier among the red paintings in the Mogollon Mountains. The naturalistically portrayed

Figure 179. Petroglyph depiction of a head, Hatch, New Mexico. New Mexico State Planning Office; photograph, Karl Kernberger.

Figure 180. Hunched, phallic anthropomorph, Three Rivers. New Mexico State Planning Office; photograph, Karl Kernberger.

Figure 181.   Jornada Style anthropomorphic representations from (a) Three Rivers; and (b) Carrizozo.

figure with a staff in Figure 182b is probably a shaman or other being with supernatural power closely affiliated with the animals flanking him. At Three Rivers, examples occur in which insects or animals holding staffs replace human beings.

In addition to the anthropomorphic theme, which plays a major role in the rock art of the eastern region, animals, birds, and insects are very important (Figs. 183–91). Although these are somewhat less complex and varied than their counterparts on Mimbres ceramics (Figs. 8, 9), they are imaginatively conceived, surpassing all other like representations in south-western rock art. The forms of these creatures take on the quality of decorative designs, and although the legs of the quadrupeds are usually bent to indicate action, the figure as a whole is static (Figs. 183, 184). Heads are in outline, and the eye is nearly always indicated. Prominent snouts and teeth are characteristic. The body may be hunched or in the simple shape of a

Figure 182. Petroglyphs showing Jornada Style personages, Three Rivers.

Figure 183. Jornada Style quadrupeds, Three Rivers. New Mexico State Planning Office; photograph, Karl Kernberger.

Figure 184. Quadrupeds from Three Rivers.

rectangle, the open interior of which on the larger figures is filled with a variety of decorative geometric patterns.

Most animals are stylized beyond the point of identification, although some of these may represent dogs or coyotes. Others, however, are clearly recognizable. Predominant among these is the mountain sheep, identified by realistically depicted horns, wide at the base and tapering through the curve to the tip. At both Hueco Tanks and Three Rivers, the body of the sheep tends toward a naturalistic rather than a rigid geometric configuration, and some of these are slightly hunched. Several are shown pierced with arrows, and at Hueco Tanks small human figures, probably hunters, also occur (Newcomb and Kirkland 1967:Plate 132, 10b, and Plate 144). Figures of rabbits appear in this art, and animals with long tails over their backs probably represent mountain lions. Some of these, however, are spotted, and jaguars may have been intended instead (Smith 1952:202–3). Dual symbolism is manifest in one large petroglyph of this figure that has rattles, stylized like those of a snake, at the end of its tail (Fig. 184).

An unusual assemblage of large animals painted in white on the soot-blackened roof of a deep rock-shelter occurs at Diablo Dam near Fort Hancock (Sutherland and Steed 1974:39–45). Among them are a deer, two canines (possibly wolves or coyotes), a cat, a large bear, and a very elaborate rendition of the horned serpent (Figs. 185–87). The serpent is shown with a forward-reaching horn above which fall three plumes, and its body is decorated with stepped designs, probably representing clouds. Bears and wolves are unusual figures, which among the Pueblos to the north are associated with medicine societies and war. Their Mexican affiliations have been pointed out by Sutherland and Steed (1974).

In addition to the figures of the animals themselves, decorative and formalized animal tracks are represented in the Jornada Style. Bear and mountain lion or wolf tracks (Fig. 167) are most commonly found, and they are thought to be connected with the supernatural powers attributed to these animals. Roadrunner tracks (Fig. 167) are also frequent. Green (1967) points out that they accompany feline tracks on arrowshaft smoothers from El Paso Phase sites.

Birds are pecked alone or in compositions involving cloud terraces and corn (Figs. 188, 189). The usual conventionalization shows the wing raised, indicating flight. There are also stylized spread-winged figures like the thunderbird or eagle, and this type may be highly ornate (Fig. 189c). The corn, cloud, and bird complex and the corn with the crooked stalk are

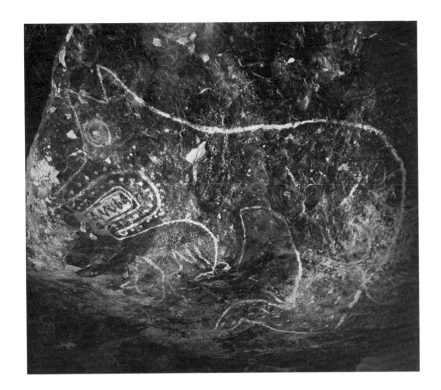

Figure 185. Canine with large teeth and curved fangs, Diablo Dam, Texas. The figure, painted in white on a soot-blackened roof, is 6 feet long. Photograph, Karl Kernberger.

Figure 186. Painting of a bear, 4 feet in length, Diablo Dam. Photograph, Karl Kernberger.

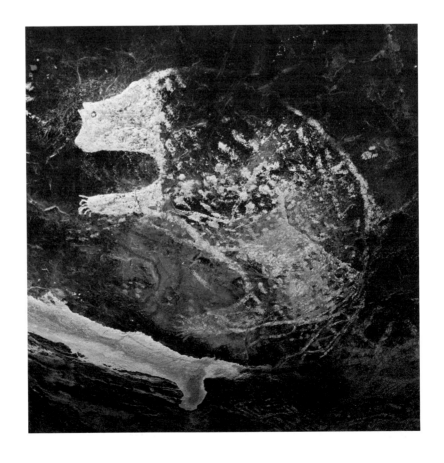

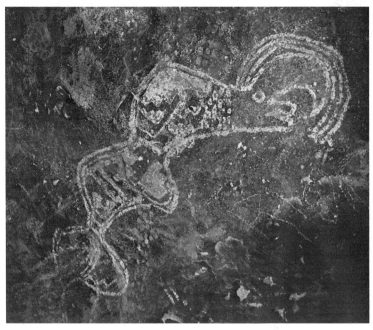

Figure 187. Eight foot long horned and plumed serpent decorated with stepped motifs possibly representing clouds, Diablo Dam, Texas. Photograph, Karl Kernberger.

Figure 188. Bird and cloud terrace, Three Rivers, New Mexico. New Mexico State Planning Office; photograph, Karl Kernberger.

229

Figure 189. Further bird motifs from Three Rivers: (a) the corn–cloud terrace–bird complex. This example is unusual in that the terrace appears on top of the corn instead of at the base; (b) a symmetrical composition with birds and terrace; (c) highly stylized thunderbird, footprint, and possible sun symbolism.

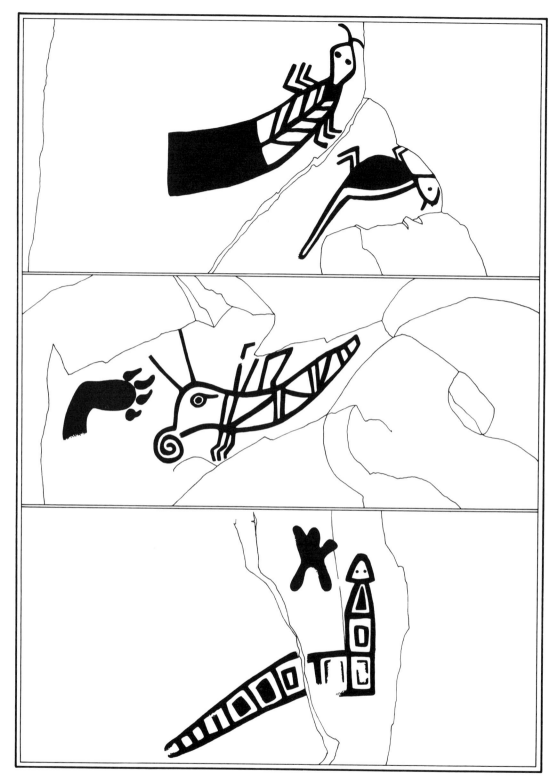

Figure 190. Snake and insects from Three Rivers. The central figure is a moth.

Figure 191. Abstract fish design, Three Rivers. Fish over a foot long. New Mexico State Planning Office; photograph, Karl Kernberger.

maintained later in this tradition in both the Rio Grande Style and its offshoot, eighteenth-century Navajo art.

Other creatures include tadpoles, snakes, abstract and realistic figures of fish, and worms and insects (Figs. 190, 191). At Three Rivers there are inchworms, a moth, butterflies, possibly a grasshopper, and others whose identity is not clear.

Following a recent discussion by Furst (1974a:132–33), who on the basis of ethnographic analogy negates the usual secular interpretation of western Mexican art, I suggest that the interpretation of Jornada Style life-forms goes beyond the mere identity of species. What we see here is not the work of prehistoric naturalists, but rather a group of figures carefully selected on the basis of their roles in the ideological structure. This hypothesis is supported by comparisons with the modern Pueblo pantheon and symbolic structure, which were in large part derived from those of the Jornada (P. Schaafsma 1972:129ff.; Schaafsma and Schaafsma 1974). Pueblo interpretation, for example, indicates that the animal tracks described previously were not made only in connection with sympathetic magic and the hunt. The power of the bear paw, which in the Pueblo world stands for the curing power of the bear,

Figure 192. Large abstract design painted in red and white, Hueco Tanks. The dynamic quality created here by the long diagonal stepped element is typical of such designs in the Jornada Style. Photograph, Karl Kernberger.

was discussed earlier in this chapter in connection with the petroglyphs of the Reserve district. The mountain lion also plays a major role in Pueblo myth and ritual, and he is represented in several different ceremonial situations (Smith 1952:202), as well as being the patron of hunters and warriors. Thus his track or his figure could have been used in any number of ritual contexts. The insects depicted may have shamanic power or participate in certain myths and rituals (Parsons 1939:191–92; Castañeda 1974:96–97). Castañeda gives an account of the meaning of the moth to the Mexican shaman. The eagle, revered in the Pueblo world as a symbol of the sky world over which he has control, is another figure that can be interpreted ethnographically. His freedom and wisdom are possible only for those living close to the sacred Sun Father, and he was personified by the ancients for boldness, alertness, and spiritual qualities (Kabotie 1949).

In addition to this significant complex of life figures, geometric motifs play an important role in the Jornada Style. The stepped cloud terrace or altar symbol is universal. Most of the geometric elements are nonrepresentational, although Hopi interpretation of Mimbres abstract designs indicates that symbolic content may be present (Kabotie 1949). Complex blanket

Figure 193. Large abstract pattern in yellow above a man-made prehistoric water catchment at Hueco Tanks. Design is over 3 feet long. Photograph, Karl Kernberger.

Figure 194. Three Rivers abstract with long-necked bird perched on corner. Photograph by Col. M. L. Crimmins, Scott Files, Peabody Museum, Harvard University.

Figure 195. Geometric pattern, Three Rivers. New Mexico State Planning Office; photograph, Karl Kernberger.

Figure 196. An example of the circle-dot motif at Three Rivers. Design approximately 6 inches in diameter. New Mexico State Planning Office; photograph, Karl Kernberger.

designs were described in connection with the torsos of the Tlaloc figures. Many of these and others (Figs. 192, 193) contain elements that could stand for clouds. There is also a variety of other, less complicated rectilinear abstracts (Figs. 194, 195). Distinctive at Three Rivers is the circle-dot motif (Fig. 196); one investigator who took the trouble to count found it to be the single most common element at this site (Yeo n.d.). Interestingly enough, its presence elsewhere is negligible, and its symbolic content has not been determined, although it occurs in various contexts in Mesoamerica (Peterson 1961:Fig. 44; Villagrá 1954:Fig 1; Toscano 1954:Fig. 19). Possibly it refers to Quetzalcoatl.

The Mexican origins of the goggle-eyed figures categorized as Tlaloc and the identity of the plumed and horned serpent and certain anthropomorphic figures as northern expressions of Quetzalcoatl are more or less assumed in the preceding discussion. It would be enlightening to explore further these possible relationships as well as other connections with Mexico that may be present. That Mexican prototypes can reasonably be sought for many of the iconographic features in the Jornada Style is suggested on the basis of a preliminary evaluation of the art itself, which contains a number of highly simplified but nevertheless apparently Mesoamerican features, and by the cultural interaction that took place after A.D. 1000 between the Desert Mogollon and the Casas Grandes region. A Mexican-Mogollon-Pueblo continuity in religion has recently been pointed out by Ellis and Hammack (1968:39), although, lacking the data base of the Jornada art style, their discussion differs somewhat from that presented here. Nevertheless, the existence of a Mexican-derived religious art complex in the prehistoric Southwest between A.D. 1050 and A.D. 1400 explains the observations of many earlier investigators regarding the apparent parallels between the religions of central Mexico and those of the ethnographic Pueblos.

The so-called Tlaloc figure in the Jornada Style is widely represented, occurring at least once in nearly every Jornada Style rock art site or site cluster. In addition to the goggles, relevant aspects of this personage are the trapezoidal head and the vertical hachuring that sometimes occurs in the lower portion of the face. The unusual representation at Alamo Mountain (Fig. 165) looks very much in proportions and stance like the crude depiction of a figure from a Mexican codex, and he is shown with a fringed kilt. A curved line from the mouth on the left could easily be interpreted as a fang, and the figure holds a short staff or similar object. Comparisons with Mexican depictions of Tlaloc suggest strongly that, in fact, it is he who is being represented throughout the Jornada Style. In Mesoamerica "Tlaloc is easily identified by the characteristic goggle eyes that were his trademark from the early Classic to the Conquest" (Furst 1974b:69–71). He is said to have worn a mask, and the rings around his eyes, originally the forms of two snakes closely associated with the rain god, represent clouds heavy with rain. Beyond this he is shown in various guises, but large fangs or canines (an attribute of the jaguar) are common, as are teeth stylized into a vertical fringelike decoration. In some representations in the codices (Peterson 1961:Fig. 31) and in ceramic decoration (Anton 1969:Plate 101), he wears a fringed kilt signifying rain, strikingly similar to that worn by the Alamo Mountain petroglyph. Di Peso's reference (1974:565) to a sleeveless netted cloud jacket as part of his attire calls to mind the examples with terraced motifs on their torsos, probably symbolizing clouds (Plate 17, Fig. 163). His general trapezoidal configuration in the Jornada Style is also paralleled by Mesoamerican examples in which his form is frequently simplified or abstracted in a like manner. The Tlaloc masks on the temple of Quetzalcoatl at Teotihuacan are good examples of this tendency toward trapezoidal abstraction (Anton 1969:Plate 105).

Tlaloc, "he who makes things grow," the rain god of Mexico, was widely worshipped, reigning as a supreme deity from the days of Teotihuacan through the Aztecs, and he was probably one of the most ancient gods of Mexico and Central America (Caso 1958:41). At Teotihuacan his representations outnumber those of Quetzalcoatl, and throughout Mexico he is represented in sculpture, painting, and ceramic art. He controlled the rain necessary for raising crops on the high central plateaus and was in charge of floods, hail, frost, and lightning. Turtles, lizards, toads, frogs, and snakes were closely connected to and often pictured with this deity. His home was on the tops of high mountains where the clouds form. He was also associated with caverns and springs, and child sacrifices were made to him.

The importance of this figure in the Jornada pantheon cannot be overemphasized. On the basis of the numbers of depictions found in the Jornada Style, it would appear that this northern Tlaloc was of supreme significance to the inhabitants of this arid region and that a cult around him was probably a major focus in the religious system of the Jornada and Mimbres people. Further insight into this aspect of Jornada religion is provided by examining the kachina cult of the Pueblos. A number of investigators have acknowledged parallels between the Tlaloc and kachina cults (Parsons 1939; Brew 1944; Beals 1944; Kelley 1966; Ellis and Hammack 1968) and have suggested that the kachina cult appears to be a variant of the Tlaloc cult. The kachinas as bringers of rain and clouds, with their homes on the tops of mountains or at water sources, bear obvious similarities. Ellis and Hammack even propose that Tlaloc can be identified with the Zuni Pautiwa: "kindly, generous, and dignified head of the Katchina village, leader of the gods, and, like Tlaloc, associated with deer" (1968:41). Further parallels can be drawn between Tlaloc's helpers, the Tlaloques, and the kachina rain spirits (Ellis and Hammack 1968:41). From a Taos myth, Parsons (1939:1018) describes the suicide of Blue Corn Girl by drowning as a parallel to Aztec sacrificial suicide to Tlalocan, home of the Rain Gods. She is also impressed by a picture of an Aztec priest impersonating the mask-wearing rain god Tlaloc, which is "strikingly Katchina-like, even to the flowing hair (a wig) and the black 'smear' on the face under the mask" (Parsons 1939:1019).

Without the evidence provided by the rock art, however, the geographic and apparent cultural gaps between central Mexico and the Pueblo world provided something of a stumbling block to this kind of thinking (Beals 1944:246). Thus the Jornada Style is important in providing positive evidence for a logical historical and cultural connection between the Tlaloc cult and the Pueblo kachina cult, the Jornada region being culturally affiliated with late developments at Casas Grandes, which were ultimately traceable to central Mexico.

Another major and widely venerated Mexican figure making an appearance in the north is Quetzalcoatl, the feathered serpent. He was frequently associated with Tlaloc in Mexico and even shared some of his characteristics. This deity, with varied and complex attributes, was recognized as the god of life, the morning, fertility, and agriculture and the patron of twins and monsters. As the god of wisdom, calendars, and learning, he was the god of civilization. He also took the form of Ehecatl, the Wind God, and at other times he may be seen combined with his twin brother Mictlantecuhtil, the Death God, thus symbolizing the duality of life and death. The cosmic counterpart of this two-faced figure is Venus, the morning and evening star (Anton 1969; Vaillant 1948). A beneficent deity at Teotihuacan, Quetzalcoatl later became an astral figure, demanding human sacrifice (Soustelle 1967:94). He occurs in the Mexican iconographic system in both anthropomorphic and serpent form, and he is also symbolized by the morning star, often in the form of an outlined cross (Villagrá 1954:80). In human form he may be bearded, and as Ehecatl he is shown with a projecting mask or bird's beak. Tozzer (1957:519) notes that the pointed hat, a Huastec feature, is among Quetzal-coatl's usual articles of attire (see Caso 1958; Soustelle 1967:104–5).

Parallels have been drawn between Quetzalcoatl and the Horned or Plumed Water Serpent of the Pueblos (Kelley 1966:109; Parsons 1939:1016; Ellis and Hammack 1968), variously referred to as Palülükon (Hopi), Kolowisi (Zuni), and Awanyu (Rio Grande). In the graphic art of the Pueblo world, he is nearly always represented as a serpent, although in myths he may take the form of a man (Dutton 1963:101–3). Ellis and Hammack (1968:41) state that he is "recognizable through personality and costume in the Hopi Sky God, Sotuqnang-u, who wears a single horn or high cone when masked and a hat shaped like a star when unmasked." In addition they mention him in connection with a wooden kachina figure used in eastern Pueblo water rituals. The Horned Serpent is the patron of rivers and irrigation, and he is identified with springs, which he inhabits. He may also live in the mountains, and he is associated with fertility and rain. At times he is a fearsome and punitive being, both controlling and causing floods and earthquakes, and human sacrifice is mentioned in this connection (Parsons 1939:184–89; Switzer n.d.). Fewkes (1906:355) refers to a cult around the Plumed Serpent at Hopi that is a form of sky or sun worship and that reportedly derived from the mythic land of Palatkwabi in the south. Ellis and Hammack (1968:41) also suggest that he is possibly connected with the eastern "Pueblo god–culture hero, Poshaiyanne, also known as Montezuma, who taught the people to farm and introduced medicine societies." In other words, he is probably as complex in concept in the Southwest as in Mexico.

As described earlier, this personage appears in the Jornada Style in various guises, both as an anthropomorph and as a serpent. The single horn, plumes, and conical cap are all part of his attire, and in one instance he is bearded. Since he is symbolized in Mexico by Venus, the morning star, it is possible that the outlined equilineal cross, so frequent in Mimbres sites, and the cross of the Three Rivers circle-dot design are part of his symbolic repertoire in the Southwest. In some sites, as in the Pueblo art discussed in the next chapter, simple crosses occur in association with serpent figures. On the whole, however, the graphic symbolism of this supernatural being appears to be more varied in the Jornada Style than among the Pueblos, perhaps reflecting closer ties with Mexican prototypes. The proposed combination of Quetzalcoatl symbolism with that of Mictlantecuhtil and Ehecatl would seem to confirm this observation. It is noteworthy, however, that Ellis and Hammack (1968:42) describe a Zuni kachina "bearing the Mexican wind symbol protruding from her chin" as Quetzalcoatl in his wind guise.

The horn almost universally has been "the insignia of supernatural power—especially shamanic power or even power of the gods" (Furst 1974a:135). Exactly when in the history of Quetzalcoatl the horn was acquired has not been determined, although it may be comparable to the conical cap. Horned beings figure prominently in Pueblo iconography and in that of western Mexico. Furst (1974a:136) has drawn an analogy between the One-Horns appearing in figurine art in Colima and the Two-Horns of Nayarit and similar horned beings in Hopi cosmology. At Hopi they relate to the Underworld and armed with spears and clubs act both as guardians for the soul in its journey through the Underworld and as defenders of the Hopi villages and initiates at Wüwüchim. Similar guardian roles are ascribed by Furst to their Mexican analogues. It is possible that the Two-Horns of the Jornada pantheon were similarly guardians; in this regard, the One-Horns represented in Mogollon Mountain rock art also come to mind. On the other hand, the presence of both single and double horns on several different modern Pueblo kachinas and on hunting supernaturals among the Rio Grande Tewa is cautionary evidence rendering any specific identification of these figures highly tentative without further information.

Other resemblances between Jornada iconography and that of Mexico are less specific in regard to the identification of particular personages but are nonetheless definite indicators that a single general ideographic system is in operation. The macabre element in Mexican art is present in several petroglyphs at Three Rivers. In Mesoamerica the skull or death's-head is often made in connection with the gods of the Underworld and as part of the iconography of certain earth goddesses. Its significance in the Jornada Style in most cases is less readily understood.

Eagles, large cats and canines, rabbits, and insects are other themes in Mexican as well as in Jornada art, and in Mexico each has its own symbolic position within the cosmos. The Pueblo significance of these and other animals, some of which were discussed previously, often closely parallels the Mexican interpretations (see also p. 296). In the later days of Indian Mexico, the eagle was associated with Huitzilopochtli, a war god, largely identified with the sun. The jaguar (its southwestern counterpart being the mountain lion) is an ancient figure in Mesoamerican symbolism, associated with a large number of supernaturals. Among other things he was the guise of Tezcatlipoca, another warrior god. The coyote was associated with dance, music, and sexual pleasure, and the rabbit with the moon and drunkenness.

As regards relationships with Mexico, however, perhaps the most important component in the Jornada Style, in addition to the Tlaloc and Quetzalcoatl figures, is the mask itself: "A common art form even in archaic times, the mask is one of the most characteristic elements of all the cultures of ancient Mexico" (Westheim 1965:93). An item of magicoreligious significance with an important place in ritual, the mask transforms men into the being it represents. Mexican sovereigns and priests had in their possession the masks of the gods, and priests, enacting the role of a god's representative, wore the masks in ceremonies. In Mexico, masks could also be worn on the chest, the headdress, the belt, and so on, thus accounting for the numbers of small masks or talismans in mask form (Westheim 1965:93–96). Undoubtedly, among the Jornada people, masks served certain parallel functions, at least in that they represented a certain class of supernaturals and had a place in the ceremonial ritual. The masks of the Pueblo kachinas serve a comparable purpose.

Not only is the presence of the mask in itself significant, but also important are general stylistic and iconographic similarities between Jornada masks and those of Mexico. The shape and proportion of many of the painted masks at Hueco Tanks and some of the petroglyphic representations elsewhere show a decided similarity with mask sculpture and painting from Teotihuacan. A distinguishing characteristic of the Teotihuacan masks is the tendency to flatten the top of the head and widen the proportions of the face. The addition of ears also lends to the impression of horizontal stretching. The Teotihuacan sculptor flattened the cubic mass enough to achieve a fine balance between the plane of the face and its plasticity, and both procedures work together toward a type of abstraction in which the spiritual quality of the mask is emphasized (Westheim 1965:142–43). Similar effects are present in the solid painted masks at Hueco Tanks, in which the horizontal dimension is stressed by abstract decoration emphasizing wide horizontal bands. Like the Mexican masks, some of these have wider than normal proportions to begin with. The blank eyes of many of the figures add to their otherworldly quality. The long smooth line of the eyebrows in the paintings is also reminiscent of Teotihuacan mask sculpture, and stepped elements and negative patterns in the lower part of the face occur in the masks of both areas.

It must be emphasized that the reference to Teotihuacan here is only a most general one. The civilization that was Teotihuacan collapsed as a political entity several hundred years before these masks appeared in the north. Nevertheless, its cultural impact was tremendous throughout Mexico for a long time after, and it is perhaps these lingerings that we see in the masks of Hueco Tanks.

A few other mask motifs are shared between the Southwest and Mexico. The protruding tongue is a common Mexican feature, and it also appears at Hueco Tanks. In the northern examples it may be divided (Fig. 174), but no cleft examples like those found in Mexico are known here. The helmet mask, with an animal's head above the face of the wearer, is common in Mexican work and appears on occasion in that of the Jornada (P. Schaafsma 1972:99; Newcomb and Kirkland 1967:Plate 145). Finally, the Jornada practice of pecking masks on rock corners may have derived from the common Mexican practice of situating mask sculpture in a similar fashion on the corners of ceremonial buildings.

CONCLUSIONS

As described earlier, the advent of the Jornada Style in the north was concurrent with changes in the cultural system, including a rise in population, concentration of population into large villages, and probable reliance on irrigation agriculture. Ceramic associations, ceremonial objects such as copper bells and stone palettes, coursed adobe pueblo construction, and the art, in which masks and Mexican-like supernatural beings are present, all indicate that after A.D. 1050 the Mimbres and Jornada people were operating within the communication network of Casas Grandes. Whatever Mexican contact with the Southwest had gone on previously was greatly intensified after this date, when Casas Grandes and the surrounding territory came under the domination of what were presumably Toltec-related *pochteca* groups (Di Peso 1966, 1968). Thus it is proposed that the latter-day Desert Mogollon, rather than being a peripheral Anasazi manifestation, as is often implied (Lehmer 1948:90; Willey 1966:199), were peripheral to the high cultures of Mesoamerica; and it is hypothesized that they constituted a culture of greater complexity than has heretofore been recognized.

The urban social structure of Casas Grandes had to be sustained by socioreligious institutions capable of integrating the large population. The contemporaneous presence of a Mexican-derived art style in the Mogollon, the contents of which suggest the influence of religious cults related to those of Mesoamerica, at a time when population aggregation was taking place and large pueblos were forming seems to indicate that socioreligious institutions such as those as Casas Grandes were also operative here. Further, on the northern Rio Grande, the post-1300 developments of large Pueblo towns occurred concomitantly with the appearance of irrigation and the Jornada-derived Rio Grande art style (Dozier 1970:39). It has been hypothesized that the Pueblo trend toward population aggregation at this time on the upper Rio Grande was facilitated by intravillage, lineage-independent integrative mechanisms like the kachina cult and related sodalities, the presence of which are manifest in the art (Chapter 8 and Schaafsma and Schaafsma 1974). This logically implies the presence at an earlier date of similar institutions in the religious structure of the Desert Mogollon. The evidence provided by the rock art, in regard to both its cultural-historical origins and its systemic context, is consistent with and helps to explain other changes in the prehistory of the Mimbres and Jornada Mogollon after the middle of the eleventh century.

8

Pueblo Rock Art
After A.D. 1300

The Pueblo IV period—that time in Pueblo history following the abandonment of vast regions of the Anasazi country on the Colorado Plateau and before Spanish cultural impact—has been referred to in southwestern archaeology as the "Regressive-Pueblo" period (Roberts 1935). As Brew (1944:241) has aptly pointed out, however, "regression" occurred in the area of occupation alone; in almost all other respects this was a period of cultural efflorescence and startling progress. Pueblo settlements shifted from villages to towns, and there was new and vigorous growth in artistic symbolism, painting methods, and religion. Later investigators have referred to the period A.D. 1325–1600 as the Rio Grande Classic Period (Wendorf and Reed 1955:149).

The developments in the arts that took place at this time, however, cannot properly be considered a renaissance, a vigorous revival of the Anasazi arts of the past. There is very little that bears upon the florescence in the arts of the preceding years, and as was described earlier, a decided degeneration is visible in much Anasazi graphic art just before A.D. 1300. Thus explanations for the changes heralding the Pueblo IV developments have been sought in "outside stimuli" (Brew 1944:244). Before considering this, however, it is relevant to review events in the Pueblo Southwest just prior to Pueblo IV times.

As described in Chapter 5, archaeological studies have demonstrated that the Anasazi settlement pattern after A.D. 1150 was characterized by trends toward population aggregation and larger villages (Hill 1970:88; Dean 1970:151; Zubrow 1971:137). These trends were accompanied by shifts in population centers, so that by the fourteenth century the Pueblos were concentrated in the vicinities of the modern villages at Hopi and Zuni, in even greater numbers in the northern Rio Grande drainage, and on the Little Colorado (Map 8). It was at this point that the efflorescence in the art occurred, and it has been proposed (Schaafsma and Schaafsma 1974) that this was due to the acceptance by the Pueblos of a new ideology and associated art complex from the Jornada Mogollon.

In commenting on the trend toward aggregation in eastern Arizona, Longacre has pointed out that the development of larger villages must have been accompanied by concomitant sociocultural changes:

> Related to these changes was a change in the nature of the organization of the community itself. Villages up to A.D. 1300 probably were more commonly composed of single localized lineages. The economic advantages accruing to larger aggregates of people in the face of environmental pressures resulted in the establishment of communities of more than a single lineage after 1300. Strong localized lineages are not conducive to a strong village integration when a village consists of several lineages. I would expect the development of integrative ties that crosscut social groups to develop within the village under these circumstances. These would be such things as the development of societies with strong ritual functions, the breakdown of the association of kiva with clan, and the assumption by the kivas of more villagewide significance (for example, by association with societies). Crosscutting integrative mechanisms such as these would promote community solidarity at the expense of the disruptive lineage strength, and this is the pattern today among the western Pueblos. (Longacre 1964:1455)

It is therefore significant that the content of the Jornada-derived Rio Grande Style art suggests the appearance of socioreligious institutions capable of successfully integrating the multilineage villages that were forming at this time in the Pueblo region (Schaafsma and Schaafsma 1974:544). The Pueblos in the Rio Grande Valley were dependent on irrigation, using water from

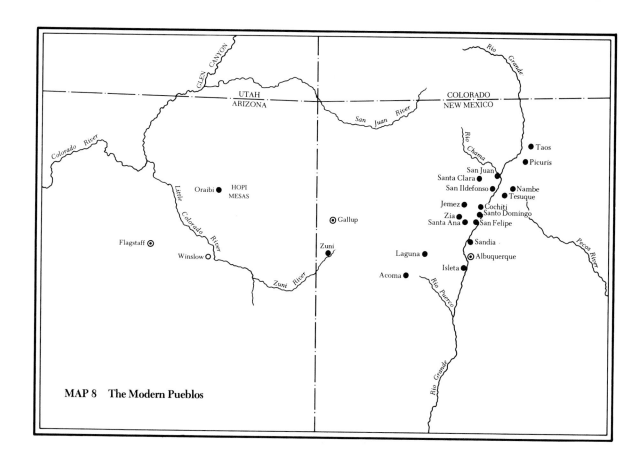

MAP 8   The Modern Pueblos

permanent streams in the manner described by Dozier (1970:131–33), who proposes that these intensive irrigation practices brought about the centralized orientation of the Rio Grande villages. He specifically suggests that nonkinship units such as sodalities or associations were needed to mobilize the people needed to operate an irrigation society. The major identifiable components of the art are related to the kachina cult and a number of sodalities such as the warrior, hunting, and curing societies, which draw their membership from the entire village and thus crosscut lineage affiliations. Once they were operative, these institutions would have furthered the trend, already in progress, of village growth and social integration (Hill 1970:99).

In contrast to the situation for the Jornada Mogollon, this period in Pueblo prehistory has been documented through numerous archaeological excavations and surveys. Wendorf and Reed (1955:149) list more than thirty excavated Rio Grande sites from the Classic Period alone (A.D. 1325–1600). Villages consisted of large multistoried pueblos arranged around a number of enclosed plazas, and masonry or coursed adobe, depending on the area, was used in their construction. Ceremonial rooms or kivas varied from subterranean rectangular or circular structures within the plazas to rooms incorporated within the pueblo roomblock. Population estimates for these villages vary from several hundred to more than a thousand occupants. The material culture of the Classic Period also experienced an unprecedented development, evident in the "elaborate decoration of pipes, elaborate axes, numerous vessel forms, carved bone tools, stone effigies, and mural paintings" (Wendorf and Reed 1955:153). This florescence in the arts and in the culture in general was still developing when it was, to quote a euphemistic phrase, "abruptly modified by the impact of European culture" (Wendorf and Reed 1955:153). The nature of this "modification"—Spanish oppression after A.D. 1600, civil and church attacks on native religion, economic exploitation, and so on—is well described by Dozier (1970).

Much of the archaeological research on the post–A.D. 1300 Pueblos has focused on the distribution of pottery types and interregional contacts. Western-originated glazewares appear in the central Pueblo province of the Rio Grande around A.D. 1325, and they began to be made locally shortly thereafter, replacing the older Anasazi Black-on-white wares. North of Santa Fe, the thick matte pottery, or Biscuit Wares, distinguish the northern Tewa province. The entire Rio Grande region (Map 9) has been broken down into a number of divisions (Mera 1940) based on linguistic groups of the seventeenth century, and these divisions reflect archaeological variation of the Classic and early Historic (1600–present) periods in regard to both ceramics and the graphic arts.

In addition to the view of this period presented in the archaeological reports, a number of firsthand accounts from the chronicles of early Spanish explorers greatly amplify our understanding of the sixteenth-century Pueblo world (Winship 1896, 1904; Villagrá 1933; Hammond and Rey 1927, 1929, 1940; Bolton 1930). An excellent collection of Spanish quotes regarding Pueblo life at that time can be found in Dutton's *Sun Father's Way* (1963:3–18). The scribe Hernán Gallegos of the Chamuscado-Rodríguez expedition (1581–82) describes a Tiwa pueblo from the Rio Grande as follows:

> We entered this pueblo and they gave us much corn. They showed us many pots and other earthenware containers very well painted. . . . The way they build their houses, which are square, is as follows. They bake [?] the clay; they build the walls narrow; they make adobes for the doorways. The lumber used is pine and willow.

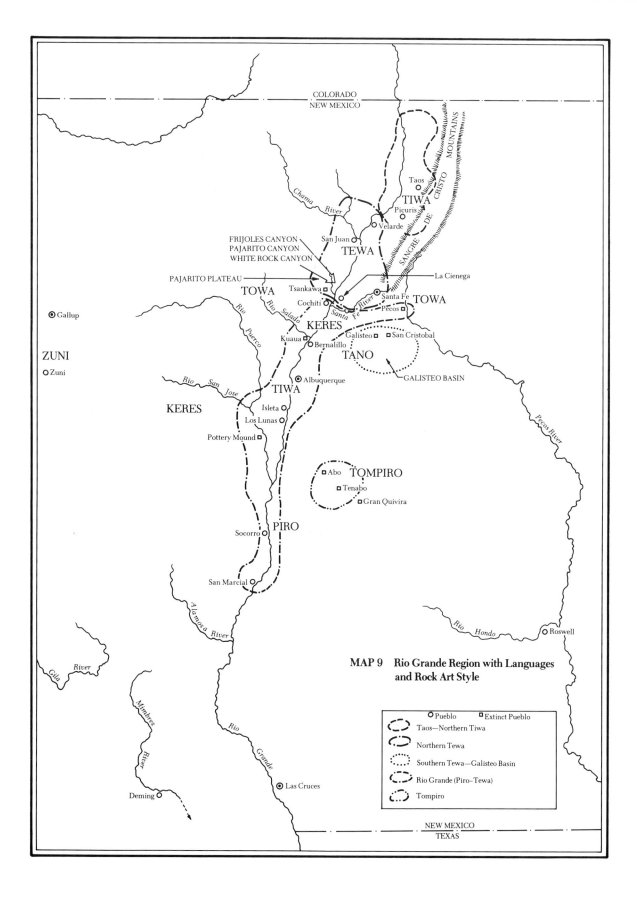

COLORADO
NEW MEXICO

Chama

River

Taos

TIWA

Picuris

Velarde

San Juan

FRIJOLES CANYON
PAJARITO CANYON
WHITE ROCK CANYON

TEWA

La Cienega

PAJARITO PLATEAU

Tsankawa

TOWA

Cochiti

Rio

Salado

Santa Fe

River

Santa Fe

TOWA

Pecos

KERES

Gallup

Rio

Puerco

Kuaua

Bernalillo

Galisteo

San Cristobal

TANO

ZUNI

Zuni

KERES

Rio

San

Jose

TIWA

Isleta

Los Lunas

Pottery Mound

Albuquerque

GALISTEO BASIN

Pecos River

Abo

TOMPIRO

Tenabo

Gran Quivira

PIRO

Socorro

San Marcial

Alamosa

River

Rio

Hondo

Roswell

Gila

River

**MAP 9 Rio Grande Region with Languages
and Rock Art Style**

Mimbres

River

Rio

Grande

Las Cruces

Deming

○ Pueblo   ▢ Extinct Pueblo

⬭ Taos—Northern Tiwa

⬭ Northern Tewa

⬭ Southern Tewa—Galisteo Basin

⬭ Rio Grande (Piro–Tewa)

⬭ Tompiro

NEW MEXICO
TEXAS

They use many timbers ten and twelve feet long. They provide them with movable ladders by means of which they climb to their quarters. They are movable wooden ladders, for when they retire at night they lift them up since they wage war with one another.

These people are clothed like the others. I wish to describe here their garments, because, for a barbarous people, it is the best attire that has been found among them. It is as follows. The men have caps, I mean on the crown of their heads, a sort of skull cap formed by their own hair. Others wear their hair long, to the shoulders, as the Indians of New Spain formerly did. Some adorn themselves with painted cotton pieces of cloth three spans long and two thirds wide, with which they cover their privy parts. Over this they wear, fastened at the shoulders, a blanket of the same material, painted with many figures and colors. It reaches to their knees like the clothes of the Mexicans. Some, in fact most of them, wear cotton shirts, hand painted and embroidered, that are very charming. They wear shoes. Below the waist the women wear cotton skirts, colored and embroidered, and above, a blanket of the same material, painted and worked like those used by the men. They wear it after the fashion of the Jewish women. They girt themselves over it with cotton sashes adorned with tassels. They comb their hair, which is long. (Dutton 1963:8–9)

In another account, Luxán of the Espejo expedition of 1582–83 mentions in reference to the Tiwa that "throughout this nation they have many masks which they use in their dances and ceremonies" (Hammond and Rey 1929:79).

Villagrá in 1610 (1933:143–44) described the Rio Grande villages as follows:

We visited a good many of these pueblos. They are all well built with straight, well-squared walls. Their towns have no defined streets. Their houses are three, five, six, and even seven stories high, with many windows and terraces. . . . The men spin and weave and the women cook, build the houses, and keep them in repair. They dress in garments of cotton cloth, and the women wear beautiful shawls of many colors. . . . The men and women alike are excellent swimmers. They are also expert in the art of painting, and are great fishermen. . . .

Various chroniclers describe the corn, beans, melons, cotton, tobacco, and native fowl, "cocks with great hanging chins," or turkeys (Winship 1896:520–22), raised by the Indians of the Rio Grande, but little mention is made of farming methods. There are, however, a few references to irrigation that are of interest in reference to the earlier discussion of irrigation practices and the implication thereof in the structure of Pueblo society (see pp. 244–45). Espejo's narrative (Bolton 1930:178) includes the following observations on the Piro, the southernmost of the Rio Grande Pueblo groups: "They have fields of maize, beans, gourds, and piciete (tobacco) in large quantities, which they cultivate like the Mexicans. Some of the fields are under irrigation, possessing very good diverting ditches, while others are dependent upon the weather." Espejo stated further that "on each bank there are sandy flats more than a league wide, of soil naturally well adapted to the raising of corn," and Luxán (Hammond and Rey 1929:73) described the entire river at some point in the Piro province as being "bordered with sown fields." Finally, in a report of 1591 by Castaño de Sosa, irrigated fields, population concentrations, and an abundance of crops are described for the Tewa pueblos:

> All these six pueblos [including Pecos] are irrigated and have irrigation ditches, a thing [which would] not [be] believed if we had not seen it with our own eyes. A very great amount of maize, beans, and other vegetables is harvested. They dress in the manner of the pueblo [Pecos] previously described. They [the five Tewa pueblos visited to date] are small pueblos, although heavily populated. The houses are of two and three stories, all with such devices as hatchways and ladders which can be lifted up. (Schroeder and Matson 1965:117)

Of considerable interest in regard to the art of the period are observations made by the various sixteenth-century chroniclers about the wall paintings. These paintings in the Piro villages are mentioned in several instances: in the narratives of Espejo (Bolton 1930:178), Villagrá (1933), and Gonzáles de Mendoza (Smith 1952:73), and twice by Hernán Gallegos (Hammond and Rey 1927:263). Espejo's comment that "The paintings of their houses, and the things which they have for balls and dancing, both as regards the music and the rest, are all very much like those of the Mexicans" is of interest in that it alludes to other aspects of ceremonial life.

Descriptions of the murals by Captain Gaspar Pérez de Villagrá of the

Oñate expedition are the most vivid, and Smith (1952:73) aptly notes that "Villagrá, although he was perhaps a more conscientious poet than a historian, and in response to his Muse frequently took full advantage of his professional license, still remains our best authority." Villagrá thus describes the paintings of a southern Piro pueblo:

> On the walls of the rooms where we were quartered were many paintings of the demons they worship as gods. Fierce and terrible were their features. It was easy to understand the meaning of these, for the god of water was near the water, the god of the mountains was near the mountains, and in like manner all those deities they adore, their gods of the hunt, crops, and other things they have. (Villagrá 1933:140)

To Villagrá we also owe the account of the paintings in the southern Tiwa pueblo variously referred to as Puaray, Puarai, Paula, and so on, in the vicinity of the modern town of Bernalillo, in which the friars left behind by Chamuscado had been murdered. The imagination of the members of Oñate's party sixteen years later, quartered in a room there, led to the misinterpretation that the paintings on the walls (viewed through a layer of newly applied whitewash) were a visual narrative of the murder. Good evidence exists (Dutton 1963:13 and Smith 1952:74–75) to show that the uneasy Spaniards were victimized by their fantasies and that the images Villagrá (1933:142) describes as "the details of the martyrdom of those saintly men, Fray Agustín, Fray Juan, and Fray Francisco," were simply a Pueblo ceremonial scene.

Espejo (Bolton 1930:182) describes Zia as a very large pueblo with "eight plazas and better houses than those previously mentioned, most of them being whitewashed and painted with colors and pictures after the Mexican custom." Finally, Smith (1952:78–80) cites other Spanish references to wall paintings at Zuni and possibly also at Acoma.

As intriguing as the Spanish accounts may be, fortunately we are not dependent for our knowledge of these murals on the brief notations of these early explorers. Excavations in Pueblo sites postdating A.D. 1300 have revealed a significant number of kiva paintings (Plate 24). The most elaborate are from the ruins of Awatovi and Kawaika-a in the Jeddito district at Hopi (Smith 1952), Pottery Mound (Hibben 1960, 1966, 1975; Vivian 1961), and Kuaua (Dutton 1963) on the Rio Grande. Although other murals in the same style have been reported from the Pajarito Plateau (Chapman 1938:148), Picuris Pueblo, Pueblo del Encierro near Cochiti (P. Schaafsma 1965), Gran

Quivira, and a site near Winslow, Arizona (Pond 1966), these are for the most part less complex than those from the Jeddito, Pottery Mound, and Kuaua sites. From each of these three, innumerable paintings have been recorded from the many superimposed layers of plaster. The largest collection is from Pottery Mound, where hundreds of paintings, dating from the fourteenth and fifteenth centuries, have been documented from seventeen different kivas (Hibben 1975).

Clearly it is in the murals, and specifically those of the Jeddito and Pottery Mound sites, that the apex of Pueblo art is to be found. Furthermore, these paintings may be regarded as the highest artistic development within the Jornada–Rio Grande tradition preserved in the archaeological record. The mural art consists of bold, dynamic design layouts adapted to the entire wall surface. Borders and framing lines are often used to break up the wall surface, or the whole wall may be treated as a single, unbounded, integrated composition. Subject matter consists of ceremonial and ritual themes into which elaborately attired humans, animals, birds, and abstract designs are incorporated. Shields, feathers, baskets, pots, jewelry, textiles, miscellaneous ceremonial items, food, and plants are also pictured. While this is a highly meaningful art, full of graphic portrayals and symbolic content, it is, at the same time, very decorative. Colors are highly varied and sensitively juxtaposed. Areas of flat solid color contrast with those broken into intricate patterns or bold designs.

The murals of the painted kiva at Kuaua are also noteworthy, although they lack the variation in color, complexity of subject matter, and sophistication in layout of the Jeddito and Pottery Mound work. Present here, however, are certain types of masked ceremonial figures that do not occur in the other kiva paintings.

Were it not for the preservation of these fragile paintings on the delicate, thin plaster layers of the prehistoric kivas, our concept of the art of the Pueblo world after A.D. 1300 would be considerably restricted. A limited range of designs from this period appears on stone slabs recovered from Kawaika-a; these are reproduced in Smith (1952:261–70), who also describes comparable material from other sites. There were parallel developments in the startling new ceramic decoration, particularly at Hopi, where a native efflorescence occurred in the decorative arts in response to the general stimulation of the period, but the other arts lack the rich representational imagery present in the murals.

The prolific rock drawings are but an echo of the mural art. The same stylistic framework prevails and ceremonial figures and themes are represented, but the rock depictions, because of the very nature of the medium, are by comparison highly simplified and often crude, and the beautiful compositional arrangements, so appropriate for kiva functions, are not to be found. Although the Rio Grande Style rock paintings and petroglyphs are not an exhaustive document of the artistic talents of the later Pueblos, they are, nevertheless, one of the more powerful rock art complexes in the Southwest.

Until recently research on this rock art was limited. Descriptions of upper Rio Grande rock art include those of Renaud (1938a, 1938b) and Sims (1949, 1950, 1963). Recognition of these petroglyphs as a definite stylistic complex resulted from a study of the petroglyphs in the Cochiti Reservoir district in 1966 (P. Schaafsma 1975. See P. Schaafsma 1972 for further discussion).

PETROGLYPHS AND ROCK PAINTINGS OF THE RIO GRANDE STYLE

As the Jornada Style replaced the Abstract Style in the Mogollon area, so Rio Grande Style rock art took precedence over earlier Anasazi work throughout the Pueblo world, both in the upper Rio Grande drainage and in regions to the west. The sociocultural implications of this change in the art and its associated ideology have been discussed. The appearance of the new art style in the fourteenth century is datable through its associations with early Pueblo IV villages in the form of both murals and rock art (Schaafsma and Schaafsma 1974:538), and also by its occurrence in the decoration of the late black-on-white ceramics and the early glazewares, the latter appearing in the central Rio Grande Pueblo region between 1325 and 1350. That the style, once adopted, spread rapidly throughout the Pueblo communication network is evidenced by its early occurrence in the farther reaches of the Pueblo domain—petroglyphs in association with the Puerco Ruin in the Little Colorado River drainage with a terminal date of 1350 (Gumerman and Skinner 1968:196) and on a Talpa Black-on-white sherd from Taos (Wetherington 1968:56) dating no later than 1400.

Along with Pueblo religion, the Rio Grande Style survived the trauma of the Spanish conquest and the later encroachment of the Anglo-American world, and it has persisted into the present. Elements of the style are painted on altars and other ceremonial articles currently in use and are present in

Figure 197. Rio Grande gorge in White Rock Canyon. The Pajarito Plateau with cliff outcrops of tuff and basalt is visible at top and left. Photograph, Laura Gilpin.

petroglyphs and rock paintings done within the twentieth century. Some of the latter, however, have begun to show the strong impact of Western art, with its emphasis on three-dimensional form and realism.

The upper Rio Grande Valley figures prominently in Pueblo culture and rock art. Like the Colorado Plateau to the west, it is in the Upper Sonoran life zone. Grassland steppe prevails in the lower elevations below Santa Fe, while the hills and mesas throughout are covered with piñon and juniper woodland (Fig. 197). In the northern reaches around Taos, sagebrush, chamisa, and grass are characteristic of the open plateau above the river canyon. The Rio Grande itself and its northern gorges are dominant features of the north-central New Mexico landscape. South of Cochiti the Rio Grande finally becomes a muddy desert river winding through arid hills and mesas. The Rio Grande drainage is bordered on the east by the high Sangre de Cristo range, whose peaks reach altitudes of more than 12,000 feet and create a dramatic backdrop. This southern extension of the Rocky Mountains ends abruptly at Santa Fe. Desert fault block mountains like the Sandias and the Manzanos lie to the south.

Volcanic activity played an important role in shaping the Rio Grande Valley itself. The Jemez Mountains, skirted by high tuff and basalt-covered plateaus, harbor the largest volcanic crater in the world, Valle Grande, and other small peaks and hills, also volcanic in origin, are numerous. Mesas with hard basalt caprock characterize the entire upper Rio Grande Valley. The black cliffs and talus boulders at the edges of these mesas, as well as the walls of volcanic dikes, are important in the history of the rock art of the region; it was these surfaces, dark with patina, that the Pueblos selected for making the rock-cut images of figures from their myths and ritual dramas (Fig. 198).

The rock art of the Rio Grande Style is similar in many respects to that of the Jornada, for we are dealing here with a continuing tradition (Fig. 199). Like the Jornada Style, the later rock art of the upper Rio Grande is characterized by ceremonial figures and prolific depictions of masks. There are also outline renditions of hunched animals with bent legs and some interior detail, thunderbirds, birds in flight or with raised wings, horned serpents, corn plants, and cloud terraces. In addition to sharing a similar element inventory with like figure types, and even specific symbolic complexes, both styles also possess certain peculiarities, such as depicting masks or faces without outlines or pecking masks on rock corners.

Within the overall similarities between the two styles, however, there are important differences in stylistic features and nuances. In Rio Grande Style rock art there is a general simplification of earlier themes. In the mask, for example, the almond-shaped eyes are replaced by simple dots or circles, and facial decoration is on the whole less common and less complicated. Eyebrows are very rarely depicted; the nose is not portrayed except for the occasional presence of a short line from the top of the center of the forehead down to eye level, which appears to be a highly conventionalized method of representing this feature. There are some rather detailed masks, however, and some of these are equatable with those of modern kachinas. Animals with abstract body decoration are less usual than in the Jornada Style, and mountain sheep do not appear. Also missing in Pueblo work are the Tlaloc

Figure 198. Rio Grande Style petroglyph on black basalt talus boulder, Rio Grande gorge, Tewa province. The river is visible in the background. New Mexico State Planning Office; photograph, Karl Kernberger.

figure and the large, complicated blanket designs so characteristic of the Jornada.

There are a number of interesting new emphases and additions. The number of horned serpents increases, and in addition to the single-horned type, which is in many cases essentially indistinguishable from its Jornada predecessor, there is a two-horned snake (Fig. 200 lower left; see also P. Schaafsma 1975:Fig. 73 c and d). Simple equilinear crosses or stars increase in numbers, and the star face makes its debut. Stars of all kinds are often juxtaposed with snake motifs; stars may be embellished with eagle feathers and claws, and they commonly occur on shields. The large, decorative shield design and the shield bearer are prominent themes in the Pueblo art of the period (Figs. 200, 201). As for human figures, some are naturalistic in configuration and resemble Jornada Style renditions, but others are conventionalized into various types with simple boxy outlines (P. Schaafsma 1975:Fig. 66). Headgear, sashes, and other simple apparel may indicate their ceremonial nature, although such embellishments are not frequent. One mythical personage occurring in the Pueblo work is the age-old Kokopelli

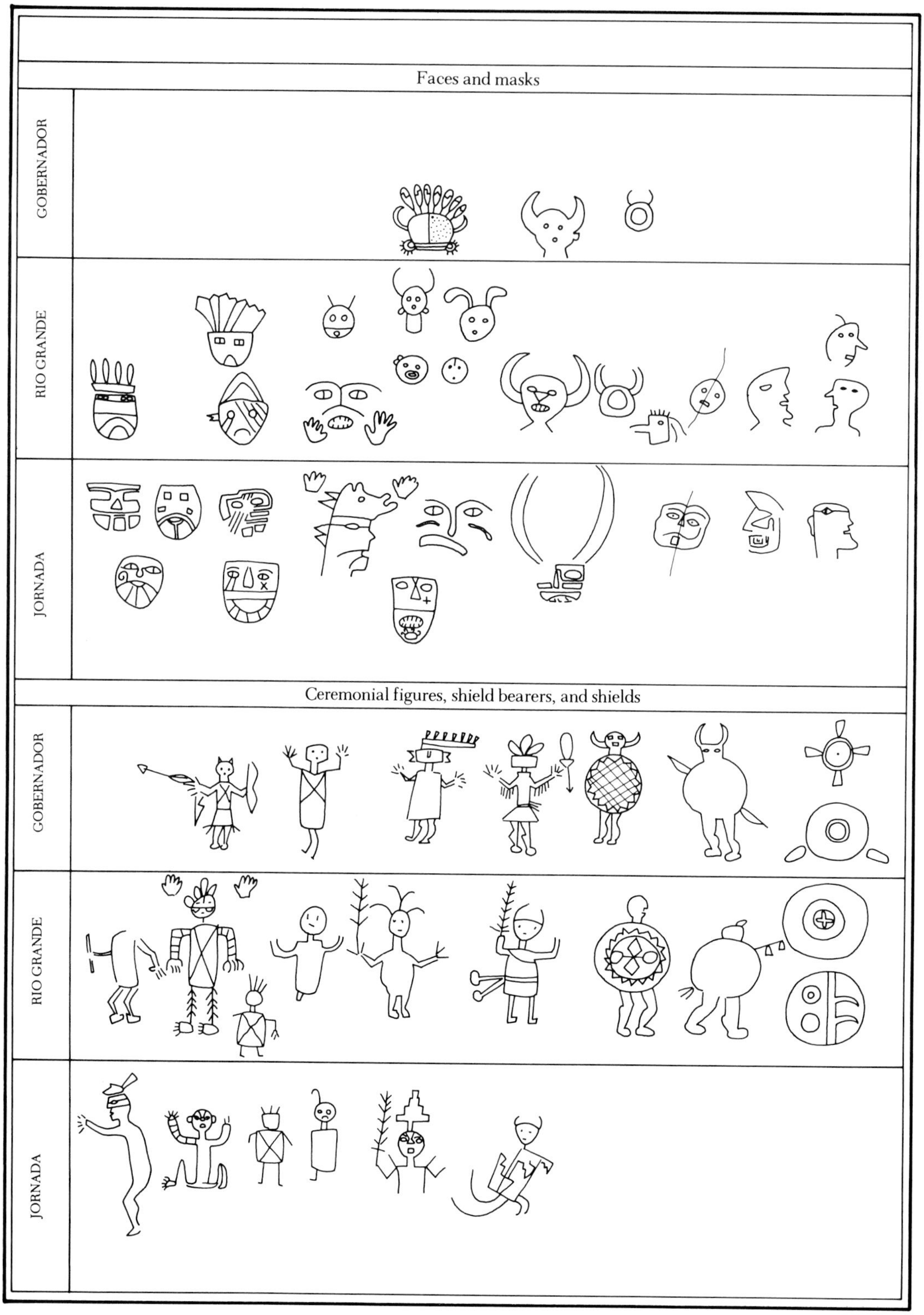

Figure 199. Selected figures illustrating stylistic continuity between the Jornada, Rio Grande, and Gobernador representational styles. Iconographic relationships are also apparent.

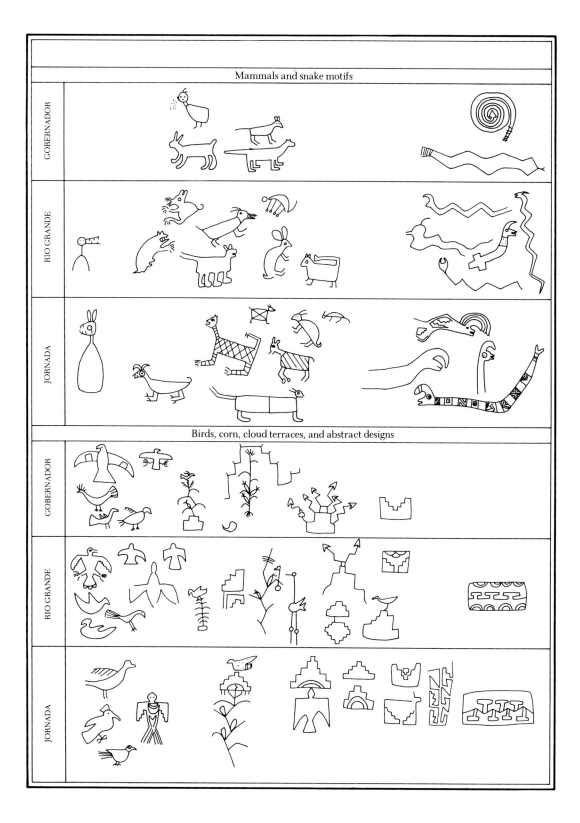

Mammals and snake motifs

GOBERNADOR

RIO GRANDE

JORNADA

Birds, corn, cloud terraces, and abstract designs

GOBERNADOR

RIO GRANDE

JORNADA

Figure 200. Birds, serpents, and shield, Rio Grande Style, Galisteo, New Mexico. New Mexico State Planning Office; photograph, Karl Kernberger.

Figure 201. Tewa petroglyphs, Rio Grande Style, north of San Juan Pueblo, New Mexico. Note the paired hourglass figures. New Mexico State Planning Office; photograph, Karl Kernberger

Figure 202. Flute player, Tenabo, New Mexico. New Mexico State Planning Office; photograph, Curtis Schaafsma.

from the Anasazi (Fig. 202), a figure whose identity is unmistakable although he is now often cast in the new style. Sometimes he lacks his flute and is shown in pursuit of maidens. Other, older Anasazi influences may be seen in the occasional retention of rectilinear and stick-figure forms in certain anthropomorphic depictions.

Petroglyphs predominate over rock paintings in the Rio Grande Style. Figures vary from deeply pecked, clearly defined elements to those composed of scattered shallow dints between which the original rock surface remains. Some of the most recent masks, as in the Cochiti Reservoir district on the Rio Grande above Cochiti Pueblo, are incised (P. Schaafsma 1975:Figs. 59, 60, 61). Paintings, limited in numbers and best known from the vicinities of the old Pueblo villages of Tenabo, Abo, and San Cristobal, all of which were abandoned in the seventeenth century, are primarily limited to the depiction of masks and ceremonial anthropomorphic figures.

A certain amount of regional variation is present within the Rio Grande Style. Regional stylistic predilections, different ideological emphases, and, to some degree, variation over time may contribute to the differences. For purposes of description, the Rio Grande region falls into five divisions (Map

9): the Abo, or Tompiro; the Galisteo Basin, or southern Tewa (often referred to as Tano); the Rio Grande Valley, which includes the Piro, southern Tiwa, Keresan, and Towa linguistic provinces; the northern Tewa; and Taos, or the northern Tiwa. The style also occurs in the western Pueblo region in the vicinities of Zuni, Hopi, and elsewhere in the Little Colorado River drainage. The style as described from these various provinces dates from the Classic Period and, in some cases where it occurs near modern pueblos, from the Historic Period; it may be as recent as the twentieth century.

The Tompiro Province

Some of the finest rock art in the Rio Grande drainage is that of the Tompiro province. These rock drawings include paintings as well as petroglyphs. The paintings are of masks and complete ceremonial figures, and they are detailed and well done. The typical mask from this region has a curved lower contour, the top is flat or nearly so, and vertical feathered headgear is common. Facial decoration tends toward the abstract, and chin and cheek markings are usual. The best examples of mask paintings are those from the vicinity of Tenabo (Fig. 203 and P. Schaafsma 1972:Fig. 111). These ethereal figures occur in groups in a small rock-shelter and are painted in thin washes of orange, red, yellow, and turquoise. The carefully delineated designs include negative or unpainted areas. One has a bird form at the mouth. The thin washes, the shape of the mask, the negative patterning, and the type of facial decoration, including the use of double dots for the eyes, are all reminiscent of painted masks from the Jornada region. The figures are life size.

Paintings from a second site near Abo are less refined but still outstanding. The personage in Figure 204 with facial streaks and half-circle mouth is typical. There are a number of ceremonial figures at this site painted in blue, green, yellow, orange, red, black, and white. Many of the small ones are extremely lifelike and some of these hold bows and spears. Larger representations have masks, kilts, and sashes (Plates 25, 26); others are painted as simple silhouettes (Fig. 205).

Like the paintings, the Abo petroglyphs are technically well executed. There are decorative eagles, flute players, corn, birds, cloud terraces, and serpents (Figs. 202, 206–8). Horned serpents pecked in fine detail with snouts, teeth, tongues, and body plumes appear. Shield bearers and star faces are also notable designs. Many of the petroglyph masks, however, are relatively crude

Figure 203. Badly weathered painted traces of masks, Tenabo. Note the delicately painted negative pattern in the chin region of the lower mask and the bird at the mouth in the upper figure. Photograph, Karl Kernberger.

Figure 204. Yellow mask with red facial markings, Abo. New Mexico State Planning Office; photograph, Curtis Schaafsma.

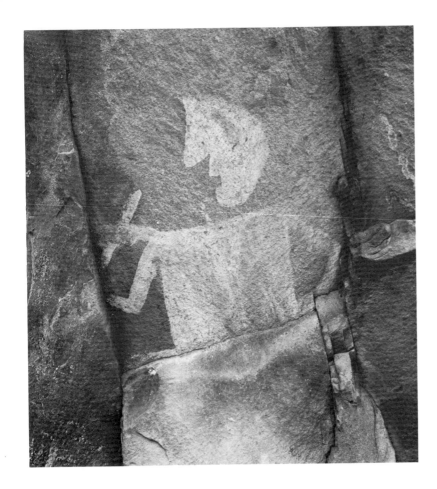

Figure 205. Stylized white silhouette of human figure, Abo. Photograph, Karl Kernberger.

Figure 206. Petroglyphs, Tenabo. New Mexico State Planning Office; photograph, Karl Kernberger.

Figure 207. Shield bearers, Tenabo.

Figure 208. Horned shield bearer with spear confronting a horned and plumed serpent, Tenabo. New Mexico State Planning Office; photograph, Curtis Schaafsma.

(P. Schaafsma 1972:Fig. 112). They resemble those from the Galisteo Basin, and some are pecked on rock angles.

The southern and eastern divisions of the Rio Grande Pueblos were abandoned or practically depopulated by the end of the seventeenth century because of various disruptive factors—raids by Navajos, Apaches, and Comanches; the Pueblo Revolt of 1680 (Mera 1940:40)—and it is likely that the rock art of the Tompiro province and much of that in the Galisteo Basin to the north dates from before this time.

The Tano Province

A number of large Tano or southern Tewa pueblos occupied the Galisteo Basin before 1680, and this geographic region, with its numerous sandstone outcrops and long volcanic dikes, is the location of several extensive Rio Grande Style petroglyph sites. Bold designs are characteristic, and variety is present in the rock art here.

Galisteo Basin masks are usually simple, but they are distinguished by their strong outlines and features (Figs. 209–11). Both here and at Abo, holes or color variation in the rock were sometimes incorporated into mask designs and undoubtedly determined exactly where the rock drawing was to be made (Fig. 212). Most Galisteo Basin masks are circular and some have open mouths and teeth that give them a fierce appearance. These may represent animals or animal priests. There are one- and two-horn personages, arrow swallowers (Sims 1963:218), and a figure with a tall pointed cap (Figs. 210, 213–15). Masks on rock angles, masks lacking outlines, and naturalistic brachycephalic heads resembling Jornada and Mimbres portrayals also occur (P. Schaafsma 1972:Fig. 123). A number of tiny but unusually lifelike human figures, not more than a few inches tall, have been documented in the rock art of this region (Fig. 216 and P. Schaafsma 1972:Fig. 131, pp. 153–54). Birds appear as do animals, including badgers, rabbits, and skunks (Fig. 217 and P. Schaafsma 1972:Figs. 126, 127). There are at least two very large depictions of bears in the Galisteo Basin art (Fig. 218); to date these have not been found elsewhere in the Rio Grande, although bear paws or tracks occur commonly in the ceremonial iconography.

Also distinctive in the Galisteo Basin are are the numerous portrayals of horned serpents. Some are the thin two-horned type. Others are thick snakes with a single horn, depicted as a full-length serpent or shortened, as the artist saw fit (Fig. 219 and P. Schaafsma 1972:Fig. 125). Cloud terraces sometimes occur at the tail, and there may be decoration on the neck. These figures have long squarish snouts and teeth and are reminiscent of the horned serpents south and east of El Paso (compare Fig. 219 with Figs. 176 and 187).

Four-pointed stars and star faces are prominent in Galisteo Basin rock art (Figs. 220–22). Stars are depicted on the body of the great bear at the San Cristobal site, and there is a definite association between stars and snakes. The composition with a plumed serpent and star face in a Pottery Mound mural (Hibben 1966:528, Fig. 12) indicates that this relationship in the rock art is intentional. Stars and star faces are also found on large shields (Fig. 223); shields and shield bearers are among the more spectacular of the Galisteo Basin designs. Some shields are actual size and are boldly decorated with vertical bands, circles, paw prints, and other figures in addition to the stars (Fig. 200). The human figure, when it occurs behind the shield, is usually portrayed in a naturalistic manner and resembles both Jornada representations and figures from the kiva murals.

Figure 209. Bear, animal masks, stars, and horned serpents in petroglyph panel at San Cristobal, Galisteo Basin, New Mexico. New Mexico State Planning Office; photograph, Karl Kernberger.

Figure 210. Masks, San Cristobal, Galisteo Basin. New Mexico State Planning Office; photograph, Karl Kernberger.

Figure 211. Animal mask and star, San Cristobal, Galisteo Basin. New Mexico State Planning Office; photograph, Karl Kernberger.

Figure 212. Masks pecked around holes in the rock which serve as mouths, Pueblo Blanco, Galisteo Basin. New Mexico State Planning Office; photograph, Karl Kernberger.

Figure 213.   Petroglyph of one-horned personage, San Cristobal, Galisteo Basin.

Figure 214.   Arrow swallower, Galisteo, New Mexico. New Mexico State Planning Office; photograph, Karl Kernberger.

Figure 215.   Masks and figure with pointed cap, San Cristobal, Galisteo Basin. New Mexico State Planning Office; photograph, Karl Kernberger.

Figure 216. Petroglyph of running human figure only a few inches tall, San Cristobal, Galisteo Basin. Photograph, David Noble.

Figure 217. Rio Grande Style petroglyphs with badger, Galisteo. New Mexico State Planning Office; photograph, Karl Kernberger.

Figure 218. Large bear petroglyph, Pueblo Blanco, Galisteo Basin. New Mexico State Planning Office; photograph, Karl Kernberger.

Figure 219. Horned serpent and shields, Pueblo Blanco, Galisteo Basin. New Mexico State Planning Office; photograph, Karl Kernberger.

271

Figure 220.   Faces and star with eagle feathers and talons. Rio Grande Style petroglyph, Galisteo, New Mexico.

Figure 221.   Star motifs in rock painting at San Cristobal, Galisteo Basin. Compare (a) with Figure 220.

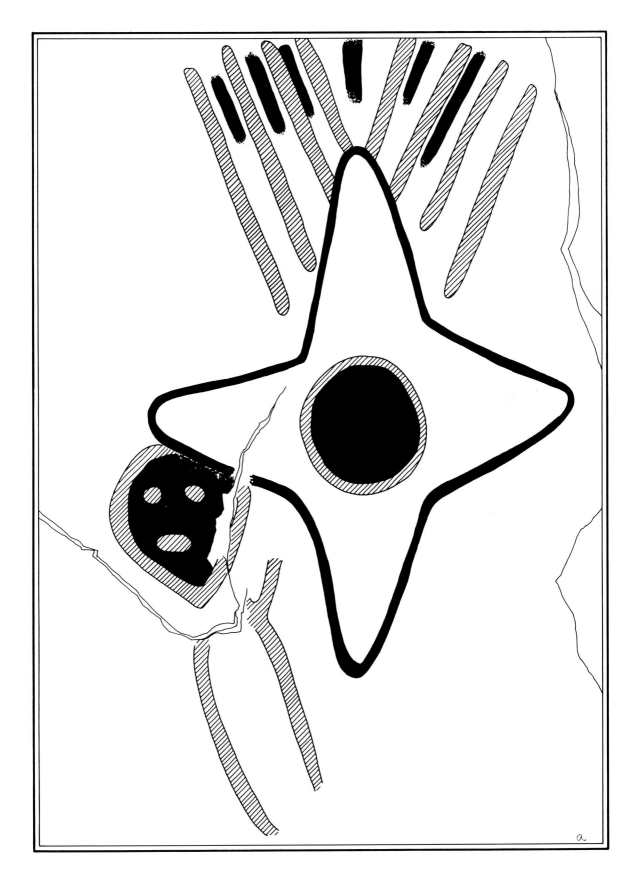

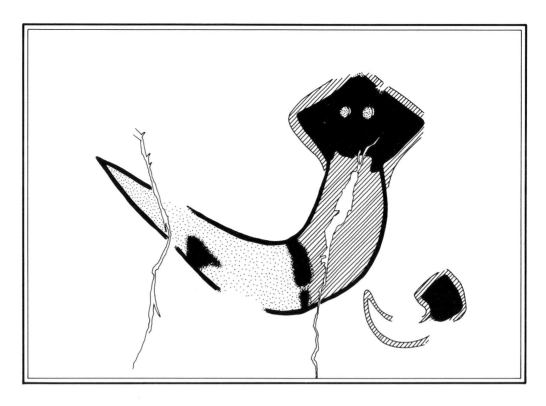

Figure 222.   These figures seem to illustrate a combined snake-star personage.

Figure 223.   Large shield bearer, Comanche Gap, Galisteo Basin. Both star and sun symbolism are present on the shield. New Mexico State Planning Office; photograph, Karl Kernberger.

The Rio Grande Valley

For the general purpose of describing Rio Grande Style rock art the Rio Grande Valley, from the Piro province in the south to the Tewa in the north, can be considered a single entity. The Piro section was abandoned by the end of the seventeenth century, but the occupancy of the southern Tiwa and Keresan sections has continued to the present, although the southern Tiwa population is now concentrated in the villages of Isleta and Sandia. Around the modern pueblos, rock art production has continued into the twentieth century. In the Rio Grande Valley, masks continue to be a major element of the Rio Grande Style (Figs. 16, 224–28). They are usually fairly simple and often small: round, rectangular, or triangular faces with eyes and mouth indicated by single dots. Elaborations may consist of simple headgear and a vertical mark on the forehead. Masks pecked on rock angles also occur in these sites. Square masks are particularly common north of Albuquerque, and many of those in White Rock Canyon north of Cochiti Pueblo (P. Schaafsma 1975) appear to have been made recently. Other modern mask depictions are detailed and resemble contemporary kachinas (Fig. 229).

Representations of the human figure are numerous. These are usually highly conventionalized, with no attempt at naturalism, and several variations of boxlike types characterize this part of the Rio Grande Valley (Figs. 230–34). Figures vary from those built around a rectangular torso to which head, arms, and legs are appended, to more integrated types defined wholly or in part by a continuous, sometimes calligraphic line. Some of the latter are distinguished by a horizontal rather than a vertical axis. Many have some suggestion of ceremonial attire. There are also a few elaborate portrayals rivaling kiva mural figures in complexity (Fig. 235). Heads of masks over blanket designs (Fig. 236) are an unusual variation on the human theme in the Keres section. Shields and shield bearers are fewer in the Rio Grande division (Fig. 237).

There is a proliferation of other elements, including hand prints, hunched animals, boxy animals, eagles and other birds, cloud terraces, and geometric designs. Presumably insects are illustrated in Figure 238. Birds of many types, often solidly pecked, are emphasized at some sites, especially in the vicinity of La Cienega (Fig. 239). Rabbits and skunks are among the quadrupeds, and the large figure of a mountain lion is characteristic of the Keresan section and the Pajarito Plateau (Figs. 240, 241). Simple snakes and two-horned serpents are commonly depicted, the latter sometimes having faces. The large and

Figure 224. Masks, cloud terrace, and deer tracks, Los Lunas, New Mexico. Photograph, Museum of New Mexico.

Figure 225. Masks, Los Lunas. Photograph, Museum of New Mexico.

276

Figure 226. Petroglyphs from Cochiti Reservoir. Photograph, Museum of New Mexico.

Figure 227. Masks on rock corners, Cochiti Reservoir. Photograph, Museum of New Mexico.

277

Figure 228.   Masks, Cochiti Reservoir. Photograph, Museum of New Mexico.

Figure 229. Modern kachina masks, Cochiti Reservoir. The top figure is the Cochiti Racing kachina. Photograph, Museum of New Mexico.

Figure 230. Bird with serpent in its mouth, masked human figure, and other elements. Cochiti Reservoir. Photograph, Museum of New Mexico.

279

Figure 231. Anthropomorph and two-horned snake, Cochiti Reservoir. Photograph, Museum of New Mexico.

Figure 232. Small anthropomorph, Cochiti Reservoir. The figure was painted with aluminum powder before photographing. Photograph, Museum of New Mexico.

Figure 233. Masks, circles, and human figure, Cochiti Reservoir. Petroglyphs were painted with aluminum powder before photographing. Photograph, Museum of New Mexico.

Figure 234. Rio Grande Style petroglyphs near Cochiti Pueblo. Photograph, Karl Kernberger.

281

Figure 235. Ceremonial figure with gourd symbolism, Pajarito Canyon, Pajarito Plateau. Photograph, Dwight S. Young, Scott Files, Peabody Museum, Harvard University.

Figure 236. Heads or masks above blanket design, Cochiti Reservoir. Photograph, Museum of New Mexico.

Figure 237. Warrior with sun shield combating horned serpent, Los Lunas. Photograph, Museum of New Mexico.

Figure 238. Depictions of insects, Cochiti Reservoir. Photograph, Museum of New Mexico.

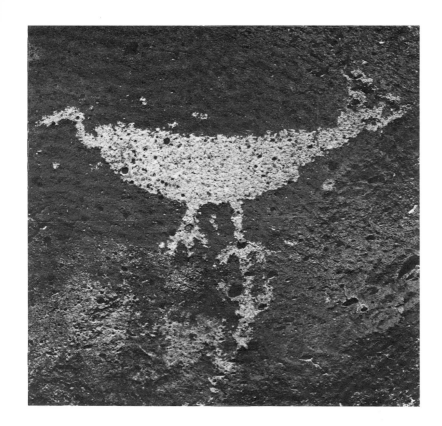

Figure 239. Turkey petroglyph, La Cieneguilla. New Mexico State Planning Office; photograph, Karl Kernberger.

Figure 240. Mountain lion, Cochiti Reservoir. Petroglyphs were painted with aluminum powder before photographing. Photograph, Museum of New Mexico.

284

Figure 241. Stars, horned serpents, fawn, mountain lion with cap, anthropomorph, and other figures on boulder at old shrine, Cochiti Reservoir. Stone retaining wall for terrace in front of boulder is visible in lower photo. Photograph, Museum of New Mexico.

well-executed designs found in White Rock Canyon probably predate many of the smaller designs found close to the modern pueblos.

The Pajarito Plateau includes both northern Keresan and Tewa sites, and a special category of graphic art occurs here in addition to the cliff face and boulder petroglyphs. These are the detailed drawings incised into the wall plaster or pecked into the rock itself inside the cavate rooms within the cliffs. Chapman (1938) made more than two hundred copies of these drawings from Frijoles Canyon. The drawings include complex textile patterns, numerous kachinas very closely resembling modern dance impersonators, and other lifelike anthropomorphs resembling those in the mural art. Hunters with bows, arrows, and spears, wearing single horns or pointed caps, are shown in these drawings. Birds were a favorite motif and range from a few rather realistic renditions to dynamic stylized designs like those found in ceramic decoration. A few animals and a number of terraces are pictured. In addition to these finely incised figures are crudely pecked horned serpents that encircle the back wall of a room and reach up to 25 feet in length. The sites themselves were occupied during the Classic Period, but the drawings, which are scratched through the smoke-blackened plaster, may have been made after the caves were abandoned.

The Northern Tewa and Tiwa Provinces

There is a dramatic reduction in the number of masks and human figures in the Tewa province between the upper part of White Rock Canyon and the

Figure 242.   Flute players, Tsankawi, Pajarito Plateau.

Rio Grande gorge north of Velarde. Here, among representations of cloud terraces, lightning arrows, birds, flute players (Fig. 242), and snakes, the shield again becomes an outstanding element (Fig. 201). There are also some very fine examples of the great horned serpent (Figs. 243, 244); the horn usually reaches backward and a tongue may be depicted in the form of a lightning arrow.

Still farther north, in the Taos district, the style becomes strictly peripheral in character. The Rio Grande Style elements are limited in number, and when they do occur it is only in simplest form. The shield bearer and horned snake are among the designs depicted here in the Rio Grande Style, where earlier Anasazi work takes precedence. The near absence of the kachina mask in the rock art is probably accounted for by the fact that the kachina cult was never adopted by these northern Tiwa.

The Western Pueblo Region

As mentioned earlier in this discussion, the Rio Grande Style is not limited to the eastern Pueblo area but is also present at an early date in the

B

Figure 243.   Serpent and star motifs, White Rock Canyon. Photograph, Dwight S. Young, Scott Files, Peabody Museum, Harvard University.

Figure 244.   Horned serpents and star symbolism, Pajarito Canyon, Pajarito Plateau.   Photograph, Dwight S. Young, Scott Files, Peabody Museum, Harvard University.

western region. Less information is available for these petroglyphs than for their Rio Grande counterparts. Pueblo IV anthropomorphs and kachina masks from Zuni (P. Schaafsma 1972:177), Hopi (Figs. 245, 246), and the Little Colorado River drainage (Pilles 1974) do not differ appreciably from those in the Rio Grande drainage. The outlined circle eyes, open mouths, and teeth of the Little Colorado River masks are most like those from the Galisteo Basin. Like the latter those from the Little Colorado occur in association with sites occupied between A.D. 1300 and A.D. 1600. Masks, animals, and birds with long, toothed beaks are predominant motifs at the Puerco Ruin on the Little Colorado. Pilles (1974:16) lists circular designs, figure eights, crescents, and squiggle mazes as other elements in Little Colorado Pueblo work after A.D. 1300. Turner (1963:6 and Figs. 8, 9) associates Glen Canyon Style 2 with Hopi revisitation of the Glen Canyon between the fourteenth century and the present and includes illustrations of kachinas, human figures, and mountain sheep, all in exemplary Rio Grande Style form.

Probably the best-known petroglyph site in the western Pueblo region is Willow Springs (Titiev 1937; Colton 1946b; Talayesva 1942), where large boulders on the Hopi Salt Trail to the deep canyon of the Little Colorado are covered with clan symbols. The site is distinctive in that symbols such as kachina masks, sun figures, bows, clouds, birds, corn plants, and animal tracks (Figs. 247–50) have been placed in linear sequences developed over a period of many years as participants in the trip have added their marks. It is said that the new symbol is made to the left of the old, and that a novice is permitted to begin a fresh row for his own work (Colton 1946b:3). Of general interest is the observation that different forms of the same symbol occur and also that different symbols stand for the same clan. The Cloud Clan, for example, may be represented by the figure of a cloud, a rainbow, lightning, a duck, a tadpole, a frog, or any aquatic animal (Colton 1946b:4). This illustrates well the flexibility allowed in denoting a given concept. Although many of these petroglyphs are recent in origin, the forms used are traditional, and they do not reflect any influence from Western art.

THE IMPACT OF WESTERN ART

Contemporary masks in White Rock Canyon, probably made by the Cochiti, were mentioned earlier. Some show a continuity with the Rio Grande Style and others reflect, in the attempt to indicate three dimensions,

Figure 245. Corn and female figure with sky symbolism, First Mesa, Arizona. Photograph, Milwaukee Public Museum.

Figure 246. Tcakwaina kachina, Second Mesa. Photograph, Scott Files, Peabody Museum, Harvard University.

290

Figure 247.   Hopi clan symbols, Willow Springs, Arizona. Photograph, Karl Kernberger.

Figure 248.   Hopi clan symbols, Willow Springs, Arizona. Photograph, Karl Kernberger.

Figure 249. Detail of sun faces, Willow Springs, Arizona. Photograph, Karl Kernberger.

Figure 250. Modern petroglyph, Willow Springs, Arizona. Photograph, Karl Kernberger.

the impact of Western art on traditional subjects (Fig. 229). Rock drawings were made within the environs of most modern pueblos until very recently, and such drawings, as at Cochiti, display the influence of both native and Western styles. Figures 245 and 246 illustrate what are probably rather recent depictions of supernaturals at Hopi. The corn and the personage with the sky symbolism in Figure 245 are traditional in presentation. Figure 246 combines aspects of both and closely resembles the Hopi drawing of Tcakwaina, a warrior being, illustrated in Fewkes (1903a:Plate IV). Even more strongly affected by Western tradition is a series of painted masks near Zuni. In these the use of three-quarter views, frontal perspective and foreshortening, and shading contributes to the illusion of three-dimensional form. Finally, there are some modern rock drawings that have little if anything to do with traditional subject matter (Fig. 289).

INTERPRETATION AND FUNCTION

Indications are that rock art sites served a variety of functions among the Pueblos. Clan symbols are sometimes pecked by Pueblo travelers to signify where they have been. Turner (1963:28), following the ethnographic documentations by Voth (1905:23) and Forde (1931:368), notes that clan symbols were used to denote the location of communal lands. Petroglyphs also occur in the immediate vicinity of Pueblo IV ruins and modern Pueblo villages. At Tsankawi, a large Pueblo IV mesa ruin on the Pajarito Plateau, petroglyphs are concentrated at what seem to have been focal points of human activity: where the main trail emerges at the top of the mesa and at what were possibly shrine or retreat areas below the cliff, spots to which prehistoric trails leading from the main village can be traced. Other carvings are relatively scattered, either along the footpaths or near the habitation areas themselves. Some of the petroglyphs in the latter kind of location may have served as territorial demarcations.

Recent Pueblo rock art is commonly found in association with shrines. Several types of shrine with associated rock drawings have been reported in the ethnographic literature by Fewkes (1891, 1906), Stevenson (1894), Parsons (1939), and Colton (1946b). Fewkes (1906:326) mentions rock art near certain Hopi shrines and says that there are holes or depressions in the heart area of certain animals, in which offerings were placed. He also describes Zuni shrines with rock art, specifically mentioning a fertility shrine where hundreds of representations are present (Fewkes 1891:9). The site described earlier at Willow Springs in north-central Arizona where Hopi clan symbols cover the trailside boulders is a major shrine that is still in use (Colton 1946b; Talayesva 1942; Titiev 1937). Stevenson (1894:110 and Plate 27) describes a circle of dry-laid masonry with a petroglyph mask as a shrine of the Knife Society at Zia. Switzer (n.d.:21–22) raises the possibility that petroglyphs of snakes may in some cases function as shrine guardians. "Stone coils" representing snakes serve this purpose at Hopi (Parsons 1939:619).

The ideology reflected in the rock art and the situation of many of the sites are compatible with the idea that many ethnographically undocumented sites, both historic and prehistoric, functioned as shrines. Rio Grande Style petroglyphs are found at springs (all of which are regarded as shrines in the Pueblo universe) and along trails to the springs. The Rio Grande Pueblos often used high points of land or small hills for ritual practices (Hewett 1938:123; Nelson 1914:70–71), and Pueblo petroglyph sites in this type of location probably serve today to denote the former presence of a shrine or sacred area. Petroglyph sites on high points of land such as the Galisteo Basin dikes are large in areal extent, and the symbolism is varied. They not only received heavy use but may have been visited for different purposes by different groups. Other rock art sites, also possibly shrines, are smaller, with more limited subject matter. These possibly were frequented for a single purpose or by only one religious organization. The site illustrated in Figure 241 on the Rio Grande below the mouth of Frijoles Canyon consists of a single, large carved boulder with war or hunting symbolism or both, fronted by a low earth platform supported by dry-laid masonry. The fact that superimposing was not as a rule practiced at any of these sites and the care with which the figures were made indicate that the images were of subsequent importance.

A study of the rich and complex iconography present in the rock art of the Rio Grande Style could fill another volume. As Kidder states in regard to the ritual designs on the clay pipes of Pecos (1932:181): "it is obvious that they reflect a mature and well-ordered symbolism, doubtless esoteric and apparently concerned with sky-beings (bird, cloud, lightning, horned serpent, etc.) potent for the bringing of rain." Beyond this point he refuses to venture. All of these things and many more are present in the rock art. In addition, we are dealing with a much more varied context, which is significant, knowing that the specific situation in which a figure is used alters its interpretation. Further, ethnographic studies have revealed that different symbols may stand for the same thing and that symbolism differs to some extent between villages and between regions. With so many variables, any interpretation of the rock art must be approached with extreme caution. A few general observations can be made about what we see here; some have already been offered in the preceding chapter to illuminate the symbolism of the Jornada Style.

The kachina cult is one of the major Pueblo institutions, represented in the art by the many masks and kachina figures. Both the supernaturals themselves and the dancers impersonating them are referred to as kachinas. Benevolent anthropomorphic supernaturals vaguely considered by the Pueblos to be ancestral, the kachinas are associated with rain and clouds and personify the power in objects such as the sun, earth, and corn. The fact that this cult, as a social institution, serves as an integrative device within the village was discussed at the beginning of this chapter. The cult is strongest and most highly developed in the western Pueblos today, but the numerous kachina representations in the Rio Grande rock art in the eastern Pueblo realm indicate its former major importance there.

Although possible at times, especially for the more recent depictions, identification of specific kachina figures in the rock art poses a number of problems. Even as documented ethnographically, kachina iconography is subject to a great deal of change and flexibility. To quote Parsons (1939:1122): "Innovations are constantly occurring in the kachina cult, which is very hospitable to novelties; new impersonations, new dances, new songs, new details of costume or array." Borrowing and invention contribute to the phenomenon of change (Anderson 1955:416). Also, in the rock art many masks are too generalized for identification. Chin and cheek markings and horns are among the commonly depicted but undiagnostic attributes that have survived throughout kachina history.

I will not attempt to list all the identifiable kachinas in the rock art, but I will mention a few. The crooked mouth (Figs. 215, 225) is a diagnostic feature of Hehea, a widely distributed kachina. Fewkes (1903a:74) expressed the opinion that "Hehea is evidently an ancient katchina, and from his appearance in many primitive ceremonies, public and secret, we may regard him as connected with very old ritual." Sims (1963:Plate A) has identified Chakwena (Tcakwaina) kachinas by the Santa Fe River below La Cienega. This group of kachinas, referred to by the same name by the Hopi, Zuni, Keres, and Tanoans, is said to have been introduced to Hopi by the Asa clan, a clan of Tanoan stock that migrated from the Rio Grande to Hopi via Zuni (Fewkes 1903a:26, 62). This kachina (Fig. 246) is said to be still impersonated on the Rio Grande as well as in the west. Star faces may represent the Star Kachina, which has warrior associations (hence its presence on shields), or the Heart of the Sky God, a figure known at Hopi as Sotuqnang-u, who also has the personality and attibutes of Quetzalcoatl. The latter explains the juxtaposition of star faces and horned serpents. The long-beaked birdlike Shalako is found in petroglyphs from the Rio Grande to the Little Colorado, suggesting that the Shalako fraternity once prevailed throughout the entire Pueblo area, although today it is best known in the west. Sims (1949:Plate I) identifies Hakto and Culawitsi (Shulawitsi), other members of the Shalako group, in the Galisteo Basin. Many other readily identifiable representations such as the racing kachina (Fig. 229 top) are relatively recent in origin.

Clowns are also represented in the rock art. Their association with serpents in the Galisteo Basin and in paintings near Abo (not illustrated) seems to be connected with March ceremonies, for example, the Ankwanti at Hopi, in which struggles between clowns and serpents take place (Sims 1949:74; Fewkes 1903a:46). Clowns are affiliated with the medicine societies, whose complex symbolism is also present in the rock art. In contrast to the kachina cult, to which belong rituals usually considered to be "beautiful" or "novel," at least at Zuni (Tedlock 1973), the medicine societies possess ritual considered "valuable" and "dangerous." These societies have considerable knowledge of psychic disciplines, magic, and psychopharmacology, which allow one to "pass through to the other side" and enter the world of the sacred, the dangerous, and the miraculous (Tedlock 1973:16). The organization of these societies at Zuni is extraordinarily complex:

> Most of the medicine societies are composed of people who once came close to death, temporarily escaped it through a society cure, and finally received a new heart and a new name in a society initiation (Bunzel 1932a:541). Eight of these societies may be grouped in pairs, the oldest pair consisting of the *Sinwana.kʷ* . . . Priestly People and their "younger brothers" the *newe.kʷe* . . . clowns. Like most of the other societies, these two are divided into orders, each with its particular capabilities for performing remarkable acts. Both societies have orders of . . . Magicians and . . . Priests of the Completed Path, of whom the latter are also called . . . Beast Priests. In addition the Priestly People have an order of . . . Fire People and the Clowns have one of . . . Big Kachina People, the latter having masks separate from those of the Kachina Society proper. (Stevenson in Tedlock 1973:28–29)

> The Clowns, sometimes augmented by Priestly People, present
> public parodies of traditional and contemporary life, but they have
> private ceremonies of a more sober nature.
>
> Another pair of societies consists of the . . . Sword Swallowers
> . . . and the . . . Big Fire People. (Tedlock 1973:2–3)

There remain also important medicine societies associated with warfare: the Cactus People, the Society of the Bow Priests, and the Shell People (Tedlock 1973:4).

It has been suggested that Arrow Swallowers (a suborder of the Big Fire People at Zuni) are depicted in certain petroglyphs in the Galisteo Basin (Sims 1963:218). Bow priests may be represented in paintings at Abo (P. Schaafsma 1972:114). The subject of bear shamans and the importance of the paw print in Pueblo ritual were discussed in the preceding chapter. Possibly it is the Beast Priests who appear in Rio Grande rock art with open mouths and teeth, or with paw prints on their faces, although paw prints may also appear on the faces of the War Gods (Smith 1952:302), the bear being associated with war as well as curing. The bear is the patron of Keresan, Zuni, and Tewa curing societies (Parsons 1939), and White (1932:Plate 12a) illustrates a large painting of a bear, not dissimilar to the southern Tewa petroglyph bears, which was painted on the wall of an Acoma chamber when a boy was made a medicine man. The mountain lion, badger (owner and master of medicinal roots), and wolf are also patrons of medicine societies at Zuni (Tedlock 1973:8), and like the bear, these same animals are associated with the War Gods (Parsons 1939:184).

War symbolism is prevalent in the rock art, particularly in the Tano region in the Galisteo Basin and in the northern Tewa province. The most obvious figures in this connection are the shield and the shield bearer. Associated with these are sky symbols that also pertain to war, such as the stars and the sun; eagle feathers, also symbolic of the sky realm, are sometimes present on shields. Depictions of warriors with shields, horns, or pointed caps, carrying clubs or other weapons, may be figures with a ritual meaning. The guardian role of the warrior in the Underworld or in connection with Wüwüchim ceremony at Hopi was discussed previously. The petroglyph scenes near Los Lunas and at Tenabo in which the shielded warriors are engaged in combat with the horned serpent (Figs. 209, 237) appear to portray a ceremony like that held in the Hopi Soyaluna kiva at winter solstice (P. Schaafsma 1968:23 and Fig. 9). Fewkes (1897a:268–72) describes a ceremony in which an effigy of the great Plumed Serpent,

Palülükonuh, puts on a threatening performance and is propitiated by the old chiefs. Following this a group of men representing malevolent powers attracts a sun shield bearer in a frenzied dance. The whole drama represents the attack of hostile powers on the sun, an event that occurs when the sun is threatened at its southern declination.

The sun not only provides power in war but is also a hunt deity. Power in the hunt also comes from mountain lions, wolves, ferrets, eagles, and hawks (Parsons 1939:187). Large figures of mountain lions occur among the petroglyphs of the Keresan province and on the Pajarito Plateau, where they may have either a war or a hunting connotation (Figs. 240, 241). In the uplands of the Parjarito Plateau, Keresan hunting shrines are marked by the sculptured stone forms of this animal.

This entire interrelated war-hunt complex in Pueblo cosmology is close in its specific symbolism to that of Huitzilopochtli, Left-Handed Humming-bird, the tribal god of the Aztecs. Huitzilopochtli was the god of the sun, war, and hunting and, in his association with the eagle, was emblematic of the sun (Peterson 1961:128). The spread of this deity in Mexico did not occur until the Aztecs themselves ascended to power in 1428 (Nicholson 1966), and it is possible that the shield bearers, stars, and other elements of the iconography relating specifically to a warrior cult are not widely manifest in the Rio Grande Style until after this date. If this is true, an ongoing interaction between Mexico and the later Pueblos is implied. Warrior symbolism, although it may be present in the earlier Jornada work, is much less prevalent.

The horned serpent, whose many attributes and place in the solstice ceremony were described earlier, is connected in one of his aspects to a cult associated with Venus and sky and sun worship—thus his depiction with stars and even cloud symbols in both the Rio Grande and Jornada styles. Within other ritual contexts, he is associated with curing and with war (Switzer n.d.:1). The Hopi Warrior–Star kachina Sotuqnang-u may be an embodiment of all these concepts.

In addition, the snake has underworld associations, and myths relate that the vast reservoir of water under the earth is controlled by the horned serpent. In connection with his Underworld aspect, the skins of skunks, weasels, and raccoons, all of which share a common ancestor with the snake and "have the same smell" (Switzer n.d.:2), are hung on the bow standard at Walpi to signify to the Snake People of the Underworld that rain is needed. Perhaps the many skunk and skunk-weasel–like figures in the petroglyphs (P.

Schaafsma 1972:Fig. 127) are connected with Snake Society activities. The skunk is also a ritual symbol for the Two-Horn Society at Hopi.

The foregoing barely begins to explore the interpretive possibilities present in the rock art of the Pueblos after A.D. 1300. What has been outlined here serves merely to point out the lines along which some of the symbols and symbol complexes may be organized, but at the same time, it illustrates the involutedness of the iconography, and hence the difficulties involved in interpretation. Overall, however, this venture into the symbolism of the rock art suggests that the panels or figure groups therein present a more unified ritual complex than first appears.

9

Navajo and
Apache Rock Art

The Athabaskan latecomers to the Southwest, the Navajos and Apaches, borrowed their ideology and art from the Pueblos and then proceeded to create within a period of a few years their own unique expression, now regarded as an integral part of the southwestern artistic heritage.

Their presence here cannot be dated with any degree of certainty earlier than A.D. 1500. Athabaskan-speakers are otherwise concentrated in northwestern North America: in Alaska, in the Canadian Northwest, and on the Pacific Coast. An Apachean movement from the north is believed to have reached the Southern Plains about 1525 (Gunnerson 1956), and migrants from this group, who very soon moved westward into the Pueblo area of central New Mexico, are believed to be ancestral to the Navajo and Apache.

According to Gunnerson (1956), various lines of evidence suggest that all Apacheans were primarily buffalo hunters in the early 1500s and that at this point they possessed a "homogeneous, Plains-oriented material culture that lacked pottery" (Gunnerson and Gunnerson 1971:7). Castañeda's account (Winship 1904:111; Hammond and Rey 1940:261) indicates that by 1540 the Apacheans had established extensive contacts with the Pueblos. They are reported to have sold buffalo skins to the pueblo of Cicuye (Pecos) and to other eastern Pueblo villages and to have spent the winters there. Other historical references from later in the sixteenth century mention further Pueblo-Apachean relationships, both hostilities and alliances (Hester 1962:21).

In these reports and others prior to 1626, the Apacheans are referred to either as Apaches or Querechos (Hester 1962:24), with no distinction between the Apache and the Navajo. In the seventeenth century several Apache groups in the Sangre de Cristo region were maintaining a semisedentary existence and raising gardens, but exactly when the Navajo emerged as an ethnic group distinct from other Apacheans and what the distinctions were at first are hazy points in southern Athabaskan culture history. At the first mention of the Navajo in a 1626 document of Fray Zárate Salmerón, as "Apaches de Nabaxu," they were living on the upper Chama River northwest of Santa Clara, where they were farming. The name "Nabaxu" is from a Tanoan word referring to "a place on the Rio Grande where a group was farming," the Spanish translation being *sementares grandes,* or "wide planted fields" (Hester 1962:21).

THE NAVAJO

Today the Navajos are the largest Indian tribe in the United States. They occupy an extensive reservation of nearly 24,000 square miles in the old Anasazi country on the Colorado Plateau, which includes much of northeastern Arizona and adjacent parts of New Mexico and Utah (Map 10). The earliest known Navajo remains, however, are to the east on the upper Chama River above Abiquiu (C. Schaafsma 1975, 1978), and these sites corroborate the historical references that mention Navajos on the upper Chama in the early 1600s (Bartlett 1932; Hodge, Hammond, and Rey 1945).

The history of Navajo and Pueblo contact, long and varied, is divisible into two periods. Initial contact dates from 1540 or earlier to 1680 and involves intermittent relationships (Hester 1971:51). During this period, agriculture was acquired by the Navajo and added to their hunting-and-gathering economy. The second period follows the Pueblo Revolt of 1680. By this time, the Navajo population was concentrated to the north and west in the upper San Juan drainage and the Gobernador District. To these mesa hinterlands some of the Pueblo Indians fled to live with the Navajos to escape Spanish oppression after the Reconquest of 1696:

> This group of people who first occupied the area along the San Juan River in the present Navajo Reservoir District and who later shifted southward into the Gobernador District were, judging from ar-

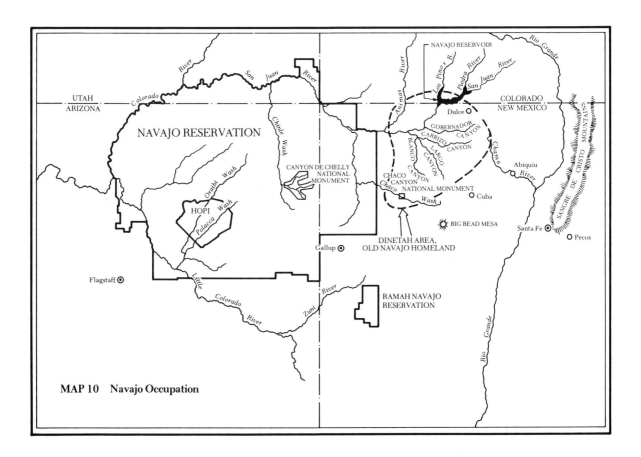

MAP 10   Navajo Occupation

chaeology and history, a mixed Indian group which formed as a
result of the unsuccessful Pueblo Revolt of 1696. In 1696 Jemez
Indians, Tewas from Santa Clara and San Ildefonso, and Keres from
Cochiti moved northward from their homes on the Rio Grande and
joined the Navajo (Forbes 1960:270–73) in order to escape Spanish
domination. It is from these four groups—Jemez, Cochiti, Tewa and
Navajo—that the 18th century inhabitants of the Gobernador seem
likely to have been descended. (Carlson 1965:100)

This period in Navajo history in northwestern New Mexico, from about 1696
to 1775, is known as the Gobernador Phase (Hester 1962:63–65). During the
early years of this phase the Navajo underwent intense Pueblo acculturation.
Intermarriage probably occurred between Navajos and Pueblos, and many of
the Pueblo people ultimately remained with the Navajos. The Navajo
practice of matrilineal descent, matrilocal residence patterns, and clan
structure are believed to derive from the Pueblos and are attributed to this

Figure 251. Eagle's Nest, Gobernador Phase Masonry Pueblito, Gobernador Canyon drainage, New Mexico. Photograph, Karl Kernberger.

period (Hester 1971:53). Archaeologically the period is recognized by forked-stick hogans along with the appearance of *pueblitos* (small masonry pueblo structures) and towers strategically situated in defensive locations on high points of land, apparently built for protection against the Utes and Comanches (Fig. 251). The settlement pattern is one of hogan clusters dispersed over a wide area and sometimes associated with the masonry *pueblitos*. In the Gobernador District there are the remains of large masonry citadels, with up to forty rooms, that probably provided protection for all the inhabitants in the locality in times of danger (Carlson 1965:100–101). Characteristic of the phase are a number of different pottery types, among which Dinetah Scored and Gobernador Polychrome are the most common, the latter being a Pueblo-derived type. In addition there are remains of eighteenth-century European trade goods. The Rabal document (Hill 1940) contains a good ethnographic account of the Gobernador Phase Navajo and describes them as using wooden implements for agriculture and growing

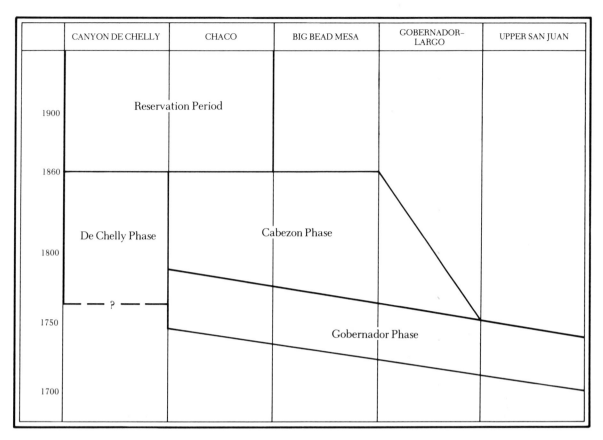

	CANYON DE CHELLY	CHACO	BIG BEAD MESA	GOBERNADOR–LARGO	UPPER SAN JUAN
1900	Reservation Period				
1860					
1800	De Chelly Phase	Cabezon Phase			
1750	?				
1700		Gobernador Phase			

Figure 252.   Chart showing approximate dates of various Navajo phases prior to the Reservation Period. (Modified after Hester 1962:Fig. 22).

maize, beans, pumpkins, and watermelons. Horses, goats, and sheep are reported, but "only the tracks of cattle" (Carlson 1965:101).

At this time many aspects of Pueblo religion, such as myths, certain ritual practices, paraphernalia, and art forms, were adopted by the Navajo. It is from this period that the first Navajo rock art is recognized. It is ceremonial in content and resembles both the Pueblo religious art of the period and modern Navajo drypainting art; in many respects, the rock drawings of the eighteenth-century Navajo may be regarded as intermediate between them.

The Gobernador Representational Style

The Gobernador Representational Style, previously referred to as simply Gobernador Phase Navajo rock art (P. Schaafsma 1963, 1966a, 1972:31–50), is known from the upper San Juan in the present Navajo Reservoir district and from the Gobernador and Largo drainages to the south (Map 10). This entire region constitutes the old Navajo homeland or the Dinetah country of Navajo legends. A small number of rock drawings from this phase of Navajo history are also present in Chaco Canyon. Approximate dates for the Gobernador Phase in each of these localities is shown in Figure 252. The phase occurred earliest in the upper San Juan, or in the northernmost district, and slightly later farther south in the Gobernador-Largo and Chaco localities, respectively. The absence of the Gobernador Representational Style, with the exception of the planetaria or star ceilings in Canyon de Chelly, is evidence that either (1) the Navajo of Canyon de Chelly were not in close communication with those to the east (considering the degree of mobility possible by this time because of the horse, this seems unlikely), or (2) the Navajo were not occupying the canyon before 1750 or so. A recent reanalysis of tree-ring dates indicates that Navajo occupation may have begun there as late as the end of the 1700s (Brugge 1967:396–98) and thus supports the second possibility.

The portrayal of religious subjects in graphic form by the Navajo seems to have resulted from adopting the practices of the resident Pueblo population, who made petroglyphs in profusion in the Rio Grande drainage and who also made kiva murals, altar paintings, and drypaintings in connection with ritual functions. As we might expect, the Gobernador Representational Style is similar in both style and content to that of the contemporary Pueblos and is thus a further manifestation of the Jornada–Rio Grande art tradition and its associated ideology (Fig. 199). As organized structures within their respective and diverse cultural systems, however, the Pueblo and Navajo religions are quite dissimilar. The various associations and sodalities characteristic of Pueblo religious oganization that serve to integrate the large village structures are absent among the Navajos. Navajo ceremonialism is directed by singers (shamans or medicine men) and is centered around curing, which Willey (1966:234) suggests is an Athabaskan focus carried over from the past. As we have seen, however, curing societies make up a major part of the religious structure of the Pueblos.

Like the Rio Grande style, eighteenth-century Navajo rock art depicts masked ceremonial human figures, shield bearers, shields, eagles, cloud terraces, birds, and corn plants (Figs. 199, 253). Occasionally masks alone are depicted, although these occur in the Navajo work in significantly smaller numbers. A comparison between Navajo supernaturals and ceremonial figures from the Pueblo kiva murals was made in an earlier study (P. Schaafsma 1963:58), where it was observed that both are outfitted with similar gear, including kilts, sashes, tassels, and necklaces. Some of their headdresses are

Plate 25. Kachina painted in red, green, and white, Abo, New Mexico. Photograph, Karl Kernberger.

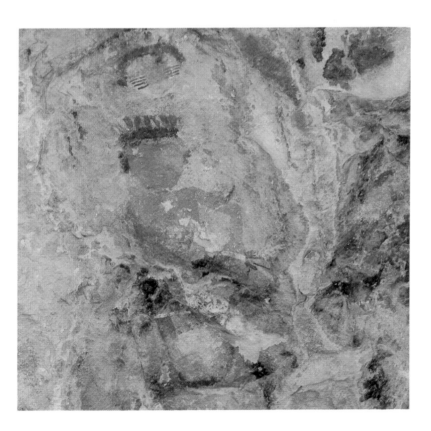

Plate 26. Mask and yellow ceremonial figure, Abo, New Mexico. Photograph, Karl Kernberger.

Plate 27. Navajo supernaturals, Largo Canyon drainage, New Mexico. Photograph, Dick Spas.

Plate 28. Night chant group, Carrizo Canyon drainage. Figures are about 10 inches tall. Photograph, Dick Spas.

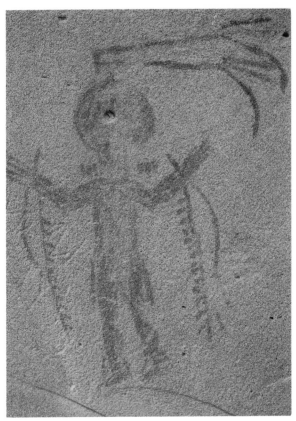

Plate 29. Navajo figure with bows, Carrizo Canyon drainage. Figure is about 8 inches tall. Photograph, Dick Spas.

Plate 30. Horned shield-bearer, Blanco Canyon, New Mexico. Figure is between 3 and 4 feet tall. Photograph, Dick Spas.

Plate 31. Navajo painting of Spanish riders, Canyon del Muerto. Photograph, Karl Kernberger.

Plate 32. Painted shield motif, probably Mescalero, Hueco Tanks, Texas. Photograph, Karl Kernberger.

Figure 253. Eighteenth-century Navajo petroglyphs, Gobernador Representational Style, Largo Canyon drainage, New Mexico. New Mexico State Planning Office; photograph, Karl Kernberger.

also the same—the horned beings of the Navajo petroglyphs being strikingly similar to Pueblo examples. Other likenesses have been pointed out by Smith (1952:322) and Wyman (in press). Some of the work in the Largo drainage is so Pueblo-like that it may be the work of Pueblo refugees (P. Schaafsma 1972:Fig. 34), but on the whole, in spite of the many Pueblo-Navajo analogies, the Gobernador Representational Style is a distinctly Navajo creation.

There is also a minor Plains element in the art of the Gobernador Phase Navajo, which would seem to reflect the earlier associations of these Apacheans. The long, feathered headdresses, absent in contemporaneous or earlier Pueblo work, are distinctly Plains-like (Fig. 254). Figures of bison are also a Plains feature, and these are sometimes depicted with heartlines (P. Schaafsma 1963:Fig. 37), a detail found with some frequency in the rock art of the High Plains (Renaud 1936:Plate 16, Fig. 3). It has been proposed (Dittert 1962 personal communication) that the Athabaskans brought the heartline with them into the Southwest, as either an Athabaskan trait or one that they acquired from Plains groups (P. Schaafsma 1963:57). Its presence in only relatively recent (after A.D. 1500) Pueblo work supports this view.

Figure 254. Supernatural with bow and rainbow approximately a foot in height, Gobernador Representational Style, Largo Canyon drainage, New Mexico. New Mexico State Planning Office; photograph, Karl Kernberger.

Paintings and carvings both are characteristic of the Gobernador Representational Style, and sites, especially the most complex ones, may consist of figures in both techniques (Fig. 12). Painting, incising, and pecking were commonly used in combination. For the most part, paintings seem to have been limited to the planetaria, the portrayal of supernaturals, and large circle motifs often referred to as shields. This interpretation for all large circles, however, is open to question. In drypaintings the sun and moon are often shown as circles both with and without feathers and horns; and there is reason to believe that these celestial beings are also present in circle form in the rock art. Paint was usually applied with brushes but on occasion was sprayed around a stencil or a hand. It is my general impression that the painted supernaturals are slightly more standardized in form than those only pecked or incised and that the sites at which painting was done were the most sacred. Many petroglyph panels from this period, however, especially in the Largo Canyon complex (which includes the Carrizo and Blanco Canyon drainages), are beautifully, carefully, and expertly executed.

Rock drawings occur in small groups sporadically located along the pale, buff-colored sandstone cliffs that characterize the canyons of the Dinetah country. They are usually found apart from, although near, habitation sites. There are also concentrations of Navajo rock art on cliffs near canyon junctions—for example, at the mouth of Todosio Canyon in Los Pinos River Canyon; at the junction of the San Juan and Los Pinos rivers, both sites now

Figure 255. Large feathered shield over 2 feet in diameter, painted in red and white, Carrizo drainage. Hand prints around this and other shields at this site (not visible in photograph) may have been put there as prayer requests. New Mexico State Planning Office; photograph, Karl Kernberger.

flooded by the waters of Navajo Lake; and in the tributaries of Largo and Carrizo canyons. Canyon junction sites frequently contain both petroglyphs and rock paintings. Panels with paintings of supernaturals and so-called shields often show signs of heavy use, as if they were the scene of ceremonial activity on many different occasions. The rock surface at such panels is often soiled in appearance, as if from much handling. Positive and negative painted hand prints associated with other designs, such as around the large circle motifs in Encierro Canyon in the Carrizo drainage (Fig. 255), may have been put there as prayer requests. Reichard (1950:558) notes that people prayed with their hands pressed into hand print impressions in a rock. Superimpositions of Navajo figures occur, and the rock was often purposely smoothed in spots, either to prepare the rock for receiving the paintings or to rub out an older one before a new one was applied. The rubbing out of paintings was definitely practiced, as is evidenced by the occasional half-destroyed paintings or smudged designs in various stages of effacement. Whether ritual obliteration was involved or whether figures were simply changed according to ceremonial requirements is not known.

It is also of interest that the major sites and many of the smaller ones occur where Rosa Representational Style petroglyphs, rock art of the Anasazi who occupied the area 800 to 1,000 years before the Navajos, are present (Fig. 7). There can be no doubt that these Rosa sites were deliberately selected by the Navajos. At this point one can only speculate on their motivation for this, but there are some indications that they felt such spots had special sanctity.

It has been hypothesized that Gobernador Phase rock art sites functioned as shrines (P. Schaafsma 1963:64–65). Their sacred nature is implicit in both the subject matter and the use patterns, and their separateness from living areas is in keeping with this interpretation. There is a small amount of ethnographic evidence to confirm the idea that rock art sites, at least in certain instances, are regarded as holy places by the Navajo (Britt 1973; Gardner 1940; P. Schaafsma 1963; Watson 1964). Sacred places are said to exist where supernatural events have occurred or where one can communicate with the supernaturals by means of prayers and offerings (Watson 1964:22). At a site from northeastern Arizona described by Gardner, there are paintings of early Anasazi origin, which the Navajo describe as records of the Sun God's teaching left by the Yeibichai. The paintings themselves have been left strictly alone, but objects of Navajo ceremonial origin were present in the shelter. The belief that rock art occurs in sacred spots may explain the Navajo relationship to the Rosa Style petroglyphs.

Most pertinent to the discussion of shrines, however, is a description of recent Navajo use of a Gobernador Phase site now inundated by the waters of Navajo Lake at the junction of the San Juan and Los Pinos rivers. The rock art at this site, in addition to a few earlier Rosa Style petroglyphs, consisted of Navajo painted and carved supernaturals, bison with heartlines, and various other figures, including deer, an owl, eagles, and a corn plant (P. Schaafsma 1963:Figs. 36, 37). The work was dominated by two large white discs outlined in red, reputed to be representations of the Twin War Gods (Fig. 256). Manuel Lucero, a former resident of the canyons, reported that the site was visited by the Navajo until the 1950s for the purpose of conducting night ceremonies, especially during dry summers when crops did poorly. "Lucero never observed the all night ceremonies, but on a clear night he could hear chanting" (P. Schaafsma 1963:60).

Newcomb (1964:26–29) mentions three specific journeys by Navajo singers to "Tohe-ha-glee (Meeting Place of Waters)," which is presumably this same site. These visits occurred during times of crisis and were made to this place where certain important Navajo supernaturals were said to reside in order to read the "Sands of Prophecy" located there where the rivers meet. Two visits occurred in the nineteenth century, one at a time of drought and a second after the return from Bosque Redondo when the people were in a state of semistarvation. The third was in 1929, when the Navajo again faced

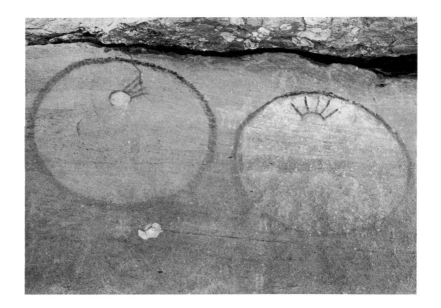

Figure 256. Paired shields, or Twin War Gods, as they formerly appeared at the junction of the Los Pinos and San Juan rivers. The figures were over 2 feet in diameter. Photograph, Laura Gilpin.

starvation after the Commissioner of Indian Affairs had instigated an extensive program of stock reduction on the reservation.

It is of further interest that this particular site is referred to in the Navajo myths. After the slaying of the monsters:

> The celebrated twins went to a place called Tho-hyel-li, the junction of the two rivers in the valley of the San Juan, where their images may yet be seen reflected in the waters. They still dwell in a mountain cavern near this place. (Matthews 1883:224)

In describing Nayenezgani, or Monster Slayer, it is said that:

> Prayers and sacrifices may be offered to him at any place, but his home is at To'yetli, the junction of the two rivers somewhere in the valley of the San Juan, and the warriors who desire his greatest favor, before setting out on the war path, go there to offer prayers and sacrifices. (Matthews 1902:20)

From the Shooting Chant we are told:

> At the place of Separating Water (possibly a meeting place at San Juan River, used by Navajo chief men until recently in emergencies to obtain oracles) it was decided to have a meeting, and Iknee, the Thunder-Bird and Water Monster were in charge. In four days, all the Gods came to the place, also the animals and the birds, and the

four holy people . . . and in the evening the two sons of the Sun came. They said that now the Monsters were killed they should plan how the people should live on this earth and the order in which ceremonies should be given. (DeJohly, B'Yash 1958:21)

Unfortunately we do not have this kind of information in connection with other rock art sites of the early Navajo, but these references to the shrine at the junction of the San Juan and Los Pinos rivers illuminate the involved significance that this and probably other major rock art sites had.

The function of other sites is more debatable. Spots where plants, minerals, and water were obtained for healing were regarded as sacred (Watson 1964:22), and rock drawings may have been made in these contexts. Navajo rock drawings may also have served mnemonic purposes in recording prayers and memorizing ritual procedure (P. Schaafsma 1963:65).

Gobernador Representational Style iconography is highly complex. Anthropomorphic figures are very important, and most of these appear to represent supernaturals. Some are bold petroglyph figures close to the Rio Grande Style (Fig. 257). More characteristic are the distinctly Navajo ye'i and other supernaturals resembling figures in the Navajo drypaintings (Plates 27, 28, Figs. 258–60, and P. Schaafsma 1963:Plates 1, 2, 4). The latter may be pecked, painted, or done in a combination of techniques. Round and rectangular heads denote male and female figures respectively. Female personages commonly wear *mantas;* males, kilts. Moccasins are present on the painted examples. Headgear includes horns, feathers, and pointed caps and may provide a clue to the identity of the being portrayed. Necklaces and streamers from the arms are details shown in the finer examples, and bows, staffs, dance wands, corn, and rattles are held in the hands of these figures, whose arms are invariably uplifted at the elbow. The calves of the legs and the feet when turned to the side indicate the direction of movement.

Supernaturals occur singly, with other elements, or in linear dance groups. The last arrangement (Plate 28, Fig. 258) resembles certain types of drypaintings, and these rock figures include some of the finest examples of the art. Although red and white are frequently used pigments in Navajo rock painting, in the dance groups blue, turquoise, ultramarine, blue-gray, orange, yellow, green, cream, and rose were also used (P. Schaafsma 1963:46).

In some cases specific personages can be identified. The War Twins, who are children of the Sun and Changing Woman (Reichard 1950:481–84), are major deities in Navajo mythology. They have many names, but the elder

Figure 257. V-necked Navajo supernaturals, Largo Canyon. New Mexico State Planning Office; photograph, Karl Kernberger.

Figure 258. Line of Night Chant figures painted in red, white, and blue. The panel, originally from the drainage of Carrizo Canyon, fell from the cliff and was subsequently removed, first to Santa Fe and then to Window Rock, Arizona. Figures approximately 16 inches tall. Photograph, Harry Hadlock.

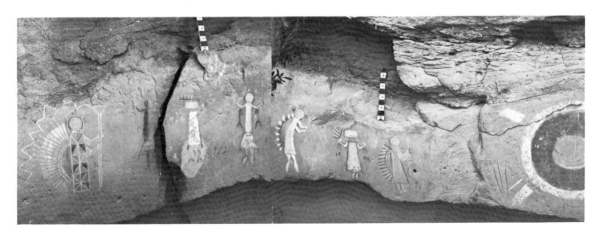

Figure 259. Painted and incised Navajo supernatural approximately 14 inches tall, Carrizo Canyon drainage. Photograph, Walter Chapelle.

Figure 260. Female God of the Night Chant, Largo Canyon drainage, New Mexico. Top of mask 16 inches across. New Mexico State Planning Office; photograph, Karl Kernberger.

twin is most often called Monster Slayer and the younger Born-for-Water. They themselves or symbols for them or their power (Newcomb and Reichard 1937:45) are present in the eighteenth-century rock art. Born-for-Water is readily identified in a Largo painting by his red color, his impersonation symbol, and the small hourglass figures scratched through the paint (Plate 27). To his right is a supernatural with a large fluffy-looking feather over his head, possibly his brother Monster Slayer, as Wyman (1960:42) mentions that this deity may wear a red plume. A similar pair appears in a group of four in Todosio Canyon on Los Pinos River (P. Schaafsma 1963:Plate 1). A third red supernatural with an inverted triangle on his face (P. Schaafsma 1963:Plate 2), an element sometimes present on Born-for-Water's mask, may represent Red God, who also has such a mask (Wyman, in press). Hourglass symbols are painted on the mask and on the ceremonial impersonators of Born-for-Water. This sign appears to be a carryover from Pueblo iconography, where it also occurs on warriors (Fig. 246 and Bunzel 1932:Plate 39b). Among both the Pueblos and the Navajos it is specifically a symbol of the scalpknot (Stevenson 1891:247). Dance impersonators of Monster Slayer are painted with a symbol of the bow. According to Reichard (1950:527):

> Monster Slayer explained the symbol as he raised his left foot toward the people: "This act represents the means I used to overcome the monsters. In days to come you shall remember the one whose name is Bow-whose-string-extends-on-one-side." The bow symbolizes the death of the monsters whose ghosts have left death or weakness behind.

Supernaturals carrying the bow may in some cases represent this deity (Fig. 254 and Plate 29). Both the hourglass and the bow also occur apart from anthropomorphic contexts in the rock art. Born-for-Water's hourglass may appear alone or is sometimes attached to corn plants (Fig. 253), and an exceptional combination of these symbols occurs in a Crow Canyon petroglyph in the Largo drainage (Fig. 261). The symbols may relate to specific activities carried out by the Twins. In the monster slaying tales, Monster Slayer downs the opponent with his bow, and Born-for-Water then scalps him.

Still another symbol of Monster Slayer is zigzag lightning (Wyman 1960:42). This symbol is present in the form of five zigzag lines on the left cheek of his mask (Stevenson 1891:Plate 115). One such set of marks has been found on a mask in the eighteenth-century rock drawings, and a set of three

Figure 261. Bow and hourglass symbols, Largo Canyon drainage. Hourglasses are approximately 4 inches tall. New Mexico State Planning Office; photograph, Karl Kernberger.

zigzag lightnings is prominent in the petroglyph panel illustrated in Figure 253.

The symbology of the Twins does not stop here. At the junction of the San Juan and Los Pinos rivers they are represented as paired circles. Similar paired shields or circle elements occur in the Carrizo drainage, and in one instance one of the pair has horns. In sandpaintings the Twins are shown on the discs of the Sun and Moon, and it is possible that these rock-painted figures are also associated with these celestial beings (Wyman 1967, personal communication). Whether all shields are affiliated with the Twins is not certain, however.

These large circles by themselves constitute some of the most striking designs in Gobernador Style art (Fig. 255). They are usually painted in red and white, but there is one turquoise painting in the Carrizo drainage. In design, they are for the most part quite simple, based on a concentric circle arrangement with a narrow band of color usually serving as an outline. There may be an additional circle in the center. Eagle feathers are sometimes painted at intervals around the rim. In some cases there are central holes that may have served as a means of attaching actual feathers or other paraphernalia for ceremonial use. The petroglyph shield in Figure 262 is a slight variant

Figure 262. Navajo hunt scene pecked over Rosa Representational Style figures, Largo Canyon drainage. New Mexico State Planning Office; photograph, Karl Kernberger.

on this basic theme. Shields such as this with zigzags may symbolize the sun. Shield bearers are also depicted (Plate 30), and some of these are horned and carry bows and quivers of mountain lion skin.

One of the most frequently depicted supernaturals in the Largo drainage is the *ghaan'ask'idii*, Humpback God (Fig. 253). These *ye'i* wear mountain sheep horns, and their humps, from which eagle feathers radiate, are said to contain seeds and mist. The figure invariably carries a staff. This personage is regarded as either a deified mountain sheep or a guardian of the sheep, and is also defined as the "god of harvest, god of plenty, god of the mist" (Reichard 1950:443–44); he is frequently present in modern drypaintings. Here again is a horned deity, horns being insignia of supernatural power. The prototype for this figure may exist in the Pueblo Mountain Sheep kachina, Panwu, who is like the Navajo Humpback in several respects: he wears mountain sheep horns, has a feathered hump, and carries a staff (Fewkes 1903:142–43, Plate 40). Historically, both the Pueblo and the Navajo personages may have roots in Kokopelli, the flute player.

In the rock art the Humpback God may occur as a single figure, especially among the petroglyphs. Figure 14 illustrates a *ghaan'ask'idii* mask situated above a high secluded ledge in Delgadito Canyon in the Carrizo drainage. In other paintings from Delgadito this personage is shown along with other supernaturals in dance groups (Fig. 258 and Plate 28). Comparisons with drypaintings indicate that this row of deities, which occurs repeatedly in the Delgadito paintings and includes, in addition to the Humpback God, Fringemouth with a divided body and pointed cap and a female *ye'i* with rectangular mask, is from the Night Chant (Stevenson 1891:Plate 123). The Night Chant myth relates that the hero of the chant was led by Mountain Sheep People, suggesting that the mountain sheep as a supernatural is particularly important in this context. The many representations of this *ye'i* in the Largo stand in contrast to its absence on the Upper San Juan, but no explanation can be offered at this time.

The female God of the Night Chant is also represented in petroglyph panels where the details of her mask (Fig. 260 and P. Schaafsma 1972:Fig. 40), including facial features and a raised nose and earpieces, identify her without question (compare Hester 1962:Fig. 43).

There are two panels from the Navajo Reservoir and others in the Largo in which Mountain Chant figures are depicted (P. Schaafsma 1963:Plate 4 and Fig. 53). Cloud symbolism is present in both of these Reservoir panels, in one as a border and in the other as background, and the supernaturals in question have tall feathered headdresses and long hair, characteristic of Mountainway sandpainting people (Wyman, in press). Finally, there are a number of beings wearing red pointed caps, a Shootingway headdress worn by almost any figure appearing in the drypaintings of the Shootingway Chant (Wyman 1967:personal communication). Caches of ceremonial paraphernalia of the Gobernador Phase Navajo suggest that the Night Chant and the Mountain Chant, as well as the Enemyway and Antelope Corralway, date back to the eighteenth century (Hester 1962:60), thus corroborating, in part, information provided by the rock drawings.

So far, the emphasis in this discussion has been on the anthropomorphic supernaturals. There are, however, a large number of petroglyph panels in which human or supernatural figures play a minor role, interact with a large number of other elements, or may be lacking entirely.

Many petroglyph panels are filled with complex symbolism that undoubtedly functions as an interrelated whole, and some are perhaps representations of scenes from myths; but the overall meaning of these is difficult to discern. In Figure 263 a large hoop or similar object is held by a horned, hunchbacked, phallic being very unusual in Navajo iconography. The panel's total meaning is not readily apparent. In a neighboring panel (Figs.

Figure 263. Eighteenth-century Navajo petroglyphs, Blanco Canyon, New Mexico. New Mexico State Planning Office; photograph, Curtis Schaafsma.

264, 17) are many well-known figures: rabbit tracks, thunder impersonated as the Thunderbird, Bat, Lizard, Dragonfly, a coiled rattlesnake, and Coyote, a mischief maker, deceiver, and symbol of excess in sexual practices who shows up in Navajo petroglyphs from time to time, but again, no interpretation is offered for the whole. The hourglass symbol of Born-for-Water is present and elaborated with a sash.

Water and corn are other themes appearing in the Gobernador Representational Style petroglyphs (Fig. 265). In this connection is the cloud terrace–corn–bird complex (Fig. 266) essentially unchanged from the Pueblo and Jornada depictions that preceded it, and the stylized corn in this instance still has a crooked stalk. In the panel in Figure 253, water is represented by the cloud terrace and the Humpback, who has moisture as well as seeds in his hump. The hourglass of Born-for-Water, the parent of all waters (Stevenson 1891:280), is attached to the corn and also occurs at the upper corner of a corn-sprouting scene nearby. Of interest here is a notation by Parsons (1940:9, note 4) that among some of the Pueblos the Little War God is represented as a corn kachina. At other sites, cloud terraces are shown with lightning arrows, which would seem to signify rain and storms (P. Schaafsma 1963:Fig. 39). The fact that arrows and lightning in modern drypaintings are heavily associated with the Shootingway Chant, however, may suggest that this symbolism is intended.

Figure 264. Navajo petroglyphs in Blanco Canyon. Panel is part of the same site illustrated in Fig. 263. Traces of hands and anthropomorphs in the Rosa Representational Style are discernible beneath the Navajo work. New Mexico State Planning Office; photograph, Curtis Schaafsma.

Figure 265. Corn plant, Largo drainage. Figure is approximately 4 feet tall. Photograph, Dick Spas.

Figure 266. Navajo bird, corn, and terrace complex, Largo Canyon drainage. Complex is about 3 feet tall. Navajo figures were pecked over anthropomorphs of the Rosa Representational Style.

There are also hunting scenes (Fig. 262). The reticulate pattern perhaps represents a hunting net. Deer, elk, and bison are pursued by a hunter carrying a bow and arrows and quivers. Hunters elsewhere are also shown with quivers. Here and in other instances these panels occur over Rosa Style work, and Rosa animals have been repecked and incorporated. In reference to our earlier discussion concerning Navajo selection of Rosa petroglyph sites as locations for their own rock drawings, this may have been a means by which the Navajo capitalized on the power or hunting magic of their predecessors, bringing it into their own realm of use. In some cases, the hunters appear to be supernaturals. Wyman (in press) notes that bison with arrows (P. Schaafsma 1963:Fig. 37) are reminiscent of scenes from the Shooting Chant in which the beasts are shot by the Holy People, who later magically restore their prey.

The horse, although thoroughly incorporated into Navajo mythology (Clark 1966), is not a major feature in Navajo art until after the Gobernador Phase, when it appears in more secular contexts. Its depiction in the artwork of the eighteenth-century Navajos is only occasional and not particularly exciting (P. Schaafsma 1963:Figs. 37 and 53).

One category of early Navajo rock art remains to be discussed: the planetaria, or star paintings, on the undersides of overhangs and ceilings of rock-shelters (Fig. 267). These are found within the region occupied by the Gobernador Phase Navajo, but they have a wider distribution than other Gobernador Phase art. Planetaria sites are also found near Cuba and Gallup, New Mexico, and Britt (1973) reports fourteen such sites from Canyon de Chelly and Canyon del Muerto, adding that a Navajo informant knows of thirty-two. Those in New Mexico probably date from the eighteenth century, but those in Canyon de Chelly could date as late as the first part of the nineteenth century (Britt 1973). They are all similar and undoubtedly functioned similarly in Navajo ceremonial practices.

The star ceilings are characterized by paintings of small, precisely painted stars in the form of crosses, which average between 3 and 5 inches across. The most typical consist simply of crossed lines, but other forms in Canyon de Chelly have been illustrated by Britt (1973:Fig. 1). As a rule, the eastern planetaria have a wider variety of color and design than the western ones. Petaled flower forms occurred in Todosio Canyon (P. Schaafsma 1963:Plate 3, Fig. 42), and negative crosses produced by spraying around a stencil are present at Dulce. The most elaborate planetarium is a large site near Cuba where elements in red, black, gray, and white, in addition to the

Figure 267. Navajo planetarium, Canyon del Muerto, Arizona. Photograph, Karl Kernberger.

standard cross, consist of single lines, asterisks, dragonflies, and crosslike flying birds, all variations on the cross element, plus eaglelike birds, circles, a few animals, and exquisite tiny red horsemen carrying lances. All are consistent in size and crisply painted.

The planetaria of Canyon de Chelly are usually in black and white, and representational elements are rare, although Britt (1973:Fig. 4) records what may be highly stylized human figures among the crosses.

These star ceilings may occur at sites at which there are also other Navajo ceremonial paintings. In many instances, however, they are isolated and particularly inaccessible. Paintings of stars may be located more than 50 feet above ground level and on the far inside surfaces of overhangs, so that the means by which the artists reached the surface are not readily apparent. As a result, some of these sites are truly awesome (Fig. 268).

From communication with the Canyon de Chelly Navajo, who live near these sites, Britt was able to learn that these paintings are still highly sacred to the Navajo and that singers visit them on behalf of patients and leave offerings (1973:11). The specific meaning of these sites is known only to certain practitioners, however; this information, along with the knowledge of

Figure 268. Cliff wall in Canyon de Chelly showing location of planetarium. Photograph, Karl Kernberger.

starlore itself, is not available to the average Navajo (Haile 1947:1; Britt 1973:5, 11–12).

Starlore, nevertheless, is important in Navajo ideology. Stars and fields of stars appear in modern drypaintings of the Big Starway, the Beadway, and the Shooting Chant, and constellations are pictured on ceremonial objects such as rattles and dance paddles. Constellations may be present in these star ceilings also, and larger stars seem to stand for those of greater brightness. The ability to recognize constellations as such, however, is rendered difficult by several factors. The constellations as defined by the Navajo do not always match those with which the Western world is familiar. Second, the shape given constellations by the Navajo has been observed to be a matter of convention rather than accuracy (Haile 1947:15). Finally, in a few cases, the stars are so closely massed that there are no discernible patterns. Numerous overpaintings seem to be responsible for such crowded ceilings.

In sum, it is clear that preserved in these rock paintings and petroglyphs are the forms and symbolic content that preceded the modern drypaintings, which may have replaced the rock art of the eighteenth century. How long drypainting has been practiced among the Navajo is not really known, although it is thought to be one of the many ceremonial practices borrowed from their early Pueblo associates. A cache of drypainting materials from a site at Big Bead Mesa to the southeast of the Dinetah region suggests that drypaintings were being made by the late 1700s (Keur 1941:62, 64).

When the first drypaintings were recorded at the end of the nineteenth century (Matthews 1887, 1902; Stevenson 1891), the style of the art had crystallized and a certain amount of standardization had occurred, so that these nineteenth-century paintings do not differ significantly from more recent ones. From the Gobernador Representational Style, we see a trend toward abstraction and geometric form. All elements have become rigid, and angularity is stressed. In particular, the supernatural anthropomorphic figure has been stretched and stylized so that in the recent art it is an elongate otherworldly being, psychically distant, divorced from human experience and profane contexts (Wyman, in press).

At the close of the Gobernador Phase in the upper San Juan and the Gobernador-Largo localities, the making of ceremonial rock art, with the possible exception of the planetaria, began to wane. Navajo rock art dealing with religious subject matter in Chaco Canyon consists primarily of miscellaneous very small groups of incised supernaturals, sketchily rendered and whimsical in quality, and in general closer to modern examples in style. In Chaco Canyon there is only one known painted panel with typical Gobernador Style supernaturals. A petroglyph site with two large pecked shields, supernaturals, moccasin prints, and deer and bison is probably Gobernador Phase in date, but I believe that most of the Chaco incisings are later in origin. Navajo rock art dealing with ceremonial themes after the end of the eighteenth century is restricted in both content and numbers of sites, and eventually secular drawings, some of which are narrative in intent, took the place of religious ones.

Later Navajo Art

The change in subject matter of the rock art at the end of the Gobernador Phase resulted not from a shift in religious ideology and symbolism but from a change in ceremonial practices. The reproduction of religious imagery after this time was largely confined to the impermanent medium of drypainting. Pressure from the encroaching Spaniards and Anglo-Americans upon the sacred world of the Navajo may have provoked this change, which may have involved adopting new values and possibly incorporating taboos that prevented the depiction of ceremonial figures in permanent form. According to Navajo mythology, "drypaintings were given to heroes by the gods who specified that they be made of impermanent material to prevent quarreling over their possession" (Mills 1959:42).

The practice of drawing on rock continued, and sacred subjects were replaced by scenes and objects from everyday life. Some of these representations are skillfully drawn and of historical interest. Many were done by sheepherders as they passed the time of day, and individual inspiration and the desire to document worldly things or events would seem to have been the motivation for many drawings that date from the nineteenth and twentieth centuries. They are best known from Chaco Canyon and Canyon de Chelly. In this work is an ever-increasing trend toward naturalism and integrated composition involving many figures, and they can be viewed as a transition to modern Navajo painting. Style definitions for Navajo rock art following the Gobernador Representational Style have not been formulated, as a thorough study of the late rock drawings has not been attempted. In a preliminary study, however, the horse motif between the late 1700s and the present is analyzed on the basis of stylistic changes (James and Davidson 1975).

In the Chaco Canyon area, Navajo rock art following the Gobernador Style usually takes the form of petroglyphs incised in the sandstone. Rather unusual rock drawings, possibly the work of one artist, show two different Navajo ceremonies, the Yeibichai Dance of the Night Chant and the Squaw Dance, a popular Enemyway ceremony (Figs. 269, 270). The figures of both are small (not more than 10 inches tall) and drawn in numerous fine, carefully controlled lines. The Yeibichai dancers are not gods but human dance impersonators depicted in a realistic, lively manner that catches the rhythm of the dance. Among the costume details are thick ruffs, kilts, and fox pelts, and in their hands the dancers hold rattles and evergreen boughs. Talking God (not shown in Fig. 268) heads the line, and the last figure is a clown with his head thrown back. A number of the masks are painted with blue-green pigment. The Squaw Dance scene is extensive and consists of a large number of men, women, and children. The women are dressed in long skirts and fringed shawls and have their hair tied up in the traditional manner. Men are wrapped in blankets and wear broad-brimmed Navajo hats. A forked-stick hogan and a horse are represented, and a number of women carry wands (Fig. 269, center).

Other interesting Chaco rock drawings appear to be records of Navajo

Figure 269. Yeibichai dancers, Chaco Canyon. New Mexico State Planning Office; photograph, Karl Kernberger.

Figure 270. Detail of an incised rock drawing of a Squaw Dance, Chaco Canyon. New Mexico State Planning Office; photograph, Karl Kernberger.

and Ute encounters. There are a number of small, shallowly incised horned horsemen with large shields and bows and arrows (Schaafsma 1972:Fig. 50). Scratched drawings of tipis with shield-bearing men on horseback nearby also appear to be a Ute scene. The elongate, stiff horses with interior hachure and barbed tails date these petroglyphs before 1800 (James and Davidson 1975). Horses and horsemen are depicted in numerous instances, and cars and trucks along with rutted roads are graphic documents of the twentieth-century Navajo in Chaco Canyon.

There are Navajo paintings and charcoal drawings as well as petroglyphs in Canyon de Chelly. With the exception of the planetaria, the ceremonial or religious subjects that occur are modern in style. Ceremonial figures include a series of very faded, pale masks with *tablitas* symbolic of clouds at a planetarium site, probably a shrine; some elongated, contemporary-looking supernaturals (Fig. 271); a polychrome mask with *tablita* in yellow, white, and red (Fig. 272); "plant people"; and a few shields, some of which are horned, perhaps representing the sun and moon. Some of these panels include figures of long elegant antelope. The latter and the designs with which they are associated, as well as certain groups of horses and riders, are reputed to be the work of Dibe Yazhi, or Little Sheep, the first Navajo artist to be identified by name, who lived in the canyons in the first half of the nineteenth century.

Among the finest rock paintings in the canyon is the Spanish cavalcade, above a high ledge in the shelter of Standing Cow Ruin in Canyon del Muerto (Fig. 273). This site is named after a handsome painting of a huge gray and white, somewhat disproportionate bull at the opposite end of the shelter. The cavalcade in red and white consists of a procession of horses and riders with long cloaks and tall broad-brimmed hats, carrying flintlock rifles. The cross on the cape is said to signify membership in the military order of St. James (Woodward in Tanner 1973:60). The figures find a balance between flat pattern and naturalism in the simplified shapes. The horses are plain white or are marked with red spots or lines, and their feet are big and round. The riders progress across the cliff face in clustered groups from left to right. This panel presumably documents the soldiers of Lieutenant Antonio Narbona, who entered Canyon de Chelly on a campaign in 1805, killing many Navajos, and who was probably responsible for the killings of a number of Navajo women, children, and old men in Massacre Cave (Grant 1974; McNitt 1972:42–44).

Farther up the canyon is a second panel of horses and other animals and Spaniards with lances (Plate 31 and Fig. 274). Figures are in soft shades of

Figure 271. Navajo antelope and supernatural, Canyon de Chelly. Photograph, Karl Kernberger.

Figure 272. Mask with tablita in yellow, white, and red, occurring with painting of antelope and supernatural (Fig. 271), Canyon de Chelly. Photograph, Karl Kernberger.

329

Figure 273. Navajo painting of Spanish cavalcade, Standing Cow Ruin, Canyon del Muerto. Photograph, Karl Kernberger.

brown, black, and white, and the antelope and a bighorn sheep are included in the group. Stylistically, the horses are typically Navajo. They are rather long and slim, their rumps are square, and they have proud curved necks and small heads. Among them are pintos, horses of a color pattern the Navajos preferred. Details of saddles, bridles, manes, tails, and feather adornments are indicated with paint and charcoal. A single white animal stands in contrast to the others in both color and style. It is a heavy creature, with curved rump and neck and very tiny head, stylized like the buffalo in drypaintings (Newcomb and Reichard 1937:Plates 23–28).

Also of historical value is the Ute Raid panel in Canyon del Muerto (Figs. 275, 276). This is an extensive mural of sketchy drawings in charcoal documenting a Ute foray into the canyon in 1858 (Grant 1974), in which Ute horsemen with shields, lances, bows and arrows, and guns encounter Navajos on foot carrying shields and weapons. The horses' bridles and the Utes' shields are given special emphasis, as they were painted in what appears to have been a thick wet charcoal medium, which contrasts with the light dry charcoal line used elsewhere. The horses have eagle feathers on their bridles, and feathers hang from the shields. A herd of sheep and cattle is also depicted here, and in the midst of battle is the inconspicuous image of Talking God!

The horses in the panels just described from Canyon de Chelly fall into a style category dating between 1800 and 1860 (James and Davidson 1975), in

Figure 274. Detail of horses and antelope, Canyon del Muerto. Animals are approximately 10 inches in length. Photograph, Karl Kernberger.

Figure 275. Charcoal drawing of an 1858 Ute raid on the Navajo, Canyon del Muerto. Shields are about 5 inches in diameter. Photograph, Karl Kernberger.

Figure 276. Detail of horse's head from the Ute Raid panel, Canyon del Muerto, showing eagle feathers attached to the bridle. Photograph, Karl Kernberger.

Figure 277. Modern incised drawing of horse and rider with dogs, Canyon del Muerto. Horse is approximately a foot long. Photograph, Karl Kernberger.

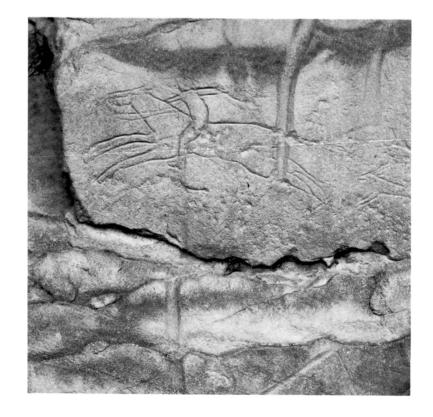

which long slim horses are depicted with more naturalism than those from the preceding period. Following this time, and especially after 1900, drawings became increasingly fluid and naturalistic (Fig. 277). Partly responsible for this change was the compulsory education for Navajo children then enforced by the government and the resulting increased familiarity of the Navajo with Western art. Twentieth-century drawings are sometimes referred to as "Navajo schoolboy art" (James and Davidson 1975:20).

Since the late eighteenth century the horse has been a favorite motif in Navajo rock art, both as a subject in its own right (Figs. 211, 212) and as part of complicated scenes in which it plays a major role. Horses in the rock drawings tend to be lithe, with long legs and with necks held in a high arch, and more often than not they are in motion. The horse of Navajo art is not always strictly an ordinary horse; it may be conceived of as a somewhat supernatural creature, a gift of the gods. Many of these drawings manifest a Navajo ideal of " 'beautiful horses—slim like a weasel'—horses such as those they believed belonged to one of their Twin War Gods" (Clark 1966:11). In the twentieth century, when Navajo artists began to paint on paper, the horse was rendered with more skill and elaboration than before and with sophisticated use of depth and perspective.

The acquisition of the horse in the early seventeenth century (Clark 1966:4) changed the life-styles of all the southern Athabaskans in the Southwest, providing them with new freedom of travel, wider contacts, and raiding ability, as well as an additional source of food. As a result, horses gave their owners "prestige and a place in society as warriors and wealthy men" (Clark 1966:9). At the same time the horse was incorporated into the folklore of the Navajo and Apache, and it played a symbolic role in the mythology of both. A pervasive and important factor in their lives and thought, it appears again and again in their art. The significance of the horse to the Navajo and Apache and its place in their myths is nowhere more thoroughly and more beautifully described than in the book *They Sang for Horses*, by La Verne Harrell Clark (1966).

THE APACHE

Several Apache groups have occupied New Mexico and Arizona for the last three centuries, and a small number of Apache rock art sites have been recorded from the Mescalero, Chiricahua, and San Carlos regions (Map 11).

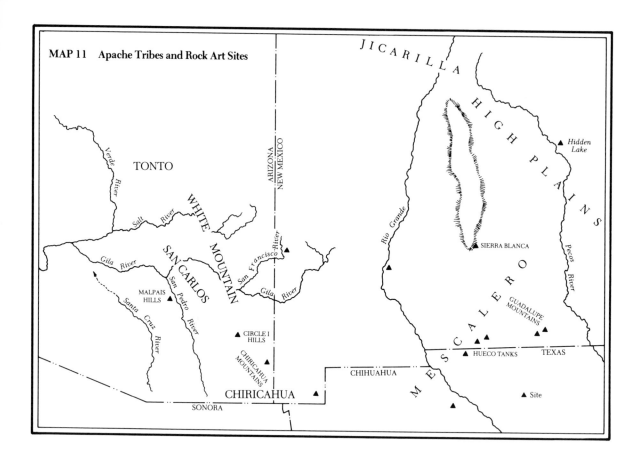

MAP 11   Apache Tribes and Rock Art Sites

Archaeology of the Apache who lived west of the Pecos and the Rio Grande is virtually unknown (Gunnerson and Gunnerson 1971:21), but many historical records refer to these groups from the late sixteenth through the nineteenth centuries (Gunnerson 1974). From the early 1600s on, the New Mexico Apaches had horses (Clark 1966:7), and with the horse they created a life-style around raiding that displaced an earlier subsistence based on a combination of bison hunting, gathering, and gardening. Gardening in particular declined in importance with the coming of the horse, and the invasion of the southern Plains by Comanches early in the 1700s denied the Mescaleros some of their best hunting grounds (Newcomb and Kirkland 1967: 189). Among these Apache groups, the Mescaleros, Jicarillas, and some others traded and spent winters with the Pueblos along the Rio Grande. Like the Navajo, they acquired and incorporated into their thinking a number of Pueblo religious beliefs and practices, perhaps including the visual expression of these beliefs in rock paintings and petroglyphs (Newcomb and Kirkland 1967:189).

In comparison with the rock art of other cultural groups discussed in this volume, very little is known about that of the Apaches. What are presumed to be Apache rock drawings in the Southwest are scattered from southern Arizona through southern New Mexico, northern Chihuahua, and West Texas. The work at these sites presents a rather miscellaneous collection of rock paintings and petroglyphs, obviously relatively recent in origin, but often so limited or undiagnostic in content and style that where other historic Indians are involved, especially in Texas and Chihuahua where Comanches ranged in the Historic Period along with the Apache, one cannot always be certain who made them.

Dry charcoal line drawings and paintings are common, and although a range of colors occurs, a heavy black pigment is characteristic. In contrast, however, at Hueco Tanks paintings attributable to the Apaches are frequently done with thick white paint (Newcomb and Kirkland 1967:199). Knowledge of the Apache petroglyphs is limited to southern New Mexico and adjacent parts of Texas (P. Schaafsma 1972:Figs. 106, 107).

As one might predict, horses and riders are frequently represented in Apache rock art. Some of the riders are shown with broad-brimmed hats and weapons like the Navajo depictions of Europeans and Americans. Others seem to represent Apaches (Fig. 278 and Newcomb and Kirkland 1967:Plates 137, 17-G). Several of these horse representations occur at desert springs or tanks that these mobile people must have frequented.

Other subject matter includes decorative shields, bison, miscellaneous small, unidentifiable animals, snakes of different kinds, some of which are based on mythological and not naturalistic interpretations, lizards, masks, and hourglass designs. Possibly the last-mentioned design in Apache art parallels in meaning its counterpart in Navajo iconography, as the symbol of Born-for-Water. Born-for-Water, more commonly referred to in literature on the Apache as Child-of-the-Water, is more important than the first-born twin, Monster Slayer or Killer-of-Enemies, among the Chiricahua and Mescalero. It is interesting in this regard that the hourglass, as a sketchily drawn figure in charcoal or as a petroglyph (Schaafsma 1972:Fig. 107), is distributed from the Guadalupe Mountains across southern New Mexico to the San Pedro River Valley in Arizona.

Major concentrations of Apache rock drawings are found in the Guadalupe Mountains and at Hueco Tanks. Other noteworthy Apache sites are located in the Circle I Hills in southeastern Arizona and on the San Pedro River to the west. The Hueco Tanks paintings (Fig. 279) are discussed in detail by Newcomb and Kirkland (1967:198–203). These are characterized by

Figure 278. Petroglyph of horse and rider and other figures, Alamo Mountain, New Mexico.

solidly portrayed figures and a liberal use of thick white paint. There are lively human figures in white with rabbit-eared or feathered headdresses in dance scenes in which sexuality is an important theme, and which Newcomb relates to certain victory celebration rites (Newcomb and Kirkland 1967:194). An alternative interpretation is that these figures depict Mountain Spirit dancers (Claire Farrer 1977, personal communication). Also at Hueco Tanks are shield motifs (Plate 32), a number of rather stodgy horses, and large white paintings of snakes, the details of which are in red, yellow, and black. There are polychrome paintings depicting nineteenth-century Americans and shield bearers that Newcomb feels may be Apache work (Newcomb and Kirkland 1967:Plates 124, 1-A; 125, 2-C and 2-D; 126, 6-A and 6-B; 127; 128, 6-E; 135, 15-C and 16-D; 137, 17-G). Newcomb emphasizes that this work is tentatively attributable to the Mescaleros on the basis of the fact that they were the principal tribe that habitually visited Hueco Tanks in historic times.

In the Guadalupe Mountains, petroglyphs, sketchy charcoal drawings, and designs in thick paint occur, and figures include horses and riders, bison, lizards, and miscellaneous small human figures and animals. There are a

Figure 279. Row of white dancing figures, Mescalero Apache, Hueco Tanks, Texas. Photograph, Karl Kernberger.

number of painted and pecked masks, some of which have horns (Figs. 280, 281), and the hourglass symbol is present. I have suggested elsewhere (P. Schaafsma 1972:124) that early Apache trade relations with the Rio Grande Pueblos may account for the mask representations, some of which resemble copies of late Pueblo work in the upper Rio Grande.

One of the most interesting Apache sites is in the Circle I Hills in southeastern Arizona, where a number of ceremonial themes are depicted. The site consists of a large panel of black and white (but now faded) shields, boldly decorated with various circle motifs and bordered with a fringe (Fig. 282). The patterns resemble those of contemporary Pueblo shields. A spotted serpentine element partially frames the group. Additional figures include a thunderbird and a lizard with a circle at the mouth. There is evidence of overpainting in yellow-green paint.

Farther west in an overhang in the Malpais Hills locality of the San Pedro Valley are more ceremonial paintings (Fig. 283). Unlike the Circle I Hills paintings, these consist of small figures scattered at random throughout the shelter, and designs occur on the ceiling as well as on the walls. Red,

Figure 280. Red and yellow sun face and petroglyphs, Mescalero Apache, Guadalupe Mountains, New Mexico. New Mexico State Planning Office; photograph, Curtis Schaffsma.

Figure 281. Crude petroglyph of a one-horned mask, Mescalero Apache, Guadalupe Mountains. Mexico State Planning Office; photograph, Curtis Schaafsma.

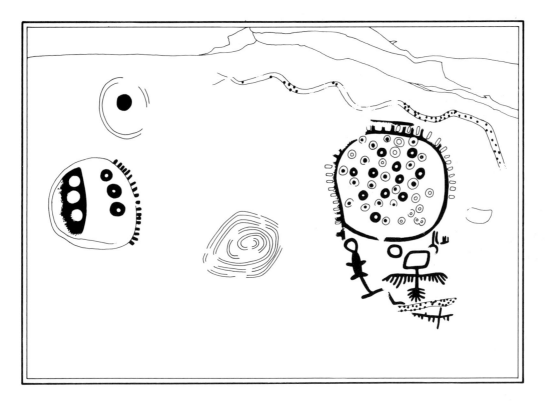

Figure 282. Black and white paintings of shields, thunderbird, lizard, and snake, Circle I Hills, Wilcox, Arizona.

green, white, black, and orange pigments were used. Elements include a small shieldlike motif with concentric circles of varied width in white, black, red, green, and the natural rock, in that order from the circumference to the center, a rectilinear lizard, and a number of black or black-and-white snakes, some of which have bifurcated red tongues. One of these last has a head depicted at both ends (Fig. 282, lower). Such a snake is mentioned by Newcomb and Reichard (1937:53) in their discussion of snakes in the Navajo Shooting Chant. They report that "No one has ever seen this snake, but almost everyone has a relative who has." There is also a fringed hourglass design (not illustrated). Possible Navajo parallels with this figure were mentioned previously. Anthropomorphs depicted here are commonly portrayed with sunburst headdress motifs, halo devices, or both. Vastokas and Vastokas (1973) have brought data to bear upon the observation that this image, predominantly an American Indian and Siberian motif, is supremely shamanistic in character and meaning. Such shamans may receive their power from the sun, and the halo may also designate visionary experience.

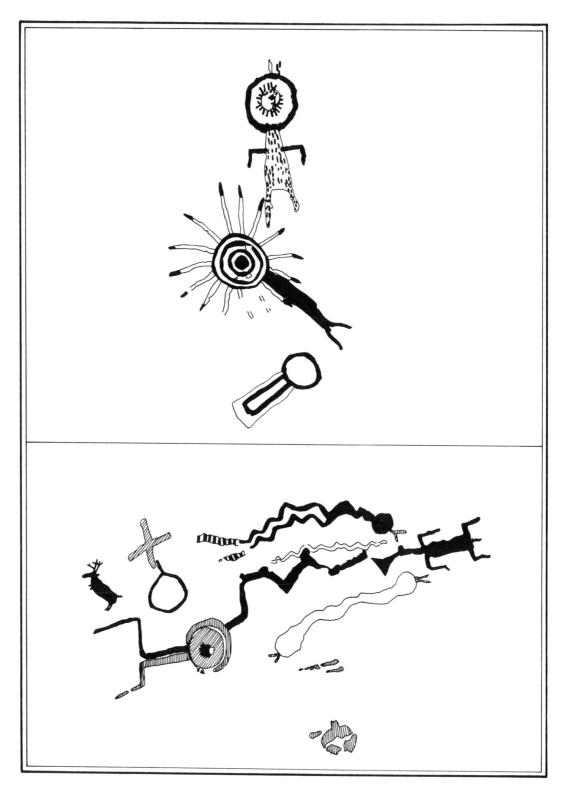

Figure 283. Details from painted ceiling, Malpais Hills, San Pedro Valley, Arizona. Figures include anthropomorphs with sunburst head motifs, and various types of mythical snakes (after drawing by Patricia Vivian).

This interpretation fits very well within the religious context of the Apache in which shamans, and specifically sun shamans, operate (Opler 1965:194). In his discussion of the Chiricahua Apache, Opler (1965:194, 203, 214) mentions shamans who obtain their power from the sun and that shamans who know the power of the sun and moon are able to look down on distant events.

The paintings described above differ considerably from rock paintings in the Sierra Blanca and Hidden Lake localities of eastern and central New Mexico, attributed by Gebhard (1957, 1958) to the Mescalero and Jicarilla. In these two sites large polychrome figures are arranged as integrated panels. Elements and design components resemble motifs commonly found in Pueblo art, yet on closer analysis the shapes employed and the manner in which they are arranged do not conform to those found elsewhere in the Southwest. The panel at Hidden Lake is dominated by three highly stylized figures—a rather monstrous insectlike being and a geometric bird about 4 feet tall, which flank an elaborate thunderbird of equal stature. In overall appearance as well as in matters of detail, these figures are truly bizarre. A terraced element and a horned serpent partially enclose the group at top and bottom, respectively. The two Sierra Blanca paintings comprise similar but less eccentric groups. Elements include horned sun faces, terraces, a deer with heartline, and hourglass-shaped anthropomorphs. Gebhard estimates that they were painted in the late nineteenth century.

One resident of Glencoe has cast some doubt on the authenticity of the Sierra Blanca group (P. Schaafsma 1972:125), but this contradicts local information obtained by Gebhard (1957:219) that indicated they date from the late 1800s and are thus probably the work of Mescaleros. Until more information is available, however, the origins of both the paintings at Hidden Lake and the Sierra Blanca should remain in question.

What significance rock paintings and petroglyph sites held for the Apache is primarily a matter of speculation. Those sites in which ritual symbolism occurs may have served, as did the Navajo sites, as a focus for religious activity. This is supported by Opler's observation that to the Apache places with markings on the walls or rocks may be considered sacred. He goes on to mention a specific cave where men go to pray, in which the sun, moon, stars, and mountain spirits are depicted on the walls (Opler 1965:312). Figures of horses and riders, on the other hand, are only occasionally associated with ceremonial designs. Perhaps they were either documentary in purpose or served to signify visits to the places where they occur.

10

Concluding Remarks

Many rock art styles can be identified in the rock drawings on cliffs and boulders throughout the Southwest. These styles were created by the people of various prehistoric and even historic cultures of the region. Some of the styles consist of little more than simple marks on stone; in others, a well-developed sense of design, both representational and abstract, is apparent.

This survey has viewed southwestern rock art primarily as an archaeological artifact. A question commonly asked about rock art is whether it really is art and to what degree an aesthetic sense is involved in its making. The opinions of investigators vary considerably, depending in part upon the rock art with which they are dealing. Heizer and Clewlow (1973:5), for example, view the Great Basin petroglyphs as a manifestation of "a 'reflex' of the uncertainties of the desert way of life" and explain the simplicity of the designs by saying the designs themselves were probably secondary to the act of making them: "In these terms Great Basin petroglyphs are not properly speaking art, but rather a minimal and wholly practical aspect of compulsive magic." Others (Grant 1967:40; Santayana 1896) believe that, to some degree, the aesthetic plays a role in *all* products of human industry. I am inclined toward the latter point of view, while at the same time noting that apparent artistic self-consciousness may vary considerably between styles or between works within a style. Grant (1967:40) states that if concern for composition, design, and craftsmanship is apparent and if the rock to be decorated is carefully chosen, then we are dealing with a form of art. From the foregoing descriptions and illustrations within this volume, we can see that this is true for many of the petroglyphs and rock paintings in the Southwest. In this sense the aesthetic intent of the prehistoric and early historic artists is readily communicable to the modern viewer. At the same time, the various styles described here are widely divergent and distinct.

The Great Basin Abstract Style, for example, emphasizes the covering of a surface with rambling patterns that are sometimes adapted to the shape of the rock, usually a boulder, being decorated. In such cases the individual element loses its importance in the context of the whole. In contrast, the late Pueblo II–Pueblo III Anasazi in the Kayenta region were concerned with producing individual representational figures, the parts of which were abstracted into pleasing, crisp, usually solid patterns. These might be arranged in striking groups, and the solidly pecked areas contrast effectively with the surrounding untouched rock. The aesthetic emphasis in the Jornada Style is on highly stylized representational figures in which abstract design quality has high priority. Artists of the Barrier Canyon Anthropomorphic Style focused primarily on the emotional impact of their work, which was achieved by a conscious emphasis on certain aspects of the anthropomorphic form. Spectral images were achieved by painting figures with elongate bodies, insignificant limbs or none at all, faces that were featureless except for large eyes, and fantastic headgear.

At the same time, it has been demonstrated that rock art was probably rarely if ever made as an end in itself. Thus this art has been viewed as an expression of the thought systems to which the artists belonged. We have also seen that art styles, once we can identify them, are sensitive indicators of cultural relationships, of systems of communication and exchange, both temporal and geographical. Art is the immediate material expression of certain aspects of the ideographic system of a particular people or culture, their myths, and their interpretation and ordering of their world. The art is one way in which this information is passed down from one generation to the next. Further clues to how people of the past thought and ordered their world are provided by knowledge of how sites were used and how they were related to other activities.

The art styles and, by extension, the ideologies of the Southwest were remarkably diverse. A number of different styles have been described from the Archaic Period alone. In the horticultural period between A.D. 1 (or slightly before) and A.D. 1300, which embraces the Hohokam, Mogollon,

Anasazi, and Fremont cultures, regionalism prevailed in the art styles and presumably also in ideological systems. Understanding and interpreting of these systems are attempted primarily through ethnographic comparisons drawn from the art and ideology of Mexico and the Pueblo Southwest. Such comparisons have proved to be particularly useful as aids to interpreting the art of the Mimbres and Jornada Mogollon. Rock art of the Pueblo world after 1300 and of the Navajo and Apache after about 1700 is amenable to relatively detailed interpretation through comparison with the ideological systems of these cultures as they now exist.

Work in the ideational dimension, that is, interpretation of the content, has really just begun in this field of study, but as it progresses one is astounded by the significance and orderliness of any design or set of images. The insights provided by Peter Furst on Mexican iconography (1972, 1974a, 1974b) and by Alexander Marshak's (1975) research on the art of Paleolithic Europe caution against simplistic interpretations of prehistoric art remains of any age or place.

More intensive studies are needed along these lines. In conjunction with more interpretive information on the content of any art style, other kinds of information need to be obtained. Fieldwork describing intrastyle differences in content between sites and how specific kinds of sites correlate spatially with other cultural remains and topographic features is essential to understanding how the rock art functioned in its overall context.

Finally, I should point out that what remains on the rocks may be in some cases only the final fragments of a prehistoric art complex (Brody 1977, personal communication). Ceremonial sites, as many of these are believed to be, may have been viewed originally in a ritual context in which other art objects, now gone, were present and at which costumed participants presided in ceremonies. At the same time, rock art, unlike the portable artifacts displayed in museums, enables us to view prehistoric art in its original, often dramatic, settings, In this it is unique.

References

AIKENS, C. MELVIN

1967 "Plains Relationships of the Fremont Culture: A Hypothesis," *American Antiquity* 32:198–209.

1972 "Fremont Culture: Restatement of Some Problems," *American Antiquity* 37:61–66.

AMBLER, JOHN RICHARD

1966 "Caldwell Village and Fremont Prehistory" (Ph.D. diss., University of Colorado, Boulder).

1969 "The Temporal Span of the Fremont," *Southwestern Lore* 34:107–17.

1970 "Just What is Fremont?" Paper presented at the Fremont Culture Symposium, Thirty-fifth Annual Meeting, Society for American Archaeology, Mexico City.

AMBLER, JOHN RICHARD, ALEXANDER J. LINDSAY, JR., AND MARY ANNE STEIN

1964 *Survey and Excavation on Cummings Mesa, Arizona and Utah, 1960–61,* Museum of Northern Arizona Bulletin 39 (Glen Canyon Series no. 5) (Flagstaff).

ANATI, EMMANUEL

1970 "The Rock Engravings of Dahthami Wells in Central Arabia," in *Bolletino del Centro Camuno di Studi Preistorici,* vol. 5, pp. 99–158 (Capo di Ponte, Italy).

ANDERSON, FRANK G.

1955 "The Pueblo Kachina Cult: A Historical Reconstruction," *Southwestern Journal of Anthropology* 11:404–19.

ANDERSON, KEITH

1971 "Excavations at Betatakin and Keet Seel," *The Kiva* 37:1–29.

ANTON, FERDINAND

1969 *Ancient Mexican Art* (London: Thames and Hudson).

BAHTI, MARK

1970 "A Cache at Huerfano Butte," *The Kiva* 36:17–22.

BARTLETT, KATHARINE

1932 "Why the Navajos Came to Arizona," *Museum Notes* 5:29–32 (Flagstaff).

BAUMHOFF, M. A., R. F. HEIZER, AND A. B. ELSASSER

1958 *Lagomarsino Petroglyph Group (Site 26-St-1) near Virginia City, Nevada,* University of California Archaeological Survey Report, no. 43, Part II (Berkeley).

BEAGLEHOLE, ERNEST

1936 *Hopi Hunting and Hunting Ritual,* Yale University Publications in Anthropology, no. 4 (New Haven).

BEALS, RALPH L.

1944 "Relations between Mesoamerica and the Southwest, in *El Norte de México y el Sur de los Estados Unidos,* Tercera Reunión de Mesa Redonda sobre Problemas Antropológicas de México y Centro América, Sociedad Mexicana de Antropología (Mexico City).

347

BECKWITH, FRANK

1931 "Some Interesting Pictographs in Nine Mile Canyon, Utah," *El Palacio* 31:216–22.

BILBO, MICHAEL J., AND KAY SUTHERLAND

1975 "Pine Springs Canyon Pictograph Site in Guadalupe Mountain National Park," *The Artifact* 13:52–56 (El Paso Archaeological Society).

BINFORD, LEWIS R.

1962 "Archaeology as Anthropology," *American Antiquity* 28:217–25.

BOHRER, VORSILA L.

1970 "Ethnobotanical Aspects of Snaketown, a Hohokam Village in Southern Arizona," *American Antiquity* 35:413–30.

BOLTON, HERBERT EUGENE

1930 *Spanish Exploration in the Southwest 1542–1706* (New York: Charles Scribner's Sons).

BOWEN, THOMAS G.

1972 "A Survey and Re-evaluation of the Trincheras Culture, Sonora, Mexico," unpublished manuscript, Department of Anthropology, University of Arizona (Tucson).

1974 "The Trincheras Culture," paper presented at La Reunión sobre Antropología e Historia del Noreste (Hermosillo, Mexico).

BRAND, DONALD D., FLORENCE M. HAWLEY, AND FRANK C. HIBBEN

1937 *Tseh So, A Small House Ruin, Chaco Canyon, New Mexico*, University of New Mexico Bulletin no. 308, Anthropology Series, vol. 2, no. 2 (Albuquerque).

BREUIL, H.

1952 *Four Hundred Centuries of Cave Art*, Centre d'Etudes et de Documentation Préhistoriques, Montinacs (Dordogne).

BREW, J. O.

1943 "On the Pueblo IV and on the Katchina-Tlaloc Relations," in *El Norte de Mexico y el Sur de los Estados Unidos*, Tercera Reunión de Mesa Redonda sobre Problemas Antropológicas de México y Centro América, Sociedad Mexicana de Antropología (Mexico City).

BRITT, CLAUDE, JR.

1973 "Early Navajo Astronomical Pictographs in Canyon de Chelly, Northeastern Arizona, USA," paper presented to the American Association for the Advancement of Science (Mexico City).

BRODY, J. J.

1977 *Mimbres Painted Pottery* (Albuquerque: University of New Mexico Press, School of American Research Southwest Indian Arts Series).

BROOK, VERNON RALPH

1971 "Some Hypotheses about Prehistoric Settlement in the Tularosa-Hueco Bolson between A.D. 1250–1350," in *Transactions of the Sixth Regional Archeological Symposium for Southeastern New Mexico and Western Texas*, pp. 63–82 (El Paso Archaeological Society).

BRUGGE, DAVID M.

1967 "Revised Dates for Navajo Hogans near Canyon de Chelly," *American Antiquity* 32:396–98.

BUNZEL, RUTH L.

1932 "Zuni Katcinas: An Analytical Study," in *Forty-seventh Annual Report of the Bureau of American Ethnology, 1929–1930*, pp. 837–1086 (Washington, D.C.: Government Printing Office).

BURTON, ROBERT JORDAN

1971 "The Pictographs and Petroglyphs of Dinosaur National Monument" (Master's thesis, University of Colorado, Boulder).

CAIN, H. T.

1950 *Petroglyphs of Central Washington* (Seattle: University of Washington Press).

CARLSON, ROY L.

1965 *Eighteenth Century Navajo Fortresses of the Gobernador District,* The Earl Morris Papers, no. 2, University of Colorado Studies, Series in Anthropology, no. 10 (Boulder).

CASO, ALFONSO

1958 *The Aztecs: People of the Sun,* trans. Lowell Dunham (Norman: University of Oklahoma Press).

CASTAÑEDA, CARLOS

1974 *Tales of Power* (New York: Simon and Schuster).

CASTLETON, KENNETH

1978 *Petroglyphs and Pictographs of Utah* (Salt Lake City: University of Utah and Utah Museum of Natural History).

CHAPMAN, KENNETH

1938 "The Cave Pictographs of the Rito de los Frijoles," in *Pajarito Plateau and its Ancient People,* by Edgar L. Hewett (Albuquerque: University of New Mexico Press).

CHRISTENSEN, ERWIN O.

1955 *Primitive Art* (New York: Viking Press).

CLARK, JOHN W., JR.

1974 *Rock Art of the Guadalupe Mountains National Park Area.* Bulletin of the Texas Archaeological Society, vol. 45 (Austin).

CLARK, LA VERNE HARRELL

1966 *They Sang for Horses* (Tucson: University of Arizona Press).

COLTON, HAROLD S.

1946a *The Sinagua,* Museum of Northern Arizona Bulletin no. 22 (Flagstaff).

1946b "Fools Names like Fools Faces—" *Plateau* 19:1–8.

COSGROVE, C. B.

1947 *Caves of the Upper Gila and Hueco Areas in New Mexico and Texas,* Papers of the Peabody Museum of Archaeology and Ethnology, vol. 24, no. 2 (Cambridge, Mass.).

COSGROVE, H. S., AND C. B. COSGROVE

1932 *The Swarts Ruin: A Typical Mimbres Site in Southwestern New Mexico,* Papers of the Peabody Museum of Archaeology and Ethnology, vol. 15, no. 1 (Cambridge, Mass.).

CRESSMAN, L. S.

1937 *Petroglyphs of Oregon,* University of Oregon Monographs, Studies in Anthropology, no. 2 (Eugene).

CRIMMINS, M. L.

1929 "An Archaeological Survey of the El Paso District," *Texas Archaeological and Paleontological Society Bulletin* 1:36–42.

CROSBY, HARRY

1975 *The Cave Paintings of Baja California* (Salt Lake City: Copley Books, Publishers Press).

CULWICK, A. T.

1931 "Ritual Use of Rock Paintings at Bahi, Tanganyika Territory," *Man* 31:33–36.

CUNNISON, I. N.

1951 *History of the Lapuala,* Rhodes-Livingston Papers, no. 21 (n.p.).

DANIELS, HELEN SLOAN

1954 "Pictographs," Appendix A in *Basketmaker II Sites near Durango, Colorado,* by Earl H. Morris and Robert F. Burgh. Carnegie Institution of Washington Publication 604 (Washington, D.C.).

DAVIS, EMMA LOU

1963 "The Desert Culture of the Western Great Basin: A Lifeway of Seasonal Transhumance," *American Antiquity* 29:202–12.

DAVIS, JOHN V., AND KAY S. TONESS

1974 *A Rock Art Inventory at Hueco Tanks State Park, Texas,* El Paso Archaeological Society Special Report, no. 12 (El Paso).

DAVIS, LESLIE

1968 "Recent Excavations at Hot Well Site (EPAS-3)," in *Transactions of the Third Regional Symposium for Southeastern New Mexico and Western Texas,* pp. 23–32 (Lubbock: South Plains Archeological Society).

DEAN, JEFFREY S.

1970 "Aspects of Tsegi Phase Social Organization: A Trial Reconstruction," in *Reconstructing Prehistoric Pueblo Societies,* ed. William A. Longacre (Albuquerque: University of New Mexico Press, School of American Research Advanced Seminar Series).

DE HARPORT, DAVID L.

1951 "An Archaeological Survey of Cañon de Chelly: Preliminary Report of the Field Sessions of 1948, 1949, and 1950," *El Palacio* 58:35–48.

1959 "An Archaeological Survey of Cañon de Chelly, Northeastern Arizona: A Puebloan Community Through Time," (Ph.D. diss., Harvard University, Cambridge, Mass.).

DE JOHLY, H. AND HATRALI B'YASH

1958 *Red Ant Myth and Shooting Chant,* recorded and retold by Mary C. Wheelwright, Museum of Navajo Ceremonial Art Bulletin, Series no. 7 (Santa Fe).

DEWDNEY, SELWYN

1959 "Stone Age Art in the Canadian Shield," *Canadian Art* 16:164–67.

DEWDNEY, SELWYN, AND KENNETH E. KIDD

1962 *Indian Rock Paintings of the Great Lakes* (Toronto: University of Toronto Press).

DICK, HERBERT W.

1965 *Bat Cave,* School of American Research Monograph no. 27 (Santa Fe).

DI PESO, CHARLES C.

1966 "Archaeology and Ethnohistory of the Northern Sierra," in *Handbook of Middle American Indians,* vol. 4, ed. R. Wauchope (Austin: University of Texas Press).

1968 "Casas Grandes and the Gran Chichimeca," *El Palacio* 75:45–61.

1974 *Casas Grandes: A Fallen Trading Center of the Gran Chichimeca,* 3 vols. (Flagstaff: Northland Press).

DOUGLAS, CHARLES L.

1972 "Analysis of Faunal Remains from Black Mesa, 1968–1970 Excavations," Appendix 3, in *Black Mesa: Archaeological Investigations on Black Mesa, the 1969–1970 Seasons,* ed. George J. Gumerman, Deborah Westfall, and Carol S. Weed. Prescott Studies in Anthropology, no. 4 (Prescott).

DOYEL, DAVID E.

1977 "Rillito and Rincon Period Settlement Systems in the Middle Santa Cruz River Valley: Alternative Models," *The Kiva* 43:93–110.

DOZIER, EDWARD P.

1970 *The Pueblo Indians of North America* (New York: Holt, Rinehart and Winston).

DURHAM, DOROTHY
1955   "Petroglyphs at Mesa de los Padillas," *El Palacio* 62:3–17.
DUTTON, BERTHA P.
1963   *Sun Father's Way: The Kiva Murals of Kuaua* (Albuquerque: University of New Mexico Press, School of American Research, Museum of New Mexico).
EDDY, FRANK W.
1961   *Excavations at Los Pinos Phase Sites in the Navajo Reservoir District,* Museum of New Mexico Papers in Anthropology, no. 4 (Santa Fe).
1966   *Prehistory in the Navajo Reservoir District,* Parts 1 and 2, Museum of New Mexico Papers in Anthropology, no. 15 (Santa Fe).
EGGAN, FRED, AND WARREN L. D'AZEVEDO
1966   "Introduction," in *The Current Status of Anthropological Research in the Great Basin: 1964,* ed. Warren L. D'Azevedo, William A. Davis, Don D. Fowler, and Wayne Suttles (Reno: Desert Research Institute).
ELIADE, MIRCEA
1964   *Shamanism: Archaic Techniques of Ecstasy,* Bollingen Series 76 (Princeton: Princeton University Press).
ELKIN. A. P.
1938   "Foreword," in *Australian Aboriginal Decorative Art,* by F. D. McCarthy (Sydney: Australian Museum).
ELLIS, FLORENCE HAWLEY, AND LAURENS HAMMACK
1968   "The Inner Sanctum of Feather Cave, A Mogollon Sun and Earth Shrine Linking Mexico and the Southwest," *American Antiquity* 33:25–44.
FERG, ALAN
1974   "Petroglyphs of the Silver Creek–Five Mile Draw Confluence Snowflake, Arizona," unpublished manuscript, Department of Anthropology, University of Arizona (Tucson).
FEWKES, JESSE WALTER
1891   "A Few Summer Ceremonials at Zuni Pueblo," *A Journal of American Ethnology and Archaeology,* vol. 1 (Cambridge, Mass.: Hougton, Mifflin and Co.).
1897a   "Tusayan Katcinas," in *Fifteenth Annual Report of the Bureau of American Ethnology,* pp. 245–313 (Washington, D.C.: Government Printing Office).
1897b   "Tusayan Totemic Signatures," *American Anthropologist* 10:1–11 (old series).
1903a   "Hopi Katcinas Drawn by Native Artists," in *Twenty-first Annual Report of the Bureau of American Ethnology,* pp. 1–126 (Washington, D.C.: Government Printing Office).
1903b   "Prehistoric Porto Rican Pictographs," *American Anthropologist* 5:441–67.
1906   "Hopi Shrines near the East Mesa, Arizona," *American Anthropologist* 8:346–75.
1912   "Casa Grande, Arizona," in *Twenty-eighth Annual Report of the Bureau of American Ethnology,* pp. 25–179 (Washington, D.C.: Government Printing Office).
1921   "Field-Work on the Mesa Verde National Park" in *Explorations and Field-Work of the Smithsonian Institution in 1920,* Smithsonian Miscellaneous Collections, vol. 72, no. 6, pp. 75–94 (Washington, D.C.).
1973   *Designs on Prehistoric Hopi Pottery* (New York: Dover Publications) (reprinted from the *Thirty-third Annual Report of the Bureau of American Ethnology,* 1919, Washington, D.C.: Government Printing Office).
FONTANA, BERNARD L., J. CAMERON GREENLEAF, AND DONNELLY D. CASSIDY
1959   "A Fortified Arizona Mountain," *The Kiva* 25:41–52.
FORBES, J. D.
1960   *Apache, Navajo, and Spaniard* (Norman: University of Oklahoma Press).

FORDE, C. D.

1931 "Hopi Agriculture and Land Ownership," *Royal Anthropological Institute* 61:357–405.

FOSBROKE, H. A., AND P. I. MAREALLE

1952 "The Engraved Rocks of Kilimanjaro," *Man* 52:244–63.

FOSTER, GENE

1954 "Petrographic Art in Glen Canyon," *Plateau* 27:6–18.

FRASSETO, M. F.

1960 "A Preliminary Report on Petroglyphs in Puerto Rico," *American Antiquity* 25:381–91.

FROBENIUS, LEO, AND DOUGLAS C. FOX

1937 *Prehistoric Rock Pictures in Europe and Africa* (New York: The Museum of Modern Art).

FURST, PETER T.

1972 "The Olmec Were-Jaguar Motif in the Light of Ethnographic Reality," in *Contemporary Archaeology*, ed. Mark P. Leone (Carbondale: Southern Illinois University Press).

1974a "Ethnographic Analogy in the Interpretation of West Mexican Art," in *The Archaeology of West Mexico*, ed. Betty Bell (Ajijic, Jalisco: West Mexican Society for Advanced Study).

1974b "Hallucinogens in Precolumbian Art," in *Art and Environment in Native America*, ed. Mary Elizabeth King and Idris R. Traylor, Jr., Special Publications, no. 7, The Museum of Texas Tech, Texas Tech University (Lubbock).

GARDNER, G. A.

1931 *Rock Paintings in Northwest Córdoba, Argentina* (Oxford: Oxford University Press).

GARDNER, W. A.

1940 "Place of the Gods," *Natural History* 45:40–43, 54–55.

GEBHARD, DAVID

1951 "The Petroglyphs of Wyoming: A Preliminary Paper," *El Palacio* 58:67–81.

1957 "Pictographs in the Sierra Blanca Mountains," *El Palacio* 64:215–21.

1958 "Hidden Lake Pictographs," *El Palacio* 65:146–50.

1960 *Prehistoric Paintings of the Diablo Region: A Preliminary Report*, Publications in Art and Science, no. 3 (Roswell: Roswell Museum and Art Center).

1962 "Prehistoric Rock Drawings at Painted Grotto, New Mexico," *El Palacio* 69:218–23.

1969 *The Rock Art of Dinwoody, Wyoming*, Catalogue for the exhibition at the Art Galleries, University of California, Santa Barbara.

GOLDMAN, IRVING

1963 *The Cubeo: Indians of the Norhtwest Amazon*, Illinois Studies in Anthropology, no. 2 (Urbana).

GOODALL, E., C. K. COOKE, AND J. D. CLARK

1959 *Prehistoric Rock Art of the Federation of Rhodesia and Nyasaland*, National Public Trust, Rhodesia and Nyasaland.

GRANT, CAMPBELL

1965 *The Rock Paintings of the Chumash: A Study of a California Indian Culture* (Berkeley: University of California Press).

1967 *Rock Art of the American Indian* (New York: Thomas Y. Crowell).

1968 *Rock Drawings of the Coso Range*, Maturango Museum Publications, no. 4 (China Lake, Ca.).

1974 *Rock Art of Baja California* (Los Angeles: Dawson's Book Shop).

1978 *Canyon de Chelly* (Tucson: University of Arizona Press).

GREEN, JOHN W.

1967 "Rock Art of the El Paso Southwest: Fusselman Canyon Petroglyph Site EPAS-44," *The Artifact* 5:1–19.

GUERNSEY, SAMUEL JAMES, AND ALFRED VINCENT KIDDER

1921 *Basket-Maker Caves of Northeastern Arizona: Report on the Explorations, 1916–1917*, Papers of the Peabody Museum of Archaeology and Ethnology, vol. 8, no. 2 (Cambridge, Mass.).

GUMERMAN, GEORGE J., AND S. ALAN SKINNER

1968 "A Synthesis of the Prehistory of the Central Little Colorado Valley, Arizona," *American Antiquity* 33:185–99.

GUNNERSON, DOLORES A.

1956 "The Southern Athabascans: Their Arrival in the Southwest," *El Palacio* 63:346–65.

1974 *The Jicarilla Apaches: A Study in Survival* (Dekalb: Northern Illinois University Press).

GUNNERSON, JAMES H.

1957 *An Archeological Survey of the Fremont Area*, University of Utah Anthropological Papers, no. 28 (Salt Lake City).

1969 *The Fremont Culture: A Study in Culture Dynamics on the Northern Anasazi Frontier*, Papers of the Peabody Museum of Archaeology and Ethnology, vol. 59, no. 2 (Cambridge, Mass.).

GUNNERSON, JAMES H., AND DOLORES A. GUNNERSON

1971 "Apachean Culture: A Study in Unity and Diversity," in *Apachean Culture History and Ethnology*, ed. Keith H. Basso and Morris E. Opler. Anthropological Papers of the University of Arizona, no. 21 (Tucson).

HAILE, BERARD

1947 *Starlore Among the Navaho* (Santa Fe: Museum of Navajo Ceremonial Art).

HAMMOND, GEORGE P., AND AGAPITO REY

1927 "The Rodríguez Expedition to New Mexico, 1581–1582 (Gallegos' Relation)" *New Mexico Historical Review* 2:239–68, 334–62.

1929 *Expedition into New Mexico Made by Antonio de Espejo 1582–1583, As Revealed in the Journal of Diego Pérez de Luxán, a Member of the Party* (Los Angeles: Quivira Society).

1940 *Narratives of the Coronado Expedition 1540–1542* (Albuquerque: University of New Mexico Press).

HARTE, N. A.

1960 *Panorama of Panama Petroglyphs, Preliminary Report on Petroglyphs of the Republic of Panama* (Curundu, Canal Zone: Private Printing).

HAURY, EMIL W.

1934 *The Canyon Creek Ruin and Cliff Dwellings of the Sierra Ancha*, Medallion Papers, no. 14 (Globe, Ariz.: Gila Pueblo).

1936 *The Mogollon Culture of Southwestern New Mexico*, Medallion Papers, no. 20 (Globe, Ariz.: Gila Pueblo).

1945a *The Excavation of Los Muertos and Neighboring Ruins in the Salt River Valley, Southern Arizona*, Papers of the Peabody Museum of Archaeology and Ethnology, vol. 24, no. 1 (Cambridge, Mass.).

1945b *Painted Cave, Northeastern Arizona*, Amerind Foundation Publication, no. 3 (Dragoon, Ariz.).

1950 *The Stratigraphy and Archaeology of Ventana Cave, Arizona* (Tucson: University of Arizona Press).

1976 *The Hohokam, Desert Farmers and Craftsmen* (Tucson: University of Arizona Press).

HAWLEY, FLORENCE

1937   "Kokopelli, of the Prehistoric Southwestern Pueblo Pantheon," *American Anthropologist* 39:644–46.

HAYDEN, JULIAN D.

1967   "A Summary Prehistory and History of the Sierra Pinacate, Sonora," *American Antiquity* 32:335–44.

1972   "Hohokam Petroglyphs of the Sierra Pinacate, Sonora, and the Hohokam Shell Expeditions," *The Kiva* 37:74–83.

HAYES, ALDEN C.

1964   *The Archeological Survey of Wetherill Mesa, Mesa Verde National Park—Colorado*, Archeological Research Series, no. 7-A, National Park Service (Washington, D.C.).

HAYES, ALDEN C., AND JAMES A. LANCASTER

1975   *Badger House Community*, Publications in Archeology 7E, Wetherill Mesa Studies, National Park Service (Washington, D.C.).

HEDGES, KEN

1973   "Rock Art in Southern California," *Pacific Coast Archaeological Society Quarterly* 9:1–28.

1975   "Southern California Rock Art as Shamanic Art," paper presented at the Second Rock Art Symposium, El Paso, Texas.

HEIZER, ROBERT F., AND MARTIN A. BAUMHOFF

1959   "Great Basin Petroglyphs and Prehistoric Game Trails," *Science* 129:904–5.

1962   *Prehistoric Rock Art of Nevada and Eastern California* (Berkeley: University of California Press).

HEIZER, ROBERT F., AND C. W. CLEWLOW, JR.

1973   *Prehistoric Rock Art of California*, vols. 1 and 2 (Ramona, Calif.: Ballena Press).

HESTER, JAMES J.

1962   *Early Navajo Migrations and Acculturation in the Southwest*, Museum of New Mexico Papers in Anthropology, no. 6 (Santa Fe).

1971   "Navajo Culture Change: From 1550 to 1960 and Beyond," in *Apachean Culture History and Ethnology*, ed. Keith H. Basso and Morris E. Opler. Anthropological Papers of the University of Arizona, no. 21 (Tucson).

HEWETT, EDGAR LEE

1938   *Pajarito Plateau and its Ancient People* (Albuquerque: University of New Mexico Press).

HEYDEN, DORIS

1975   "An Interpretation of the Cave Pyramid Underneath the Pyramid of the Sun in Teotihuacan, Mexico," *American Antiquity* 40:131–47.

HIBBEN, FRANK C.

1960   "Prehispanic Paintings at Pottery Mound," *Archaeology* 13:267–74.

1966   "A Possible Pyramidal Structure and Other Mexican Influences at Pottery Mound, New Mexico," *American Antiquity* 31:522–29.

1975   *Kiva Art of the Anasazi at Pottery Mound* (Las Vegas, Nev.: KC Publications).

HILL, JAMES N.

1970   *Broken K Pueblo: Prehistoric Social Organization in the American Southwest*, Anthropological Papers of the University of Arizona, no. 18 (Tucson).

HILL, W. W.

1940   "Some Navaho Culture Changes during Two Centuries," Smithsonian Miscellaneous Collection, vol. 100, pp. 395–416 (Washington, D.C.).

HINTON, THOMAS B.

1955   "A Survey of Archaeological Sites in the Altar Valley, Sonora," *The Kiva* 21:1–12.

HODGE, F. W., G. P. HAMMOND, AND AGAPITO REY

1945 *Fray Alonso de Benavides' Revised Memorial of 1634* (Albuquerque: University of New Mexico Press).

HOUGH, WALTER

1907 *Antiquities of the Upper Gila and Salt River Valleys in Arizona and New Mexico,* Bureau of American Ethnology Bulletin no. 35 (Washington, D.C.: Government Printing Office).

HOWARD, E. B.

1932 "Caves along the Slopes of the Guadalupe Mountains," *Texas Archaeological and Paleontological Society* 4:7–19.

HUCKERBY, T.

1914 "Petroglyphs of St Vincent, British West Indies," *American Anthropologist* 16:238–44.

IRWIN-WILLIAMS, CYNTHIA

1967 "Picosa: The Elementary Southwestern Culture," *American Antiquity* 32:441–57.

1973 *The Oshara Tradition: Origins of Anasazi Culture,* Eastern New Mexico University Contributions in Anthropology, vol. 5, no. 1 (Portales).

JACKSON, A. T.

1938 *Picture-Writing of Texas Indians,* University of Texas Anthropological Papers, vol. 2 (Austin).

JAEGER, EDMUND C.

1957 *The North American Deserts* (Stanford: Stanford University Press).

JAMES, CHARLES D. III, AND HOWARD N. DAVIDSON

1975 "Style Changes of the Horse Motif in Navajo Rock Art, A Preliminary Analysis," paper presented at the Second Rock Art Symposium, El Paso, Texas.

JENNINGS, JESSE D.

1953 "Danger Cave: A Progress Summary," *El Palacio* 60:179–213.

JERNIGAN, E. WESLEY

1978 *Jewelry of the Prehistoric Southwest* (Albuquerque: University of New Mexico Press, School of American Research Southwest Indian Arts Series).

JOHNSON, ALFRED E.

1963 "The Trincheras Culture of Northern Sonora," *American Antiquity* 29:174–86.

JUDD, NEIL M.

1926 *Archeological Observations North of the Rio Colorado,* Bureau of American Ethnology Bulletin no. 82 (Washington, D.C.: Government Printing Office).

1954 *The Material Culture of Pueblo Bonito,* Smithsonian Miscellaneous Collections, vol. 124, whole volume (Washington, D.C.)

KABOTIE, FRED

1949 *Designs from the Ancient Mimbreños with a Hopi Interpretation* (San Francisco: Grabhorn Press).

KEARNS, TIMOTHY M.

1973 "Abiotic Resources," in *An Archaeological Survey of the Orme Reservoir,* assembled by Veletta Canouts and Mark Grady. Manuscript prepared for the U.S. Bureau of Reclamation, Central Arizona Project, on file at Arizona State Museum, University of Arizona (Tucson).

KELLER, DONALD R., RICHARD V. AHLSTROM, AND DANA HARTMAN

1974 "Final Report for Surface Cleanup of Cultural Sites in Grand Gulch, Archaeological Investigation, Bureau of Land Management, Denver Service Center and Monticello District, San Juan County Utah, Contract No. 52500-CT4-558," unpublished manuscript.

KELLEY, J. CHARLES

1951 "A Bravo Valley Aspect Component of the Lower Rio Conchos Valley, Chihuahua, Mexico," *American Antiquity* 32:114–19.

1966 "Mesoamerica and the Southwestern United States," in *Handbook of Middle American Indians*, vol. 4, ed. Robert Wauchope (Austin: University of Texas Press).

KEUR, DOROTHY

1941 *Big Bead Mesa: An Archaeological Study of Navaho Acculturation 1745–1812*, Memoirs of the Society for American Archaeology, no. 1 (Menasha, Wis.).

KIDDER, ALFRED VINCENT

1927 "Southwestern Archaeological Conference," *Science* 66:489–91.

1932 *The Artifacts of Pecos*, Papers of the Southwestern Expedition, no. 6, Phillips Academy (New Haven: Yale University Press).

KIDDER, ALFRED VINCENT, AND SAMUEL J. GUERNSEY

1919 *Archeological Explorations in Northeastern Arizona*, Bureau of American Ethnology Bulletin no. 65 (Washington, D.C.: Government Printing Office).

KLUCKHOHN, CLYDE

1939 "Subsistence Remains," in *Preliminary Report on the 1937 Excavations, Bc 50–51, Chaco Canyon, New Mexico*, ed. Clyde Kluckhohn and Paul Reiter, University of New Mexico Bulletin 345 (Albuquerque).

KLUCKHOHN, CLYDE, AND DOROTHEA LEIGHTON

1956 *The Navajo* (Cambridge, Mass.: Harvard University Press).

KRONE, MILTON F.

1974 "Little Peaks Site Report," *The Artifact*, 12:9–25.

KSICA, M.

1960 *Rock Pictures in Central Asia*, Science and Life, no. 3 (Brno, Czechoslovakia).

LAMBERT, MARJORIE F.

1957 "A Rare Stone Humpbacked Figurine from Pecos Pueblo, New Mexico," *El Palacio* 64:93–107.

1967 "A Kokopelli Effigy Pitcher from Northwestern New Mexico," *American Antiquity* 32:398–401.

LAMBERT, MARJORIE F., AND J. RICHARD AMBLER

1965 *A Survey and Excavation of Caves in Hidalgo County, New Mexico*, School of American Research Monograph no. 25 (Santa Fe).

LANG, RICHARD W.

1976 "An Archaeological Survey of the Upper San Cristobal Arroyo Drainage, in the Galisteo Basin, Santa Fe County, New Mexico," unpublished manuscript, School of American Research (Santa Fe).

LARSON, STEPHEN M.

1972 "The Tumamoc Hill Site near Tucson, Arizona," *The Kiva* 38:95–101.

LE BLANC, STEVEN A.

1975 *Mimbres Archeological Center: Preliminary Report of the First Season of Excavation, 1974* (Los Angeles: University of California Institute of Archaeology).

1976 *Mimbres Archeological Center: Preliminary Report on the Second Season of Excavation, 1975* (Los Angeles: University of California Institute of Archaeology).

LEHMER, DONALD J.

1948 *The Jornada Branch of the Mogollon*, University of Arizona Bulletin, vol. 19, no. 2 (Social Science Bulletin 17) (Tucson).

LIPE, WILLIAM D.

1960 *1958 Excavations, Glen Canyon Area*, University of Utah Anthropological Papers, no. 44 (Glen Canyon Series no. 11) (Salt Lake City).

1970 "Anasazi Communities in the Red Rock Plateau," in *Reconstructing Prehistoric Pueblo Societies*, ed. William A. Longacre (Albuquerque: University of New Mexico Press, School of American Research Advanced Seminar Series).

LIPE, WILLIAM D., FLOYD W. SHARROCK, DAVID S. DIBBLE, AND
KEITH M. ANDERSON

1960 *1959 Excavations, Glen Canyon Area*, University of Utah Anthropological Papers, no. 49 (Glen Canyon Series no. 13) (Salt Lake City).

LISTER, ROBERT H.

1958 *Archaeological Excavations in the Northern Sierra Madre Occidental, Chihuahua and Sonora, Mexico*, University of Colorado Studies, Series in Anthropology, no. 7 (Boulder).

1964 *Contributions to Mesa Verde Archaeology: I, Site 499, Mesa Verde National Park, Colorado*, University of Colorado Studies, Series in Anthropology, no. 9 (Boulder).

1966 *Contributions to Mesa Verde Archaeology: III, Site 866, and the Cultural Sequence at Four Villages in the Far View Group, Mesa Verde National Park, Colorado*, University of Colorado Studies, Series in Anthropology, no. 12 (Boulder).

LOMMEL, ANDREAS

1976 *Rock Paintings of the Australian North-West* (Graz, Austria: Akademische Druck-und Verlagsanstalt).

LONG, PAUL, JR.

1966 *Archaeological Excavations in Lower Glen Canyon, Utah, 1959–1960*, Museum of Northern Arizona Bulletin no. 42 (Glen Canyon Series no. 7) (Flagstaff).

LONGACRE, WILLIAM A.

1964 "Archaeology as Anthropology: A Case Study," *Science* 144:1454–55.

LUMHOLTZ, CARL

1900 *Symbolism of the Huichol Indians*, Memoirs of the American Museum of Natural History, vol. 3, no. 1 (New York).

1912 *New Trails in Mexico* (New York: Charles Scribner's Sons).

MALLERY, GARRICK

1886 "Pictographs of the North American Indians," in *Fourth Annual Report of the Bureau of American Ethnology* (Washington, D.C.: Government Printing Office).

1893 "Picture-Writing of the American Indians," in *Tenth Annual Report of the Bureau of American Ethnology* (Washington, D.C.: Government Printing Office).

MARSHACK, ALEXANDER

1975 "Exploring the Mind of Ice Age Man," *National Geographic*, 147:64–89.

MARSHALL, MICHAEL P.

1973 "Background Information on the Jornada Culture Area," in *Technical Manual, 1973 Survey of the Tularosa Basin*, pp. 49–119 (Three Rivers: Human Systems Research, Inc.).

MARTIN, PAUL S.

1943 *The SU Site: Excavations at a Mogollon Village Western New Mexico, Second Season 1941*, Field Museum of Natural History, Anthropological Series, vol. 32, no. 1 (Chicago).

MARTIN, PAUL S., AND FRED PLOG

1973 *The Archaeology of Arizona: A Study of the Southwest Region* (Garden City, N.Y.: Doubleday and Natural History Press).

MARTIN, PAUL S., JOHN B. RINALDO, AND ERNST ANTEVS

1949 "Cochise and Mogollon Sites: Pine Lawn Valley, Western New Mexico," *Fieldiana: Anthropology* 38:1–232.

MARTIN, PAUL S., JOHN B. RINALDO, ELAINE BLUHM, HUGH C. CUTLER, AND ROGER GRANGE, JR.

1952   "Mogollon Cultural Continuity and Change: The Stratigraphic Analysis of Tularosa and Cordova Caves," *Fieldiana: Anthropology* 40:1–528.

MARTIN, PAUL S., JOHN B. RINALDO, AND MARJORIE KELLEY

1940   *The SU Site: Excavations at a Mogollon Village Western New Mexico, 1939*, Field Museum of Natural History, Anthropological Series, vol. 32, no. 1 (Chicago).

MARTINEAU, LA VAN

1973   *The Rocks Begin to Speak* (Las Vegas, Nev.: KC Publications).

MARWITT, JOHN P.

1970   *Median Village and Fremont Culture Regional Variation*, University of Utah Anthropological Papers, no. 95 (Salt Lake City).

MATTHEWS, WASHINGTON

1883   "A Part of Navajo's Mythology," *American Antiquarian* 5:207–24.

1887   "The Mountain Chant: A Navajo Ceremony," in *Fifth Annual Report of the Bureau of American Ethnology, 1883–1884* (Washington, D.C.: Government Printing Office).

1902   *The Night Chant, a Navaho Ceremony*, Memoirs of the American Museum of Natural History, vol. 6 (New York).

MC CARTHY, F. C.

1938   *Australian Aboriginal Decorative Art* (Sydney: Australian Museum).

MC NITT, FRANK

1972   *Navajo Wars* (Albuquerque: University of New Mexico Press).

MEADE, GEORGE R.

1968   *Rock Art North of the Mexican-American Border: An Annotated Bibliography*, Colorado State College Museum Occasional Publications in Anthropology, Archaeology Series, no. 5 (Greely, Colo.).

MEIGHAN, CLEMENT W.

1969   *Indian Art and History, the Testimony of Prehispanic Rock Paintings in Baja California* (Los Angeles: Dawson's Book Shop).

MERA, H. P.

1938   *Reconnaissance and Excavation in Southeastern New Mexico*, American Anthropological Association Memoir no. 51 (Menasha, Wis.).

1940   *Population Changes in The Rio Grande Glaze-Paint Area*, Laboratory of Anthropology Technical Series Bulletin no. 9 (Santa Fe).

MILLS, GEORGE

1959   *Navaho Art and Culture* (Colorado Springs: Taylor Museum).

MOORE, DAVID R.

1971   "Australian Aboriginal Rock Art: Its Relevance to the European Palaeolithic," *Bollettino del Centro Camuno di Studi Preistorici*, vol. 7 (Capo di Ponte, Italy).

MORI, FABRIZIO

1972   *Rock Art of the Tadrart Acadus (Libyan Sahara)* (Graz, Austria: Akademische Druck- und Verlagsanstalt).

MORRIS, EARL H.

1939   *Archeological Studies in the La Plata District, Southwestern Colorado and Northwestern New Mexico*, Carnegie Institution of Washington, Publication 519 (Washington, D.C.).

1951   "Basketmaker III Human Figurines from Northeastern Arizona," *American Antiquity* 17:33–40.

MORRIS, EARL H., AND ROBERT F. BURGH

1954   *Basketmaker II Sites Near Durango, Colorado*, Carnegie Institution of Washington, Publication 604 (Washington, D.C.).

MORSS, NOEL

1931   *The Ancient Culture of the Fremont River in Utah,* Papers of the Peabody Museum of Archaeology and Ethnology, vol. 12, no. 3 (Cambridge, Mass.).

1954   *Clay Figurines of the American Southwest,* Papers of the Peabody Museum of Archaeology and Ethnology, vol. 49, no. 1 (Cambridge, Mass.).

MOUNTJOY, JOSEPH B.

1974a   "San Blas Complex Ecology," in *The Archaeology of West Mexico,* ed. Betty Bell (Ajijic, Jalisco: West Mexican Society for Advanced Study).

1974b   *Some Hypotheses regarding the Petroglyphs of West Mexico,* Mesoamerican Studies, no. 9, University Museum, Southern Illinois University (Carbondale).

NELSON, N. C.

1914   *Pueblo Ruins of the Galisteo Basin, New Mexico,* American Museum of Natural History, Anthropological Papers, vol. 15, Part 1 (New York).

NEWCOMB, FRANC JOHNSON

1964   *Hosteen Klah: Navaho Medicine Man and Sand Painter* (Norman: University of Oklahoma Press).

NEWCOMB, FRANC JOHNSON, AND GLADYS REICHARD

1937   *Sandpaintings of the Navajo Shooting Chant* (New York: J. J. Augustin).

NEWCOMB, W. W., JR., AND FORREST KIRKLAND

1967   *The Rock Art of Texas Indians* (Austin: University of Texas Press).

NICHOLSON, HENRY B.

1966   "Religion in Pre-Hispanic Central Mexico," in *Handbook of Middle American Indians,* vol. 10, ed. Robert Wauchope (Austin: University of Texas Press).

OKLADNIKOV, A. P.

1969   "The Petroglyphs of Siberia," *Scientific American* 221:74–82.

OPLER, M. E.

1965   *An Apache Life-way: The Economic, Social, and Religious Institutions of the Chiricahua Indians* (New York: Cooper Square Publishers).

PAGER, HARALD

1975   *Stone Age Myth and Magic, as Documented in the Rock Paintings of South Africa* (Graz, Austria: Akademische Druck- und Verlagsanstalt).

PARSONS, ELSIE CLEWS

1938   "The Humpbacked Flute Player of the Southwest," *American Anthropologist* 40:337–38.

1939   *Pueblo Indian Religion* (Chicago: University of Chicago Press).

1940   *Taos Tales,* Memoirs of the American Folk-Lore Society, vol. 34 (New York: J. J. Augustin).

PEDERSON, A.

1963   *Las Pinturas Rupestres de La Región del Parque Nacional Nahuel Huapi (Provincia del Neuquén) y sus Posibles Proyecciones Prehistóricas,* Primer Congreso del Area Araucana Argentina Realizado en San Martín de los Andes (Neuquén) del 18 al 24 de Febrero de 1961, tomo 2 (Buenos Aires).

PETERSON, FREDERICK

1961   *Ancient Mexico* (London: George Allen and Unwin).

PILLES, PETER J., JR.

1974   "Petroglyphs of the Little Colorado River Valley, Arizona," unpublished manuscript, Museum of Northern Arizona (Flagstaff).

POLLAK-ELTZ, A. AND H. STRAKA BULL

1975   *Venezuelan Petroglyphs* (Graz, Austria: Akademische Druck- und Verlagsanstalt).

POND, GORDON

1966 "A Painted Kiva Near Winslow, Arizona," *American Antiquity* 31:555–58.

POWELL, J. W.

1883 "Picture Writing," in *Transactions of the Anthropological Society of Washington*, Smithsonian Institution Miscellaneous Collections, vol. 25 (Washington, D.C.).

REAGAN, ALBERT B.

1931 "Ruins and Pictographs in Nine Mile Canyon, Utah," *Transactions of the Illinois State Academy of Science* 24:369–70.

1933 "Indian Pictures in Ashley and Dry Fork Valleys, in Northeastern Utah," *Art and Archaeology* 34:201–5, 210.

1935 "Petroglyphs Show that the Ancients of the Southwest Wore Masks," *American Anthropologist* 37:707–8.

REICHARD, GLADYS A.

1933 *Melanesian Design: A Study of Style in Wood and Tortoiseshell Carving*, vols. 1 and 2 (New York: Columbia University Press).

1950 *Navaho Religion: A Study of Symbolism*, vols. 1 and 2, Bollingen Series 18 (New York: Stratford Press).

REINHART, THEODORE R.

1967 "The Rio Rancho Phase: A Preliminary Report on Early Basketmaker Culture in the Middle Rio Grande Valley, New Mexico," *American Antiquity* 32:458–70.

RENAUD, E. B.

1936 *Pictographs and Petroglyphs of the Western High Plains*, University of Denver Archaeological Survey, 8th report (Denver).

1938a *Petroglyphs of North Central New Mexico*, University of Denver Archaeological Survey, 11th report (Denver).

1938b "The Snake Among the Petroglyphs from North Central New Mexico," *Southwestern Lore* 4:42–47.

1948 "Kokopelli: A Study in Pueblo Mythology," *Southwestern Lore* 14:25–40.

RICHERT, ROLAND

1964 *Excavation of a Portion of the East Ruin, Aztec Ruins National Monument, New Mexico*, Southwestern Monuments Association Technical Series 4 (Globe, Ariz.).

RITTER, DALE W., AND ERIC W. RITTER

1976 "Prehistoric Pictography in North America of Medical Significance," in *Medical Anthropology*, ed. F. X. Grolley, S. J. Harold, and B. Haley (The Hague: Mouton).

ROBERTS, FRANK H. H., JR.

1935 "A Survey of Southwestern Archaeology," *American Anthropologist* 37:1–35.

ROHN, ARTHUR H.

1971 *Mug House, Mesa Verde National Park—Colorado*, Archaeological Research Series no. 7-D, National Park Service (Washington, D.C.).

RUSSELL, FRANK

1908 "The Pima Indians," in *Twenty-sixth Annual Report of the Bureau of American Ethnology* (Washington, D.C.: Government Printing Office).

SAHAGÚN, BERNARDINO DE

1969 *Historia general de las Cosas de Nueva España*, annotated by Angel María Garibay (Mexico City: Editorial Porrua).

SANTAYANA, GEORGE

1896 *The Sense of Beauty* (New York: Charles Scribners' Sons).

SAYLES, E. B.

1945 *The San Simon Branch: Excavations at Cave Creek and in the San Simon Valley: I: Material Culture*, Medallion Papers, no. 34 (Globe, Ariz.: Gila Pueblo).

SCHAAFSMA, CURTIS F.

1973 "Chaco Canyon Revisited," unpublished manuscript, Department of Anthropology, University of New Mexico (Albuquerque).

1974 *The Hatch Site: Archaeological Salvage Excavations on Interstate Highway 25, Dona Ana County, New Mexico*, Laboratory of Anthropology Notes 96 (Santa Fe).

1975 "Final Report on a Survey of Abiquiu Reservoir, National Park Service Contract no. CX 700050240," unpublished manuscript, School of American Research (Santa Fe).

1978 "Archaeological Studies in the Abiquiu Reservoir District," *Discovery*, School of American Research, Santa Fe, pp. 41–69.

SCHAAFSMA, POLLY

1963 *Rock Art in the Navajo Reservoir District*, Museum of New Mexico Papers in Anthropology, no. 7 (Santa Fe).

1965 "Kiva Murals from Pueblo del Encierro (LA 70)," *El Palacio* 72:6–16.

1966a *Early Navaho Rock Paintings and Carvings* (Santa Fe: Museum of Navaho Ceremonial Art).

1966b "A Survey of Tsegi Canyon Art," unpublished manuscript, National Park Service Region 3 Office (Santa Fe).

1968 "The Los Lunas Petroglyphs," *El Palacio* 75:13–24.

1971 *The Rock Art of Utah*, Papers of the Peabody Museum of Archaeology and Ethnology, vol. 65 (Cambridge, Mass.).

1972 *Rock Art in New Mexico* (Santa Fe: State Planning Office).

1974 "Petroglyphs and Rock Paintings at Inscription House, Appendix 12," in *Inscription House: Excavations and Observations*, ed. Albert E. Ward (Flagstaff: Museum of Northern Arizona).

1975 *Rock Art in the Cochiti Reservoir District*, Museum of New Mexico Papers in Anthropology, no. 16 (Santa Fe).

SCHAAFSMA, POLLY, AND CURTIS F. SCHAAFSMA

1974 "Evidence for the Origins of the Pueblo Katchina Cult as Suggested by Southwestern Rock Art," *American Antiquity* 39:535–45.

SCHAPIRO, MEYER

1953 "Style," in *Anthropology Today*, ed. A. L. Kroeber (Chicago: University of Chicago Press).

SCHROEDER, ALBERT H.

1964 "Comments on Johnson's 'The Trincheras Culture of Northern Sonora,'" *American Antiquity* 30:104–6.

SCHROEDER, ALBERT H., AND DAN S. MATSON

1965 *A Colony on the Move: Gaspar Castaño de Sosa's Journal 1590–1591* (Santa Fe: School of American Research).

SCHROEDL, ALAN R.

1977 "The Grand Canyon Figurine Complex," *American Antiquity* 42:254–65.

SERVICE, ELMAN R.

1971 *Primitive Social Organization*, 2d ed. (New York: Random House).

SHARROCK, FLOYD W., KEITH M. ANDERSON, DON D. FOWLER, AND DAVID S. DIBBLE

1961 *1960 Excavations, Glen Canyon Area*, University of Utah Anthropological Papers, no. 52 (Glen Canyon Series no. 14) (Salt Lake City).

SHARROCK, FLOYD W., KENT C. DAY, AND DAVID S. DIBBLE

1963 *1961 Excavations, Glen Canyon Area*, University of Utah Anthropological Papers, no. 63 (Glen Canyon Series no. 18) (Salt Lake City).

SHUMATE, M.

1960 *Pictographs in Central Montana: Part II*, Montana State University Anthropology and Sociology Papers, no. 21 (Missoula).

SIMS, AGNES C.

1949 "Migration Story in Stone," *El Palacio* 56:67–76.

1950 *San Cristobal Petroglyphs* (Santa Fe: Southwest Editions).

1963 "Rock Carvings, A Record of Folk History," in *Sun Father's Way,* ed. Bertha P. Dutton (Albuquerque: University of New Mexico Press).

SMITH, HOWARD NORMAN, JR.

1974 "A Survey and Stylistic Analysis of Rock Art in the San Juan Basin, Northwestern New Mexico," (Master's thesis, Eastern New Mexico University, Portales).

SMITH, WATSON

1952 *Kiva Mural Decorations at Awatovi and Kawaika-a,* Papers of the Peabody Museum of Archaeology and Ethnology, vol. 37 (Cambridge, Mass.).

SNYDER, ERNEST E.

1966 "Petroglyphs of the South Mountains of Arizona," *American Antiquity* 31:705–9.

SOUSTELLE, JACQUES

1967 *Arts of Ancient Mexico* (New York: Viking Press).

SPIER, LESLIE

1921 "The Sun Dance of the Plains Indians: Its Development and Diffusion," in *Anthropological Papers of the American Museum of Natural History,* vol. 16, Part VII (New York).

STEEN, CHARLIE R.

1966 *Excavations at Tse Ta'a, Canyon de Chelly National Monument, Arizona,* Archaeological Research Series no. 9, National Park Service (Washington, D.C.).

STEVENSON, JAMES

1891 "Ceremonial of Hasjelti Dailjis and Mythical Sand Painting of the Navajo Indians," in *Eighth Annual Report of the Bureau of American Ethnology,* pp. 229–85 (Washington, D.C.: Government Printing Office).

STEVENSON, MATILDA COXE

1894 "The Sia," in *Eleventh Annual Report of the Bureau of American Ethnology,* pp. 1–157 (Washington, D.C.: Government Printing Office).

STEWARD, JULIAN

1929 "Petroglyphs of California and Adjoining States," in *University of California Publications in American Archaeology and Ethnology,* vol. 24 (Berkeley).

1937 "Petroglyphs of the United States," *Smithsonian Annual Report for 1936* (Washington, D.C.)

1941 "Archeological Reconnaissance of Southern Utah," in *Bureau of American Ethnology Bulletin no. 128* (Washington, D.C.).

STRUEVER, STUART

1972 "The Hopewell Interaction Sphere in Riverine-Western Great Lakes Culture History," in *Contemporary Archaeology,* ed. Mark P. Leone (Carbondale: Southern Illinois University Press).

SUHM, DEE ANN AND EDWARD B. JELKS, EDS.

1962 *Handbook of Texas Archeology: Type Descriptions,* Texas Memorial Museum Bulletin 4 (Austin).

SUTHERLAND, KAY, AND PAUL STEED

1974 "The Fort Hancock Rock Art Site Number One," *The Artifact* 12:1–64.

SWAUGER, JAMES L.

1962 "Canadian Rock Drawings," *Pennsylvania Archaeologist* 32:84–89.

1974 *Rock Art of the Upper Ohio Valley* (Graz, Austria: Akademische Druck- und Verlagsanstalt).

SWITZER, RONALD R.

n.d. *The Origin and Significance of Snake-Lightning Cults in the Pueblo Southwest,* El Paso Archaeological Society Special Report, no. 2 (El Paso).

TALAYESVA, DON

1942 *Sun Chief,* ed. L. W. Simmons (New Haven: Yale University Press).

TANNER, CLARA LEE

1973 *Southwest Indian Painting,* 2d ed. (Tucson: University of Arizona Press).

TANNER, CLARA LEE, AND FLORENCE CONNOLLY

1938 "Petroglyphs in the Southwest," *The Kiva* 3:13–16.

TEDLOCK, DENNIS

1973 "In Search of the Miraculous at Zuni," paper prepared for the Ninth International Congress of Anthropological and Ethnological Sciences (n.p.).

TITIEV, MISCHA

1937 "A Hopi Salt Expedition," *American Anthropologist* 39:244–58.

TONESS, KAY, AND MACK HILL

1972 "An Unrecorded Rock Art Cave at Hueco Tanks State Park," *The Artifact* 10:1–14.

TOSCANO, SALVADOR

1954 *Los Murales Prehispánicos* (Mexico City: Artes de México).

TOZZER, ALFRED M.

1957 *Chichen Itza and Its Cenote of Sacrifice: A Comparative Study of Contemporaneous Maya and Toltec,* Memoirs of the Peabody Museum of Archaeology and Ethnology, vols. 11 and 12 (Cambridge, Mass.).

TURNER, CHRISTY G., II

1963 *Petrographs of the Glen Canyon Region,* Museum of Northern Arizona Bulletin no. 38 (Glen Canyon Series no. 4) (Flagstaff).

1971 "Revised Dating for Early Rock Art of the Glen Canyon Region," *American Antiquity* 36:469–71.

UCKO, PETER J., AND ANDRÉE ROSENFELD

1967 *Paleolithic Cave Art* (New York: McGraw-Hill Book Co.)

UNDERHILL, RUTH M.

1946 *Papago Indian Religion* (New York: Columbia University Press).

VAILLANT, G. C.

1948 *The Aztecs of Mexico* (Suffolk: Penguin Books).

VASTOKAS, JOAN M., AND ROMAS K. VASTOKAS

1973 *Sacred Art of the Algonkians: A Study of the Peterborough Petroglyphs* (Peterborough, Ontario: Mansard Press).

VILLAGRÁ, AGUSTÍN

1954 *Las Pinturas de Tetitla, Atetelco e Ixtapantongo* (Mexico City: Artes de México).

VILLAGRÁ, GASPAR PÉREZ DE

1933 *History of New Mexico,* trans. Gilberto Espinosa (Los Angeles: Quivira Society).

VIVIAN, PATRICIA B.

1961 "Kachina: The Study of Pueblo Animism and Anthropomorphism with the Ceremonial Wall Paintings of Pottery Mound and the Jeddito" (Master's thesis, University of Iowa, Ames).

VIVIAN, GORDON, AND TOM W. MATHEWS

1964   *Kin Kletso: A Pueblo III Community in Chaco Canyon, New Mexico*, Southwestern Monuments Association Technical Series 6, Part 1 (Globe, Ariz.).

VIVIAN, R. GWINN

1965   "An Archaeological Survey of the Lower Gila River, Arizona," *The Kiva* 30:95–146.

VON DER OSTEN, E.

1946   "Las pictografías de Cueva Pintador," *Acta Venezolana*, vol. 1, no. 4 (Caracas).

VON WERLHOF, J. C.

1965   *Rock Art of Owens Valley, California*, University of California Archaeological Survey Report, no. 65 (Berkeley).

VON WINNING, HASSO

1974   "A Duck Hunter from West Mexico," *The Masterkey* 48:72–73.

VOTH, H. R.

1905   *The Traditions of the Hopi*, Field Columbian Museum Publication 96, Anthropological Series vol. 8 (Chicago).

WAKANKAR, V. S.

1962   *Painted Rock Shelters of India* (Rome: ICCPPH).

1976   *Bhimbetka: The Prehistoric Paradise*, Prachya Pratibha vol. 3, no. 2.

WASLEY, WILLIAM W., AND ALFRED E. JOHNSON

1965   *Salvage Archeology in Painted Rocks Reservoir, Western Arizona*, Anthropological Papers of the University of Arizona, no. 9 (Tucson).

WATSON, EDITHA L.

1964   *Navajo Sacred Places*, Navajoland Publications, Series 5 (Window Rock).

WAUER, ROLAND

1965   "Pictograph Site in Cave Valley, Zion National Park, Utah," in *University of Utah Anthropological Papers*, no. 75 (Salt Lake City).

WELLMANN, K. F.

1970   "Kokopelli of Indian Paleology: Hunchbacked Rain Priest, Hunting Magician, and Don Juan of the old Southwest," *Journal of the American Medical Association* 212:1678–82.

1975   "Some Observations on the Bird Motif in North American Indian Rock Art," paper presented at the symposium on American Indian Rock Art (El Paso, Texas).

In press   *A Survey of North American Indian Rock Art* (to be published by Akademische Druck- und Verlagsanstalt, Graz, Austria).

WENDORF, FRED, AND ERIK K. REED

1955   "An Alternative Reconstruction of Northern Rio Grande Prehistory," *El Palacio* 62:131–73.

WESTHEIM, PAUL

1965   *The Art of Ancient Mexico* (Garden City, N.Y.: Doubleday and Co.).

WETHERINGTON, RONALD K.

1968   *Excavations at Pot Creek Pueblo*, Fort Burgwin Research Center Paper, no. 6 (Taos, N.M.).

WHEAT, JOE BEN

1955   *Mogollon Culture Prior to A.D. 1000*, Memoirs of the Society for American Archaeology, no. 10 (Salt Lake City).

WHITE, CHERYL

1965   "The Petroglyphs of Saguaro National Monument, Tucson, Arizona," unpublished manuscript, Department of Anthropology, University of Arizona (Tucson).

WHITE, LESLIE A.

1932   "The Acoma Indians," in *Forty-seventh Annual Report of the Bureau of American Ethnology*, pp. 23–190 (Washington, D.C.: Government Printing Office).

WILLEY, GORDON R.

1966.   *An Introduction to American Archaeology*, vol. 1 (Englewood Cliffs, N.J.: Prentice-Hall).

WINSHIP, GEORGE PARKER

1896   "The Coronado Expedition 1540–1542," in *Fourteenth Annual Report of the Bureau of American Ethnology 1892–1893*, pp. 339–613 (Washington, D.C.: Government Printing Office).

1904   *The Journey of Coronado, 1540–1542*, trans. and ed. (New York: Allerton Book Co.).

WOODBURY, ANGUS MUNN

1965   *Notes on the Human Ecology of Glen Canyon*, University of Utah Anthropological Papers, no. 74 (Glen Canyon Series no. 26) (Salt Lake City).

WOODBURY, RICHARD B.

1954   *Prehistoric Stone Implements of Northeastern Arizona*, Reports of the Awatovi Expedition no. 6, Papers of the Peabody Museum of Archaeology and Ethnology, vol. 34 (Cambridge, Mass.).

WORMINGTON, H. M.

1951   *Prehistoric Indians of the Southwest*, Denver Museum of Natural History Popular Series, no. 7, 2d ed. (Denver).

1955   *A Reappraisal of the Fremont Culture*, Denver Museum of Natural History Proceedings, no. 1 (Denver).

WYMAN, LELAND C.

1960   *Navaho Sandpainting* (Colorado Springs, Colo.: Taylor Museum).

In press   *Southwest Indian Drypainting* (Albuquerque: University of New Mexico Press, School of American Research Southwest Indian Arts Series).

YEO, HERBERT W.

n.d.   "The Petroglyphs of Three Rivers," unpublished manuscript, Museum of New Mexico (Santa Fe).

ZAHNISER, JACK L.

1965   "Archaeological Survey of Saguaro National Monument," unpublished manuscript, Saguaro National Monument (Tucson).

1970   "The Archaeological Resources of Saguaro National Monument," *The Kiva* 35:105–20.

ZUBROW, EZRA

1971   "Carrying Capacity and Dynamic Equilibrium in the Prehistoric Southwest," *American Antiquity* 36:127–38.

Lists of Illustrations

PLATES

1. Paintings in the Great Gallery
2. Mural of painted handprints, Painted Cave
3. Superimposed paintings in Painted Grotto
4. Barrier Canyon Style composition west of Green River, Utah
5. Barrier Canyon Style paintings, Sego, Utah
6. The "Holy Ghost" panel, Great Gallery
7. The Bird Site, the Maze, Utah
8. Right-hand side, main panel, the Bird Site
9. Basketmaker II paintings, Painted Cave
10. Basketmaker anthropomorphs, Canyon del Muerto
11. Anasazi paintings, Canyon del Muerto
12. Anthropomorphs, Ceremonial Cave
13. Walking couple, Ceremonial Cave
14. Rows of human figures, Ceremonial Cave
15. Fluteplayers under rainbows with birds, Pictograph Cave
16. Clay paintings, Fluteplayer Cave, Tsegi Canyon
17. Classic Tlaloc or Rain God figure, Vado, New Mexico
18. Mask with star or cross symbolism, Hueco Tanks
19. Solid type masks with tall conical caps, Hueco Tanks
20. Solid type masks, Cave Kiva, Hueco Tanks
21. Solid type mask in red and orange, Hueco Tanks
22. Red mask with earrings and elaborate headgear, Hueco Tanks
23. Red and yellow "long" mask, Hueco Tanks
24. Fifteenth-century mural painting from Pottery Mound
25. Kachina painted in red, green, and white, Abo
26. Mask and yellow ceremonial figure, Abo, New Mexico
27. Navajo supernaturals, Largo Canyon drainage
28. Night chant group, Carrizo Canyon drainage
29. Navajo figure with bows, Carrizo Canyon drainage
30. Horned shield-bearer, Blanco Canyon
31. Navajo painting of Spanish riders, Canyon del Muerto
32. Painted shield motif, Hueco Tanks

FIGURES

1. Petroglyph by hunter-gatherers — 2
2. Navajo horsemen and deer — 2
3. Anthropomorphic figures and animals — 4
4. Chihuahuan Polychrome Abstract Style paintings — 4
5. White hand prints, Tsegi Phase — 11
6. Concentric circles painted in white — 12
7. Rosa and Gobernador Representational Style — 14
8. Bighorn sheep, Jornada Style — 16

9. Bighorn sheep on Mimbres bowl 16
10. Space-time chart of
    Southwestern rock art styles 18–19
11. Chart of southwestern chronology 20
12. Painted and incised Navajo
    supernaturals 27
13. Detail of anthropomorphs in
    Plate 1 27
14. Seventeenth-century Navajo
    horned mask 29
15. Detail of Anasazi flute-playing
    animal 29
16. Pueblo IV face on corner of
    basalt boulder 30
17. Eighteenth-century Navajo bat 30
18. Masks, bear paw, and historic
    lettering 31
19. Curvilinear abstract designs 37
20. Large abstract petroglyph designs 38
21. Anthropomorphic petroglyph
    figure 39
22. Curvilinear abstract designs and
    gridiron 40
23. Abstract Style petroglyphs on dike 44
24. Abstract Style petroglyphs with
    barred and bisected ovals 44
25. Abstract Style petroglyphs and
    representational forms 46
26. Abstract Style petroglyphs in
    northern Rio Grande Valley 48
27. Barred Abstract Style element 48
28. Chihuahuan Polychrome Abstract
    Style designs 50
29. Chihuahuan Polychrome Abstract
    paintings 51
30. Detailed view of Painted Grotto 53
31. Abstract Style, Grand Gulch 53
32. Chihuahuan Polychrome Abstract
    Style 54
33. Panel in Candelaria Painted Style 57
34. Diablo Dam Petroglyph Style 58
35. Anthropomorphs and spear points 59
36. Canyon of the Colorado Plateau 62
37. The Maze, Green River drainage,
    Utah 62
38. Spectral human forms, Sego, Utah 63
39. Anthropomorphic figures,
    Great Gallery 63
40. Pair of Barrier Canyon
    Style figures 64

41. Detail of Sego anthropomorph 65
42. Paintings in Horseshoe (Barrier)
    Canyon 65
43. Mummylike figures, Great Gallery
    mural 67
44. Detail of anthropomorphic figures 67
45. Group composition, Great Gallery 68
46. Mountain sheep, dog, and conflict 68
47. Isolated composition, the Bird Site 69
48. Anthropomorph, the Bird Site 69
49. Glen Canyon Linear Style
    petroglyphs 74
50. Petroglyphs of bighorn sheep 75
51. Rillito Red-on-brown plate 84
52. Sacaton Red-on-buff bowl 84
53. Petroglyph-covered boulders,
    Painted Rocks State Park 85
54. Hohokam petroglyphs 85
55. Gila Petroglyph Style figure 86
56. Hohokam quadrupeds 86
57. Gila Petroglyph Style designs 87
58. Santan Mountain petroglyphs 87
59. Bows and arrows 88
60. Gila Petroglyph Style elements
    and design complexes 89
61. Abstract elements and snakes 90
62. Gila Petroglyph Style figures 92
63. Hohokam birds, lizards, and spiral 92
64. Line of human figures 93
65. Hohokam hunting scene 93
66. Spirals and other circle motifs 94
67. Dancers, animals, and hunting
    scene 95
68. Cerro las Trincheras, Magdalena
    River Valley 100
69. Spirals and curvilinear motifs, Cerro
    las Trincheras 102
70. Quadrupeds, Cerro las Trincheras 102
71. Canyon del Muerto from
    Antelope House Overlook 106
72. Basketmaker II paintings 110
73. San Juan Anthropomorphic Style
    paintings 112
74. Paired Basketmaker anthropo-
    morphs 113
75. San Juan Anthropomorphic Style
    petroglyphs 114
76. Detail of anthropomorphs 115
77. San Juan Anthropomorphic Style
    petroglyphs 116

78. San Juan Anthropomorphic Style with yucca plant 116
79. Paired anthropomorphs 118–19
80. Anthropomorphic petroglyphs 120
81. Human figures, Chinle Representational Style 123
82. Human figures and birds, Chinle Representational Style 123
83. Anthropomorphic figure, Chinle Representational Style 124
84. Red and white seated stick figures 124
85. Seated flute player under rainbow 125
86. Small human figures with birds on heads 126
87. Small birds and row of human figures 127
88. Red and white painting of birds in flight 127
89. Line of tiny red masks and anthropomorphs 129
90. Anthropomorphs, Rosa Representational Style 130
91. Family group, Rosa Representational Style 130
92. Petroglyphs, Mancos Canyon 132
93. Cave Valley Style anthropomorph and flute player 133
94. Eroded bedrock petroglyphs, stick figures and sandal tracks 137
95. Late Anasazi petroglyphs, Pictograph Point 137
96. Kayenta Representational Style and earlier Anasazi work 138
97. Late Anasazi petroglyphs, Chaco Canyon 138
98. Late Anasazi petroglyphs, Chaco Canyon 139
99. Reclining humpbacked flute player 139
100. Reclining humpbacked flute players 140
101. Phallic hunters 142
102. Abstract wall painting, Spruce Tree House 142
103. Bighorn sheep, Kayenta Representational Style 144
104. Rectangular scrolls or spirals 144
105. Clay paintings, Tsegi Painted Style 145
106. Clay paintings, Tsegi Painted Style 147
107. Five-foot-long flute player 147
108. Shield figures known as Bat Woman 149
109. Negative image of anthropomorphic figure 149
110. White circle motifs, Tsegi Painted Style 151
111. Concentric circles and anthropomorphs 152
112. Petroglyphs of deer and bighorn sheep 154
113. Maze and other rectilinear design petroglyphs 156
114. Abstract elements, tadpoles, lizard man 156
115. Petroglyphs, Petrified Forest National Monument 157
116. Anthropomorph, footprints, and elk 157
117. Snake, lizards, and quadrupeds 158
118. Petroglyphs, Cave of Life 159
119. Fremont dates by region 165
120. Fremont anthropomorphs and animals 167
121. Anthropomorphic figures, Southern San Rafael Style 167
122. Pecked and incised Fremont anthropomorphs 168
123. Mountain sheep, Southern San Rafael Style 169
124. Shields and anthropomorphic figures 169
125. Horned anthropomorphs holding shields 170
126. Horned shield bearers and bighorn sheep 170
127. Anthropomorphic figures, Classic Vernal Style 172
128. Anthropomorphic figures in ceremonial attire 172
129. Large anthropomorphic figures, Classic Vernal Style 173
130. Horned human figures, Classic Vernal Style 173
131. Anthropomorph, Classic Vernal Style 173
132. Shield figures and other anthropomorphs 174

133. Abstract shield figure, Classic Vernal Style 174
134. Fremont petroglyphs, Dinosaur National Monument 175
135. Hunt scene and antlered anthropomorphs 177
136. Hunting scene, Northern San Rafael Style 177
137. Bighorn sheep, anthropomorphs, and abstract elements 178
138. Petroglyphs, Northern San Rafael Style 178
139. Cooks Peak, southern New Mexico 185
140. Rock art styles in the Mogollon area 186
141. Mogollon Red Style paintings on the San Francisco River 188
142. Simple stick figure and zigzag design 188
143. Mogollon Red zigzag and parallel lines 189
144. Small Mogollon Red designs on rock overhang 189
145. Large red circular element 192
146. Reserve Petroglyph Style, Tularosa Canyon 193
147. Elements of the Reserve Petroglyph Style 193
148. Large Mogollon quadrupeds 194
149. Outlined cross, zigzag, and spiral element 194
150. Bear track petroglyph, Apache Creek 195
151. Seated Mimbres figure and mountain sheep 200
152. Face or mask, Cooks Peak 200
153. Tlaloc blanket design near Cooks Peak 201
154. Large ogrelike being, Cooks Peak 202
155. Bearded Anthropomorphic figure 202
156. Turtles, Cooks Peak 204
157. Rattlesnake, Cooks Peak 204
158. Tadpoles carved in bedrock, Cooks Peak 205
159. Mimbres fish, Cooks Peak 206
160. Mimbres burden basket, Cooks Peak 206
161. Human footprints carved in sequence 207
162. Decorative bear tracks 207
163. Classic Tlaloc, Hueco Tanks 208
164. Mimbres-like blanket design and Tlaloc eyes 209
165. Petroglyph depiction of Tlaloc 209
166. Masks and faces at Three Rivers, New Mexico 210
167. Jornada Style faces and masks 212–13
168. Horned ceremonial masks and bird 214
169. Jornada Style mask and other designs 214
170. "Long mask" and other Jornada Style petroglyphs 215
171. Face lacking outline, Three Rivers, New Mexico 215
172. Mask or face with ceremonial decoration 216
173. Solid mask from Cave Kiva, Hueco Tanks 216
174. Red mask combining solid and linear painting 218
175. View of Cave Kiva, Hueco Tanks 218
176. Horned serpents, Hueco Mountains 219
177. Mask with abstract decoration and conical cap 220
178. Profile head with forward-reaching horn 221
179. Petroglyph depiction of head 222
180. Hunched, phallic anthropomorph 222
181. Jornada Style anthropomorphic representations 223
182. Jornada Style personages, Three Rivers, Carrizozo 224
183. Jornada Style quadrupeds 225
184. Quadrupeds from Three Rivers 226
185. Canine with large teeth and curved fangs 228
186. Bear, Diablo Dam 228
187. Horned and plumed serpent 229
188. Bird and cloud terrace 229
189. Bird motifs, Three Rivers 230
190. Snake and insects, Three Rivers 231
191. Abstract fish design, Three Rivers 232
192. Large abstract design, Hueco Tanks 233

193. Large abstract pattern, Hueco Tanks 234
194. Three Rivers abstract with long-necked bird 234
195. Geometric pattern, Three Rivers 234
196. Circle-dot motif, Three Rivers 235
197. Rio Grande gorge in White Rock Canyon 253
198. Rio Grande Style petroglyph 255
199. Figure types and iconography in rock art 256–57
200. Birds, serpents, and shield, Rio Grande Style 258
201. Tewa petroglyphs, Rio Grande Style 258
202. Flute player, Tenabo, New Mexico 259
203. Badly weathered traces of masks, Tenabo 261
204. Yellow mask with red facial markings, Abo 261
205. Stylized white silhouette of human figure, Abo 262
206. Petroglyphs, Tenabo 262
207. Shield bearers, Tenabo 263
208. Horned shield bearer with spear, Tenabo 264
209. Petroglyph panel at San Cristobal 266
210. Masks, San Cristobal 266
211. Animal mask and star, San Cristobal 267
212. Masks pecked around holes in rock 267
213. One-horned personage, San Cristobal 268
214. Arrow swallower, Galisteo 269
215. Masks and figure with pointed cap, San Cristobal 269
216. Running human figure, San Cristobal 270
217. Petroglyphs with badger, Galisteo 270
218. Large bear petroglyph, Pueblo Blanco 271
219. Horned serpent and shields, Pueblo Blanco 271
220. Petroglyph, Galisteo 272
221. Star and mask, San Cristobal 273

222. Star and mask, San Cristobal 274
223. Large shield bearer, Comanche Gap 274
224. Mask, cloud terrace, and deer tracks, Los Lunas 276
225. Masks, Los Lunas 276
226. Petroglyphs, Cochiti Reservoir 277
227. Masks on rock corners, Cochiti Reservoir 277
228. Masks, Cochiti Reservoir 278
229. Modern kachina masks, Cochiti Reservoir 279
230. Bird with serpent in mouth, Cochiti Reservoir 279
231. Anthropomorph and two-horned snake, Cochiti Reservoir 280
232. Small anthropomorph, Cochiti Reservoir 280
233. Masks, circles, and human figure, Cochiti Reservoir 281
234. Rio Grande Style petroglyphs near Cochiti Pueblo 281
235. Ceremonial figure, Pajarito Canyon 282
236. Heads or masks above blanket design, Cochiti Reservoir 282
237. Warrior with sun shield combating Horned Serpent 283
238. Depictions of insects, Cochiti Reservoir 283
239. Turkey petroglyph, La Cieneguilla 284
240. Mountain lion, Cochiti Reservoir 284
241. Figures on boulder at old shrine, Cochiti Reservoir 285
242. Flute players, Tsankawi, Pajarito Plateau 286–87
243. Serpent and star motifs, White Rock Canyon 288
244. Horned serpents, Pajarito Canyon 288
245. Corn and female figure with sky symbolism 290
246. Tcakwaina kachina, Second Mesa 290
247. Hopi clan symbols, Willow Springs, Arizona 291
248. Hopi clan symbols, Willow Springs, Arizona 291

249. Detail of sun faces, Willow Springs   292
250. Modern petroglyph, Willow Springs   292
251. Eagle's Nest, Gobernador Phase Masonry Pueblito   304
252. Approximate dates of Navajo phases   305
253. Eighteenth-century Navajo petroglyphs   307
254. Supernatural with bow and rainbow   308
255. Large feathered shield, Carrizo drainage   309
256. Paired shields or Twin War Gods   311
257. V-necked Navajo supernaturals   313
258. Line of Night Chant figures   313
259. Navajo supernatural, Carrizo Canyon   314
260. Female God of the Night Chant   314
261. Bow and hourglass symbols, Largo Canyon   316
262. Navajo hunt scene, Largo Canyon   317
263. Eighteenth-century Navajo petroglyphs   319
264. Navajo petroglyphs in Blanco Canyon   320
265. Corn plant, Largo drainage   320
266. Navajo bird, corn, and terrace complex   321
267. Navajo planetarium, Canyon del Muerto   323
268. Planetarium site, Canyon de Chelly   324
269. Yeibichai dancers, Chaco Canyon   327
270. Detail, Squaw Dance, Chaco Canyon   327
271. Navajo antelope and supernatural   329
272. Mask with tablita, Canyon de Chelly   329
273. Spanish cavalcade, Standing Cow Ruin   330
274. Detail of horses and antelope, Canyon del Muerto   331
275. Charcoal drawing of 1858 Ute raid   331

276. Detail of Ute Raid panel   332
277. Modern incised drawing of horse and rider   332
278. Horse and rider and other figures   336
279. Row of white dancing figures, Mescalero Apache   337
280. Red and yellow sun face, Mescalero Apache   338
281. One-horned mask, Mescalero Apache   338
282. Shields, thunderbird, lizard, and snake   339
283. Details from painted ceiling, Malpais Hills   340

MAPS

1. Major Subareal Divisions of the Early Prehistoric Farming Southwest   22
2. Rock Art Styles Thought to be Archaic in Origin   35
3. Basketmaker and Glen Canyon Linear Style Rock Art Distribution   73
4. The Hohokam and Related Areas   82
5. Anasazi Area with Prehistoric Regions   108
6. The Fremont Area and Prehistoric Cultural Regions   164
7. Mogollon Area and Rock Art Style Regions   184
8. The Modern Pueblos   245
9. Rio Grande Region with Languages and Rock Art Styles   247
10. Navajo Occupation   303
11. Apache Tribes and Rock Art Sites   334

TABLES

1. Sequences of Periods and Phases of the Hohokam   42
2. Bone Counts for Bighorn Sheep and Deer from Excavations in Anasazi Regions or Districts   151–52

Index

Abiquiu, 302
Abo, 259, 260, 265, 296, 297
abstract figures, 3, 83, 91, 133, 155, 161, 176. *See also* Abstract Style
Abstract Style, 36, 41, 43, 45, 55, 56, 61, 76, 77, 78, 88, 197, 203, 252; Barrier Canyon Style, 54; Chihuahuan Polychrome Style, 49, 52, 54, 55; Great Basin, 9, 42, 43, 47, 49, 55, 79, 121, 153, 179, 196, 344. *See also* abstract figures
Acoma, 250, 297
Africa, 9, 60
agriculture, 17, 21, 81, 107, 121, 163, 183, 185, 249
Ahlstrom, Richard V., 52
Aikens, C. Melvin, 166, 179
Alamo Mountain, 47, 208, 236
Alamo Hueco Mts., 50
Alaska, 301
Albuquerque, N.M., 275
Alma Plain, 190
Altar Valley, 82, 99, 101
Amargosa culture, 34, 41, 79
Amazon Basin, 72
Ambler, J. Richard, 52, 163, 165
amphibian figures, 83, 203
Anasazi Culture, 15, 21, 26, 47, 72, 105, 106, 163, 168, 171, 180, 186, 191, 195, 242, 243, 252, 259, 286, 302, 309, 344, 345; Arboles Phase, 128; Basketmaker I, 107; Basketmaker II, 107, 108–121, 128, 132, 160; Basketmaker III, 117, 121–134; Black-on-white, 246; Piedra Phase, 128; Pueblo I, 128, 131; Pueblo II, 121–134, 135–162; Pueblo III, 107, 134–162; Pueblo IV, 107, 108; Sambrito Phase, 128; San Juan Anthropomorphic Style of, 109–124, 132; Tsegi Phase, 145, 146, 148
Anderson, Keith, 148, 295
Animas Valley, 128
Antevs, Ernest, 183, 185
anthropomorphic figures, 3, 45, 52, 54, 55, 56, 61, 71, 75, 91, 99, 101, 110, 111, 112, 114, 115, 117, 119, 122, 128, 131, 132, 135, 136, 143, 146, 148, 155, 162, 166, 171, 176, 179, 191, 197, 217, 223, 259, 285, 289, 295, 312, 318, 339
Anton, Ferdinand, 217, 236, 238
Apache Creek, 191, 195

Apaches, 1, 15, 21, 23, 47, 187, 264, 301–341, 345
Archaic Period, 34, 52, 55, 56, 61, 70, 77, 78, 79, 109, 160, 179, 344. *See also* Western Archaic
Arizona, 3, 5, 17, 21, 23, 32, 34, 36, 43, 71, 76, 79, 105, 131, 135, 155, 162, 333, 335, 337; Hohokam in, 81–103; Mogollon in, 183–242; Navajo in, 302–310; Pueblo in, 244, 294
Arrow Grotto, 11
Arroyo Hondo, 47
Asa clan, 295
Athabaskan culture, 21, 187, 301, 302, 306, 333
Australia, 9, 52, 76, 77
Awatovi, 26, 221, 250
Aztecs, 236, 237, 298

B'Yash, Hatrali, 312
Bahti, Mark, 98
Barrier Canyon, 66, 168
Barrier Canyon Style, 109, 115, 117, 180, 181, 344. *See also* Representational Style
Barrier Creek, 70
Bartlett, Katharine, 302
Basketmaker, 54, 165, 180, 181; Los Pinos, 120–121; San Juan, 70, 75, 79. *See also* Anasazi culture
Basketmaker I. *See* Anasazi culture
Basketmaker II, 47, 49, 75, 180. *See also* Anasazi culture
Basketmaker III, 49. *See also* Anasazi culture
Bat Cave, 183
Baumhoff, M. A., 3, 7, 9, 36, 41, 76, 77, 88
Beaglehole, Ernest, 153
Beals, Ralph L., 237
Beckwith, Frank, 166
Bernalillo, N.M., 250
Big Bead Mesa, 325
Big Bend River, 55
Bilbo, Michael J., 56
Binford, Lewis R., 8
bird figures, 61, 66, 70, 71, 83, 91, 125, 131, 132, 133, 143, 155, 160, 179, 223, 265, 275, 285, 306
Bird Site, 66
Biscuit Wares, 246
Black Mesa, 148
Blanco Canyon, 308
Bloomfield, N.M., 117, 119, 136

Bohrer, Vorsila L., 82, 98
Bolton, Herbert Eugene, 246, 249, 250
Bosque Redondo, 310
Bowen, Thomas G., 100, 101
Breuil, H., 5
Brew, J. O., 237, 243
Britt, Claude, 322, 323, 324
Brody, J. J., 199, 345
Brook, Vernon R., 197
Brugge, David M., 306
Bunzel, Ruth L., 315
Burgh, Robert F., 128
Burton, Robert Jordan, 7, 171, 175
Butler Wash, 70, 75, 111, 112, 114, 117
Buttress Canyon, 111

Caborca, 101
Cain, H. T., 13
California, 9, 34, 42, 71, 77, 79
Canada, 301
Candelaria Peaks, 56
Canyon de Chelly, 111, 112, 114, 122, 126, 129,
    131, 132, 133, 135, 145, 306, 322, 323, 326, 328
Canyon del Muerto, 15, 111, 112, 115, 322, 328,
    330
Capitol Reef National Monument, 166
Carrizo Canyon, 308, 309
Carrizo River, 316, 317
Carlson, Roy L., 303, 304, 305
Carrizozo, N.M., 45
Casas Grandes, 198, 235, 237, 242
Caso, Alfonso, 236, 238
Cassidy, Donnelly D., 97
Castañeda, Carlos, 233, 301
Castleton, Kenneth, 166
Cave Creek, 184
Central America, 71, 236
ceramics, 21, 47, 81, 94, 186
Cerro las Trincheras, 101
Chaco Canyon, 134, 306, 325, 326, 328
Chalchihuites, 103
Chama River, 302
Chapman, Kenneth, 250, 285
Chihuahua, 3, 15, 21, 34, 43, 56, 77, 78, 183,
    196, 198, 335
Chihuahuan Desert, 21, 43, 49, 55, 76, 183
Chinle, 111, 145
Chiricahua, 333, 335, 341
Christensen, Erwin O., 60
Chupadero Black-on-white, 198
Chupicuaro, 103
Circle I Hills, 335, 337
Clark, La Verne Harrell, 15, 322, 333, 334
Clewlow, C. W., Jr., 7, 13, 42, 343
Cochise Culture, 34, 43, 81, 99, 183. See also
    Mogollon Culture
Cochiti, 250, 289, 293
Cochiti Dam, 5
Cochiti Pueblo, 5, 253, 259, 275

Cochiti Reservoir, 252, 259
Colima, 239
Colorado, 5, 34, 49, 128, 171
Colorado Desert, Calif., 41, 43, 76
Colorado Plateau, 14, 21, 32, 61, 70, 76, 105, 108,
    160, 161, 163, 180, 243, 253, 302
Colorado River, 41, 61, 66, 72, 79, 105, 131
Colton, Harold S., 161, 289, 293, 294
Comanches, 264, 304, 334
Connolly, Florence, 83, 91
Continental Divide, 105
Cora-Huichol, 134
Cordova Cave, 184, 186
Cornudas Mts., 208
Cooks Peak, 201
Cosgrove, C. B., 199
Coso Range, 76
Cowboy Cave, 70
Cressman, L. S., 7
Crimmins, M. L., 6
Crow Canyon, 315
Cuba, N.M., 322
Cubeo tribe, 72
curvilinear figures, 41, 45, 47, 49, 50, 52, 74, 77,
    88, 160, 171, 191, 289

Daniels, Helen Sloan, 128
dating methods, 13–17, 41, 47, 75, 94, 163, 165
Davidson, Howard N., 326, 328, 330, 333
Davis, Emma Lou, 17, 33
Davis, John V., 60, 211, 217
Davis, Leslie, 197
Davis Gulch, 168
De Harport, David L., 111
De Johly, H., 312
Dean, Jeffrey S., 135, 146, 244
Delgadito Canyon, 317, 318
Desert Culture, 17, 33, 34. See also Western
    Archaic
Di Peso, Charles C., 197, 198, 236, 242
Diablo Dam, 56, 227
Dick, Herbert W., 183
Dinetah, 306, 308, 325
Dinetah Scored, 304
Dinosaur National Monument, 171, 175, 176
Dittert, E., 307
Douglas, Charles L., 148
Doyel, David E., 94
Dozier, Edward P., 242, 245, 246
Dry Fork Valley, 166, 171, 176
Dulce, N.M., 322
Durham, Dorothy, 160
Dutton, Bertha P., 134, 238, 246, 248, 250
dyes, 25, 26, 49, 52, 61, 128, 131, 146, 162, 211,
    260, 335, 336, 339

Eddy, Frank W., 120, 128
El Paso, 55, 79, 197, 201, 265
El Paso Polychrome, 198

Eliade, Mircea, 71
Elkin, A. P., 77
Ellis, Florence Hawley, 11, 119, 236, 237, 238, 239
Elsasser, A. B., 7
Encierro Canyon, 309
Escalante River, 168
Europe, 5, 9, 60

Fall, A. B., 6
Farrer, Claire, 336
Ferg, Alan, 72, 73
Fewkes, Jesse Walter, 7, 11, 96, 141, 238, 293, 294, 295, 297, 317
Flagstaff, Ariz., 161
Fontana, Bernard L., 97
Forbes, J. D., 303
Forde, C. D., 293
Forestdale, 187
Fort Hancock, 55, 56, 61, 227
Foster, Gene, 143
Fox, Douglas C., 9
Fremont Culture, 21, 61, 71, 79, 109, 117, 162, 345; Classic Vernal Style of, 171, 175, 176; Great Salt Lake, 163; Northern San Rafael Style of, 176; Parowan, 163; San Rafael, 61, 163; Southern San Rafael Style of, 166, 168, 171, 175, 176, 179, 180; Sevier, 163, 176; Uinta, 163, 171, 176, 179, 180
Fremont River, 166
Frijoles Canyon, 285, 294
Frobenius, Leo, 9
Furst, Peter T., 56, 71, 134, 136, 232, 236, 239, 345

Galisteo Basin, 47, 49, 260, 264, 265, 289, 294, 296, 297
Gardner, W. A., 310
Gebhard, David, 52, 341
Gila Basin, 91
Gila Bend, 94, 96, 98, 99
Gila Cliff Dwelling, 190, 191
Gila Petroglyph Style, 83–96
Gila Plain, 94
Gila River, 97, 187
Gila-Salt site, 91, 94
Glen Canyon, 5, 72, 75, 111, 143, 145, 153, 289
Glen Canyon Linear Style, 109, 114, 135, 148. See also Representational Style
Glencoe, 341
Gobernador District, 302, 304. See also Navajos
Goldman, Irving, 72
Gran Quivira, 250
Grand Canyon, 70, 99
Grand Gulch, 52, 145
Grant, Campbell, 3, 7, 9, 13, 15, 42, 70, 76, 111, 112, 122, 125, 126, 133, 134, 328, 330, 343
Great Basin, 36, 42, 76, 77, 78, 163, 176, 343
Great Gallery, 66, 70

Great Plains, 12
Great Salt Lake, 179, 180
Green, John W., 227
Green River, 54, 64, 66, 176
Greenleaf, J. Cameron, 97
gridiron figures, 41, 45, 49, 74, 191
Growler Mts., 36, 41, 42
Guadalupe Mts., 49, 52, 55, 183, 335, 336
Guernsey, Samuel James, 110, 112, 143
Gulf of California, 52, 99, 101
Gummerman, George, 252
Gunnerson, Dolores A., 61, 301, 334
Gunnerson, James H., 165, 166, 175, 180, 301, 334

Haile, Berard, 324
Hakataya, 21
Hammack, Laurens, 11, 119, 236, 237, 238, 239
Hammond, George P., 246, 248, 249, 301, 302
hand print figures, 119, 126, 135, 146, 148, 153, 158, 179, 275, 309
Hartman, Dana, 52
Harvard Peabody Museum, 166
Haury, Emil W., 7, 81, 96, 100, 103, 111, 112, 162, 185
Hawley, Florence, 141
Hayden, Julian D., 36, 41, 42, 98, 99, 101
Hayes, Alden C., 148, 153, 161
headgear figures, 60, 61, 73, 75, 110, 112, 117, 125, 132, 171, 179, 190, 255, 275, 312
Hedges, Ken, 3, 7, 10, 41, 43, 71, 76
Heizer, Robert F., 3, 7, 9, 13, 36, 41, 42, 76, 77, 88, 343
Hester, James J., 301, 302, 303, 304, 318
Hewett, Edgar Lee, 294
Heyden, Doris, 12
Hibben, Frank C., 25, 250, 251, 265
Hidalgo County, 50
Hidden Lake, 341
Hidden Valley, 128, 132
High Plains, 307
Hill, James N., 244, 245
Hill, Mack, 217
Hill, W. W., 304
Hinton, Thomas B., 101
Hodge, F. W., 302
Hohokam Culture, 9, 15, 17, 21, 41, 42, 81, 105, 155, 163, 191, 344; Classic Period of, 82, 94, 97; Colonial Period of, 82; Gila Petroglyph Style of, 83–96; Mesoamerican influence, 81, 82, 90; Pioneer Period of, 103; River clan, 100; Sedentary Period of, 83
Hopi Pueblo, 140, 141, 158, 160, 244, 251, 260, 289, 293, 294
Hopis, 11, 26, 99, 109, 148, 233, 239, 295, 296, 297
Horse Canyon, 66
Horseshoe Canyon, 66, 168
Hot Well site, 197
Hough, Walter, 195
Hueco Mts., 211

Hueco Phase, 34, 43, 79
Hueco Tanks, 201, 211, 217, 219, 227, 240, 241, 335, 336
Huichol, 90, 134
human figures, 55, 60, 61, 70, 73, 83, 91, 111, 155, 160, 168, 191, 255, 289, 306, 312

insect figures, 83, 223, 275
Irwin-Williams, Cynthia, 33, 34, 36, 43, 79, 107
Isleta Pueblo, 275

Jackson, A. T., 43, 56
Jaeger, Edmund C., 41
James, Charles D. III, 326, 328, 330, 333
Jeddito District, 250, 251
Jelks, Edward B., EDS, 56, 61
Jemez Mts., 254
Jennings, Jesse D., 36
Jernigan, E. Wesley, 103, 117
Jicarillas, 334, 341
Johnson, Alfred E., 82, 83, 96, 99, 100, 101
Jornada, 255, 260, 265
Jornada Mogollon, 161, 244, 245, 345. *See also* Mogollon Culture
Jornada Style, 158, 252, 254, 295, 298, 306, 319, 344. *See also* Representational Style
Judd, Neil M., 131

Kabotie, Fred, 233
kachinas. *See* Pueblos
Kanab, 128
Kanab Creek, 117
Kawaika-a, 26, 250, 251
Kayenta, 134, 135, 136, 143–153, 155, 161, 171, 344
Kearns, Timothy M., 9, 83, 96, 97, 98
Keller, Donald R., 52
Kelley, J. Charles, 185, 197, 237, 238
Keres, 275, 295
Keresan, 19, 260, 275, 285, 297, 298
Keur, Dorothy, 325
Kidder, Alfred Vincent, 107, 110, 112, 143, 294
Kirkland, Forrest, 7, 15, 55, 61, 71, 211, 217, 219, 227, 334, 335, 336
Klee, Paul, 74
Kluckhohn, Clyde, 153
Kokopelli, 125, 136, 140, 141, 221, 255, 317
Kuaua, 250, 251

La Cienega, 275, 295
Laguna Creek, 110
Lake Roberts, 191
Lambert, Marjorie F., 52, 141
Lancaster, James A., 148
Lang, Richard W., 47, 49, 122
Largo Canyon, 128, 308, 309, 315, 325
Largo River, 305, 307, 315, 317, 318
Larson, Stephen M., 97
Le Blanc, Steven A., 197

Lehmer, Donald J., 34, 43, 79, 186, 187, 196, 197, 242
Lipe, William D., 109
Lister, Robert H., 198
Little Colorado River, 72, 75, 105, 155–162, 244, 252, 260, 289, 296
Long, Paul, Jr., 111
Longacre, William A., 244
Los Lunas, 297
Los Pinos River, 128, 308, 310, 312, 315, 316
Lower Sonoran, 21, 196
Lumholtz, Carl, 90, 101

Magdalena Basin, 82
Magdalena Valley, 99, 101
Malpais Hills, 337
mammal figures, 15, 56, 60, 64, 66, 70, 71, 72, 73, 83, 128, 131, 143, 146, 148, 155, 158, 191, 275
Mancos Canyon, 131
Manzano Mts., 254
Marsh Pass, 110, 111
Marshak, Alexander, 345
Marshall, Michael P., 187
Martin, Paul S., 6, 17, 34, 183, 184, 185, 195, 196
Martineau, LaVan, 13
Marwitt, John P., 163, 165
Massacre Cave, 15, 328
Matson, Dan S., 249
Matthews, Washington, 311, 325
Maze, 64, 66, 70, 71
McCarthy, F. C., 52, 77, 78
McNitt, Frank, 328
Mera, H. P., 55, 246, 264
Mesa Verde, 128, 131, 134, 141, 143, 148, 153, 155, 161
Mescaleros, 333, 334, 335, 336, 341
Mesoamerican society, 81, 82, 90, 198, 217, 235, 236, 240, 242
Mexico, 12, 81, 101, 134, 298, 345; Mogollon in, 183–242
Mills, George, 326
Mimbres, 7, 186, 237, 265, 345. *See also* Mogollon Culture
Mimbres Valley, 187, 197, 199, 201
Moab, 171
Mogollon Culture, 15, 21, 43, 45, 47, 52, 158, 163, 252, 344; Cochise Culture influence, 183, 185; Desert, 187, 191, 196–199, 203, 235, 242; El Paso Phase, 187, 198, 201, 227; Jornada Style of, 186, 187, 190, 191, 192, 196, 197, 198, 199–242, 244; Medio Period, 198; Mimbres, 186, 192, 197, 198, 199, 201, 203, 217, 223, 233, 237, 239, 242; Mountain, 187; Red, 187–196; Reserve Petroglyph Style of, 187–196; San Andres, 187; Viejo Period, 198
Mogollon Mts., 221, 239
Montezuma, 238
Monument Valley, 143
Moore, David R., 9, 76, 77

Morris, Earl H., 358
Morss, Noel, 7, 166
Mountjoy, Joseph B., 90, 91, 103
Muddy River, 105
Museum of New Mexico, Santa Fe, 166

Navajo Canyon, 146
Navajo Lake, 309
Navajo Reservoir, 120, 128, 305, 318
Navajos, 1, 10, 11, 15, 21, 111, 187, 264, 301, 345; Gobernador Phase, 303, 304, 310, 318, 325; Gobernador Representational Style, 305–325, 326
Nayarit, 103, 239
Nelson, N. C., 294
Nevada, 9, 34, 42, 77, 105, 121, 153, 161, 176
New Mexico, 3, 5, 15, 17, 21, 23, 32, 34, 43, 45, 47, 49, 50, 52, 76, 77, 79, 105, 128, 160, 253, 301, 303, 322; Apache in, 333–335; Mogollon in, 183–242; Navajo in, 302–310
Newcomb, W. W., Jr., 7, 15, 55, 61, 71, 211, 217, 219, 227, 241, 310, 315, 330, 334, 335, 336, 339
Nicholson, Henry B., 298
Nine Mile Canyon, 166, 176, 179
Northern Sector, 34
Nusbaum, Jesse, 166

Ontario, 71
Opler, M. E., 341

Painted Grotto, 52, 55
Painted Rocks State Park, 96, 98, 99
Paiutes, 135
Pajarito Plateau, 250, 275, 285, 293, 298
Papagos, 96, 99
Papaguería, 82, 99, 100
Parowan Gap, 179
Parsons, Elsie Clews, 134, 141, 195, 233, 237, 238, 293, 294, 295, 297, 298, 319
pecked surfaces, 28–32, 36, 45, 56, 72, 83, 166, 227, 275, 308
Pecos Classification, 107
Pecos, 294, 301
Pecos River, 56, 70, 79, 105, 334
Peterson, Frederick, 235, 236, 298
Petrified Forest, 155
Phoenix, Ariz., 91
Picauris Pueblo, 250
Pictograph Canyon, 191
Picture Rocks, 91, 96
Pilles, Peter J., Jr., 72, 75, 155, 289
Pimas, 96, 98
Pine Lawn, 184, 185
Pine River, 5
Piro, 249, 250, 260, 275
Plains, 12, 307, 334
Plains of San Agustin, 183
Plog, Fred, 6, 17, 34, 184, 185, 195, 196
Point of Pines, 187

Polychrome Painting, 191
Pond, Gordon, 251
Pottery Mound, 26, 250, 251, 265
Pueblo I. See Anasazi
Pueblo II, 171, 344. See also Anasazi
Pueblo III, 171, 344. See also Anasazi
Pueblo IV, 15, 243, 252, 289, 293. See also Anasazi
Pueblo del Encierro, 250
Pueblos, 1, 7, 10, 11, 12, 15, 21, 47, 70, 119, 134, 135, 146, 148, 153, 158, 160, 161, 179, 187, 192, 219, 221, 227, 236, 237, 238, 239, 301, 302, 303, 306, 307, 319, 334, 337, 345; Classic Period, 243, 245, 246, 260, 285; Historic Period, 246, 260; kachina cult, 245, 254, 275, 289, 295, 296; Revolt of 1680, 264, 302; Rio Grande Style of, 244, 251, 252–289, 294, 297, 298. See also Rio Grande Style.
Puerco Ruin, 252, 289

Quetzalcoatl, 91, 198, 203, 217, 235, 236, 237, 238, 239, 240, 296

Reagan, Albert, 166
Reed, Erik K., 243, 245, 246
Reichard, Gladys A., 78, 309, 312, 315, 317, 330, 339
Reinhart, Theodore R., 49
Renaud, E. B., 13, 252, 307
representational figures, 3, 78, 83, 91, 197. See also Representational Style
Representational Style, 55–80; Barrier Canyon Anthropomorphic Style, 61, 70, 72, 76, 79; Candelaria Painted Style, 60; Cave Valley Style, 122, 129, 131–134, 179; Chinle Style, 122–127, 129, 133; Diablo Dam Petroglyph Style, 56, 60, 61, 79; Glen Canyon Linear Petroglyph Style, 72, 74, 75, 79. See also Glen Canyon Linear Style; Gobernador Style, 305–325, 326; Great Basin Style, 79; Jornada Style, 43, 47, 56; Kayenta Style, 143, 153; Pecos River Style, 55, 79; Rosa Style, 128–131, 133, 309, 322; Virgin Style, 153
reptile figures, 73, 83, 91, 136, 146, 160, 168, 179, 191, 197, 275
Reserve, 186, 190, 191, 233
Reserve Petroglyph Style. See Mogollon Culture
Rey, Agapito, 246, 248, 249, 301, 302
Rinaldo, John B., 183, 185
Rio Grande, 5, 55, 56, 120, 121, 122, 160, 196, 242, 244, 250, 254, 259, 306, 334, 337
Rio Grande Style, 134, 158, 160, 161, 312. See also Pueblos
Rio Grande Valley, 32, 47, 49, 77, 105, 183, 203, 244, 246, 249, 252, 253, 260, 275–285, 294, 295
Ritter, Dale W., 179
Ritter, Eric W., 179
Roberts, Frank H. H., Jr., 243
Rocky Mts., 254
Rosenfeld, Andrée, 5, 9

Russell, Frank, 96, 98

Sacramento Mts., 183, 211
Saguaro National Monument, 91
Sahagún, Bernardino De, 12
Salado, 161
Salado Polychrome, 162
Salmon Ruins, 136
Salt River, 97
San Blas, 103
San Carlos, 333
San Cristobal, 47, 259, 265
San Diego Mts., 211, 219
San Francisco River, 187, 190, 191
San José River, 47
San Juan Anthropomorphic Style, 109–124, 181. *See also* Anasazi
San Juan River, 5, 21, 49, 52, 72, 75, 105, 109, 112, 114, 117, 120, 122, 128, 133, 135, 136, 145, 161, 302, 305, 306, 308, 310, 312, 316, 318, 325
San Pedro Phase, 81
San Pedro Valley, 335, 337
San Simon, 184, 187, 190
Sand Island, 75
Sandia Mts., 254
Sandia Pueblo, 275
Sangre de Cristo Mts., 254, 302
Santa Clara, 302
Santa Cruz Phase, 103
Santa Cruz Valley, 94, 97
Santa Fe, N.M., 246, 253, 254
Santa Fe River, 295
Santan Mt., 96, 98
Santayana, George, 343
Sayles, E. B., 184
Schaafsma, Curtis F., 8, 161, 187, 196, 232, 242, 244, 302
Schaafsma, Polly, 5, 7, 43, 47, 49, 51, 52, 61, 70, 71, 72, 117, 120, 128, 131, 143, 146, 153, 160, 161, 166, 168, 171, 175, 176, 187, 190, 191, 192, 197, 199, 219, 221, 232, 241, 242, 244, 250, 252, 255, 260, 264, 265, 275, 289, 297, 299, 305, 306, 307, 310, 312, 318, 319, 322, 328, 335, 337, 341
Schapiro, Meyer, 7
Schroeder, Albert H., 100, 249
Schroedl, Alan R., 70
Scott, Donald, 166
Sedlmayr, Jacobo, 96
Service, Elman R., 52
shamans, 10, 56, 71, 72, 73, 133, 153, 179–191, 192, 233, 306, 339
Sierra Ancha, 161, 162
Sierra Blanca Range, 183, 341
Sierra Madre Occidental, 183
Sierra Pincate, 41
Silver City, N.M., 191
Sims, Agnes C., 252, 295, 296, 297
Sinagua, 161
Sinaloa, 103

Skinner, S. Alan, 252
Smith, Howard Norman, Jr., 125, 128
Smith, Watson, 26, 221, 227, 249, 250, 251, 297, 307
Snake Gulch, 117
Snaketown, 98
Snyder, Ernest E., 83, 97
Sonoita, 101
Sonora, 41, 43, 82, 99, 101, 183
Sonoran Desert, 98
Soustelle, Jacques, 238
South America, 71
South Mts., 97
Southern Sector, 34, 43. *See also* Cochise Culture
Spanish influence, 15, 60, 246, 250, 252, 302, 325
Spier, Leslie, 13
Steed, Paul, 56, 227
Steen, Charlie, R., 162
Stevenson, James, 293, 294, 296, 315, 318, 319, 325
Steward, Julian, 7, 36, 41, 42, 83, 131
Struever, Stuart, 8
Suhm, Dee Ann, 56, 61
Sutherland, Kay, 56, 227
Swarts Ruin, 187
Switzer, Ronald R., 238, 294, 298

Talayesva, Don, 99, 289, 294
Talpa Black-on-white, 252
Tanner, Clara Lee, 83, 91, 328
Tano, 264–265, 295, 297
Tanque Verde Mts., 98
Taos, 252, 253, 286
Taos Pueblo, 237
Tedlock, Dennis, 296, 297
Tenabo, 259, 260, 297
Teotihuacan, 236, 238, 240, 241
Tewa, 239, 246, 249, 260, 264, 275, 285–286, 297
Texas, 3, 15, 17, 21, 34, 43, 49, 56, 70, 76, 78, 183–242, 335
Three Rivers, N.M., 6, 211, 221, 223, 227, 235, 239, 240
Tinaja Romero, 41, 42
Titiev, Mischa, 289, 294
Tiwa, 246, 248, 250, 260, 275, 285–286
Tlaloc, 198, 203, 208, 235, 236, 237, 238, 240, 254
Todosio Canyon, 308, 315, 322
Toltecs, 198, 242
Tompiro Province, 260–264
Toness, Kay S., 60, 217
tools, 47; for pecking, 28–31
Toscano, Salvador, 235
Towa, 260
Tozzer, Alfred M., 238
Trincheras Culture, 99, 100, 101
Tsegi Canyon, 111, 143, 145, 146, 161
Tucson, Ariz., 82, 83, 91, 94, 96, 97
Tucson Mt., 91, 98

Tularosa Basin, 197, 203
Tularosa Cave, 184, 186, 195
Tularosa River, 191
Tumamoc Hill, 96, 98, 101
Turner, Christy G. II, 5, 7, 28, 72, 74, 75, 135, 143, 289, 293
Turner-Look site, 180

Ucko, Peter J., 5, 9
Underhill, Ruth M., 99
Upper Sonoran, 52, 196, 253
Utah, 3, 5, 21, 34, 49, 52, 54, 55, 61, 70, 71, 72, 76, 77, 78, 79, 117, 131, 135, 153, 162, 302; Fremont in, 163–242
Utes, 15, 304, 328, 330

Vaillant, G. C., 238
Valle Grande, 254
Vastokas, Joan M., 10, 71, 73, 339
Vastokas, Romas K., 10, 71, 73, 339
Velarde, 286
Verde Valley, 97
Villagrá, Agustín, 235, 238, 246
Villagrá, Gaspar Pérez de, 249, 250
Virgin Kayenta, 131, 135, 153
Vivian, Patricia B., 83, 99, 250
Von Werlhof, J. C., 7, 42, 76
Von Winning, Hasso, 134
Voth, H. R., 293

Walpi, 298
Wasatch Plateau, 163, 176
Wasley, William W., 83, 96

Watson, Editha L., 310, 312
Wauer, Roland, 131
weapon figures, 15, 56, 60, 61, 66, 179
Wellmann, K. F., 10, 71, 134, 140, 141
Wendorf, Fred, 243, 245, 246
Western Archaic, 17, 33, 34, 36, 49, 55, 71, 77, 107, 183, 191. See also Desert Culture
Western Sector, 34, 36, 79
Westheim, Paul, 240
Wetherington, Ronald K., 252
Wheat, Joe Ben, 34, 79, 184
White, Cheryl, 9, 83, 91, 94, 97, 98
White, Leslie A., 297
White Rock Canyon, 275, 285, 289
Willey, Gordon R., 21, 33, 184, 242, 306
Willow Springs, 289, 294
Winchester Mts., 190
Winship, George Parker, 246, 249, 301
Winslow, Ariz., 251
Woodbury, Angus Mann, 143, 148
Woodward, J., 328
Wormington, H. M., 166, 171, 175, 180
Wyman, Leland C., 307, 315, 318, 322, 325
Wyoming, 71

Yeo, Herbert W., 235
Yumas, 21, 99

Zahniser, Jack L., 9, 98
Zia Pueblo, 250, 294
Zubrow, Ezra, 244
Zuni Pueblo, 134, 158, 160, 244, 250, 260, 293
Zunis, 134, 237, 239, 289, 295, 296, 297